"Atwood has compiled the data, stories, and arguments about gun culture in American you are looking for, all in one book.

—Rob Wilson-Black
PhD, CEO, *Sojourners*

"As a faith leader and gun owner himself, Reverend Atwood grounds his opposition to gun violence in theology and facts, appealing to the broader faith community to use its moral authority to stop the killing by guns of more than 2,500 children and teens in 2014 alone."

—Marian Wright Edelman
President, Children's Defense Fund

"As always, Jim Atwood does his homework. The book is well-researched and full of stories and statistics that make for compelling reading. His most powerful contribution is when he names and calls out the Gundamentalists (a term I find equally disturbing and descriptive) and lays out a prescription on how we can take them on. Read the book; share it with friends at church or at work; then form a small group to stand up, take action, and be counted."

—Rick Ufford-Chase
Co-Director of PCUSA Stony Point Conference Center
and Author of "Faithful Resistance."

GUNDAMENTALISM
and Where It Is Taking America

GUNDAMENTALISM
and Where It Is Taking America

by **James E. Atwood**

Including Discussion Questions
by Jan Orr-Harter

 CASCADE *Books* • Eugene, Oregon

GUNDAMENTALISM AND WHERE IT IS TAKING AMERICA

Cascade Books
An Imprint of Wipf and Stock Publishers
199 W. 8th Ave., Suite 3
Eugene, OR 97401

www.wipfandstock.com

PAPERBACK ISBN: 978-1-5326-0544-4
HARDCOVER ISBN: 978-1-5326-0546-8
EBOOK ISBN: 978-1-5326-0545-1

Cataloguing-in-Publication data:

Names: Atwood, James E.

Title: Gundamentalism and where it is taking America / James E. Atwood.

Description: Eugene, OR: Cascade Books, 2017 | Includes bibliographical references.

Identifiers: ISBN 978-1-5326-0544-4 (paperback) | ISBN 978-1-5326-0546-8 (hardcover) | ISBN 978-1-5326-0545-1 (ebook)

Subjects: LCSH: 1. Religion and politics—United States. | 2. Firearms—Law and legislation—United States. | Gun control—United States. | I. Title.

Classification: BL2525 .A90 2017 (paperback) | CALL NUMBER (ebook)

Manufactured in the U.S.A.   01/25/17

To those uncountable millions of loved ones and friends—members of the saddest club in America—the victims of gun violence.

Contents

Preface

For fifty-eight years I have enjoyed owning guns. For forty-one of those years I have worked to prevent their misuse and gun violence. I'm an American who stands in two worlds—with those who use guns for sport and with those who have offered too many prayers at funerals of gun victims. America faces a national epidemic of unnecessary gun deaths. I write this book because 33,000 of our citizens die every year at the barrels of guns, through murder, suicide, and accident. That translates to approximately 90 families every day who grieve that their child, parent, sibling, or loved one is one more senseless victim of gun violence. Their grief is not for a day, but for a lifetime. Too many Americans are dying because too many guns are readily accessible to *anyone* who wants one. This is not the only path for America. We do *not* have to live this way.

I title this book *Gundamentalism and Where It Is Taking America,* to highlight the dangerous role guns are playing in our psyches and culture. We are face-to-face with a small religious cult comprised of a tight-knit tribe of gun extremists who require greater numbers of weapons to feel secure and are buttressed by a mammoth gun and ammunition industry that refuses any compromise.

Nevertheless, for the vast silent majority of gun owners who are tired of the violence and those of us who work tirelessly to prevent gun violence, there is colossal space for reasonable compromise. Working together, we can create sensible gun regulations that respect two constitutional rights that must be part of our national conversation. I refer to the right to keep and bear arms and the right to live in domestic tranquility wherein we can pursue life, liberty, and happiness free of gun violence.

This book describes our current gun explosion estimated to be at 350,000,000 and its sociological consequences; our history, and how we got to this point; while also exploring some reasonable compromises that can save lives, perhaps the life of someone you love.

The problem is that this quasi-religious ideology of gundamentalism has created a cowardly army of politicians in state and national legislatures who are bought and paid for by the gun and ammunition industries, of whom they are terrified. So I write this book to call for courage from the American public, from gun owners and those who are not. I issue a call for spiritual backbone from faith communities across this nation that should be out front fighting an obscene pandemic of gun deaths. We must work together step-by-step and law-by-law to change the direction gundamentalism is taking our country. We do not want to go there and we do not have to live this way.

It's a great privilege to travel far and wide to speak about this issue, especially since a strong social movement has taken root. But, I confess my frustration when I run across so many people who think they can learn all they need to know about gun violence at a pot-luck supper.

In March of this year, one of my hosts at Kansas Wesleyan University understood the many faceted nature of the subject and challenged his students to grasp its far-reaching ramifications. He asked them, "If we are going to understand America's unique problem of gun violence, what academic disciplines need to be part of the conversation?" He then used all the space on the board to write down their answers: psychology, philosophy, medicine, sociology, history, religion and theology, government and politics, law, law enforcement, women's studies, education, criminology, statistics, and community organization.

This book will by no means exhaust this multi-faceted subject, nor am I an expert in any of the above fields. I name them only to demonstrate the effects gun violence has on almost every aspect of our lives. Each of the above disciplines is at least accessed and acknowledged in the following pages as I discuss where extremist gun lovers want to take America. I trust the reader will want to do more than skim the contents, but delve into the causes of our epidemic and then go to work to put an end to what I consider America's greatest spiritual, ethical, and moral problem.

The prophet summed up the essentials of living in a simple question: "What does the Lord require of you, but to do justice, love mercy, and walk humbly with your God?" (Mic 6:8). What small successes I have had in my life and ministry are because I share each day with Roxana, my helpmate and partner for fifty-seven years, who looks at life through Micah's lenses.

For that, I am grateful to God. Our daughter and son, Mebane and David, their spouses Alan and Robin, and our four grandchildren, Atwood, Roxana the Lesser, Oliver, and Ellen light up our lives with their love and compassion for others, and their commitments to peace and justice help keep us on the path.

Only a fool would consider writing a book about a national calamity and offer a few suggestions on how we can solve it, without plans to ask countless kindred spirits and wise friends and colleagues for their insights. Once more, I have been the beneficiary of the wisdom and common sense of family, friends, and trusted colleagues. The first person I contacted for advice and counsel was the one whom I have known longer than anyone else in the world —Walter Owensby, an elementary school classmate from Detroit. He has spent the majority of his years working for peace and God's justice in the Middle East. He was enormously helpful and made numerous suggestions that make the book more readable. Thanks, Walt!

I'm in great debt to the members of Trinity Presbyterian Church of Harrisonburg, Virginia, and their pastor, the Rev. Stephanie Sorge Wing, and particularly to those of Shalom House Church. Their faithfulness in studying peace and justice concerns in bimonthly meetings, sponsoring monthly vigils at the courthouse, protests at NRA Headquarters and lobbying our legislators, kept my feet to the fire for the simple reason that they *do* justice, *love* mercy, and *walk* humbly with God. I'm especially grateful for a new friend in Harrisonburg, Rabbi Joe Blair, who helped me understand the biblical concept of avoiding the spilling of blood.

For years I have received countless emails, letters, and articles from Thornton Parker, John Jackson, Laura Sloan, Jack Mathison, and from my son and daughter. Each has a knack for deciphering what everybody needs to know about the absurdity of America's violence. They will, no doubt, recognize much of what I included in this volume.

My special thanks to Alonzo Johnson, Josh Horwitz, J. Herbert Nelson, Katie Day, Martin Copenhaver, Rick Ufford-Chase, Marian Wright Edleman, Rob Wilson-Black, and my niece, Renee Toporcysek, each of whom read the manuscript, and graciously assured me "the book needs to be written."

Jan Orr-Harter always shows up to lend a hand. Just as she wrote study questions for my first book, she has done the same for this one. Once again, her wisdom and commitments to Shalom enhance the book. Discussion and faith groups will be grateful for her capacity to get to the heart of things with a well-crafted question. Thanks, Jan!

I'm especially thankful for my middle-school friend, Preston Striebig, who has many talents, not the least of which is art. He created the drawing that begins chapter 9 and now has his first copyright. Special thanks to cartoonist Dave Granlund, whose provocative cartoon closes chapter 14.

My copy editor, Heather Wilson, works with kindness and the patience of Job, and once again has done her magic, presenting Wipf and Stock with a beautifully edited copy. It is not only *what* Heather did, but *how* she did it, that makes me thankful. Although he caused me extra work, I'm thankful too for Wipf and Stock's Rodney Clapp who can spot a line that needs documentation a mile away.

In addition to the above, the following made valuable suggestions and contributions: Wendell Primus, Pauline Endo, Randy Benn, Andy and Colin Goddard, Ladd Everett, Chelsea White, Lori Haas, Nardyne Jeffries, Joe Vince, Andy Sale, Jim Kellet, Charles Lotts, Charles Shank, Richard Armstrong, Bill Marlowe, Gini Reese, Charles Hall, Midge Curry, Alma Noble, Arnold Brooks, Jimmie Mohler, Bill and Ramona Sanders, Eugenia Parker, and Don Oxley. Many thanks for your help.

James E. Atwood
Harrisonburg, Virginia

1

What Do You Believe About Guns?

My first gun was a twelve-gauge shotgun I bought from a Sears Roebuck catalog in 1958. I used it in Southeastern North Carolina to hunt quail, rabbits, and deer. When I traveled to Japan in 1965 to work as a missionary with the United Church of Christ in Japan, I took it along because a colleague told me Japan had good duck and pheasant hunting. In the seventies I bought another gun, a rifle more suited for deer hunting, which became my favorite outdoor sport. I waited expectantly for every November to roll around so I could get out in the woods and stake out a deer stand.

It was fun preparing for my hunting trip; sighting in my rifle; picking out a deer stand; and then on opening day, getting up long before dawn to find my way through the brush and the brambles to the spot where I hoped a deer with a big rack would venture. Hunting gave me a lot of pleasure. I kept my guns in good working order until my eightieth year when it became clear my endurance and balance were slipping and I had to give an honest answer to a troubling question.

Was it safe for an old man, who had to carefully measure his steps through fallen trees, thick brush, briar patches, and uneven ground, to make his way to a deer stand or to track a wounded deer through the woods, to carry a loaded rifle that could fire a bullet a mile or more? There has never been a hunter who hasn't fallen in such terrain, but when an octogenarian stumbles and falls with a loaded rifle, it is another story altogether. My body was sending me a message I could not ignore. It was not easy parting with a sport that gave me many hours of fun and relaxation for over fifty years.

In the fall of 2014, I sold my four hunting guns to four different men, one of whom was a friend, and two had concealed carry permits. I insisted that the other man whom I did not know have a background check. He protested: "I am a law-abiding citizen and a background check is not necessary." However, he agreed to have one because he wanted my gun.

For four decades I have been an advocate for background checks, which have stopped over two million gun purchases by dangerous people since the Brady Bill was enacted in 1993. In the foreseeable future when Congress finally comes to its senses and passes background checks on all guns sold, which 90 percent of the American people support, it will mean a few extra steps for gun buyers, but that is not a *real* hardship and will save lives. Whenever states put strong gun laws in place gun deaths decline. That is a simple fact I will stress throughout this volume.

Neither I nor my colleagues who work to prevent gun violence can be called, "gun grabbers," the derisive term used by gun extremists to describe anyone who raises a question or two about gun safety or enacting reasonable gun laws that would save lives without infringing upon anyone's Second Amendment rights. My denomination, the Presbyterian Church, USA, other ecumenical and interfaith bodies, and non-profit organizations engaged in preventing gun violence are not opposed to hunting, sports shooting, or defensive gun ownership. One caveat: we support a ban on assault weapons, which, with the use of a large magazine, can shoot up to one hundred rounds in a minute and are the weapon of choice for mass murderers.

Because I am a Christian, my highest priority is to discern God's will and then to follow it as best I can. I refuse to participate in the biblical gymnastics that claims God's blessing on anything that will go "boom." It is clear to me that such manipulation of the Scriptures elevates guns to the status of another absolute or ultimate value that requires one to be loyal to both God and guns. My faith in God means God alone is the world's *only* absolute. God and God's law of love is the only ultimate and absolute value to which a believer can pledge allegiance. To be beholden or obligated to any other person, idea, or entity that masquerades as an ultimate value is to serve a false god or an idol. My faith will not permit something made with human hands to have an *unconditional priority* in my heart or mind. Does that mean I hate guns and or gun owners? Obviously not. I enjoyed them for fifty-six years, and I can truthfully say, "Thanks for the memories!"

Although my firearms were all long guns and used for hunting, I have many friends who own handguns for personal protection. Although I have reservations about the efficacy of defensive guns that will become clear in this book, for the most part, we see eye-to-eye on gun rights and responsibilities. When our discussions first began, however, and my friends learned I was on the board of the Coalition to Stop Gun Violence (CSGV), they were suspicious and wondered if I were a "closet gun-grabber."

I can still hear the skeptical voice of another Presbyterian minister who, like myself, was an avid hunter: "Just *what* do you believe about guns anyway?" Actually, his question is even more relevant today because of the bloody year we had in 2015, with more mass shootings than days on the calendar. This book is to help you examine *your* beliefs about guns. With 350,000,000 of them around, there are 90 deaths, intentional and unintentional, every day. Ten of these deaths are children.

I have often heard, "those deaths are the price of freedom." Most gun owners reject that kind of patriotism. But such gullible pronouncements should prompt all of us to wrestle with the complex question of what we believe about guns in our society today. To dismiss the question with a shrug of the shoulders is irresponsible; so is answering it with a slogan or a bumper sticker quote. Complex questions deserve thoughtful answers.

Who would deny the issue is complex? On the one hand, the Supreme Court has declared the Second Amendment guarantees an individual the right to have a gun with limitations; the Federal Bureau of Investigation (FBI) estimates there are 350,000,000 guns in America, which assures their presence for generations, even centuries; law enforcement and first-responders need weapons to protect themselves and the public. Farmers and ranchers need protection from wild animals and/or to dispose of predators or pests. Millions of people hunt in order to feed their families, while others love to shoot skeet, or go plinking with the family. Moreover, millions of Americans are afraid of the violence that is on parade on the front pages of our newspapers and on TV; they want defensive guns for protection.

One of my church members in Wallace, North Carolina, told me how his gun literally saved his life. He worked for the State Bureau of Health and was assigned to visit a particular farm and make plans to remove the carcasses of several cattle that became ill and died in open pasture. The stench was unbearable throughout the region. He parked his truck and headed for the pasture, but returned to get his gun just in case something untoward happened. He was glad he did. He was soon surrounded by a pack of wild dogs that followed the stench. They began to circle him in menacing fashion. He drew his gun and shot one of the dogs and drove the others away. His gun saved his life.

Millions of youth love to shoot hoops (basketball) because it's fun. Millions of others shoot guns for the same reason. They *are* fun to shoot. Target shooting is an international sport in both summer and winter Olympics. I have dozens of friends who were members of high school rifle teams.

Skeet is an enjoyable outdoor sport. Even some luxury cruise lines offer it as an option for their customers. Many families go to the woods for plinking (shooting at tin cans, bottles, or other targets). Like any hobby, it can be carried to the extreme where one shoots at public property just for the fun of it. Who has not seen road signs in national forests literally riddled with bullets? Few, however, know of the world's most expensive "plink." Just north of Fairbanks, Alaska, Daniel Lewis, just for the fun of it, took aim at a section of the trans-Alaska pipeline and pulled the trigger. His single shot caused 286,000 gallons of oil to gush out of the pipeline at the cost of $20 million.[1]

On the other hand, for more than four decades America's gun fatalities have never dipped below 32,000. In this book I use 33,000 because that was the number killed last year and appears likely to repeat itself. We are reading about more mass shootings in churches, shopping malls, schools, and nightclubs. In 2013, 153 times crazed shooters opened fire in houses of worship. Ten children die every day through gun homicides or accidents; the mentally ill and terrorists can pick up an assault rifle with no questions asked at America's five thousand gun shows. Dozens of absurd laws protect the sale of guns instead of the people who are killed by them. Gun violence costs the nation over $229 billion per year.[2]

And far too many people die in utterly bizarre gun deaths. In May 2014, a fifty-three year-old Huntsville, Alabama man shot his thirty-four-year-old wife, three dogs, and a pet parrot because "they talked too much."[3]

On October 20, 2015, in Albuquerque, New Mexico, on Interstate Highway 40, Iliana "Lilly" Rose Garcia, four years old, was fatally shot when Tony Torrez opened fire on the vehicle in which she was riding. She,

1. Young, "Bullet Hole Causes Huge Alaskan Oil Spill," 1.
2. Follman, "The True Cost of Gun Violence in America."
3. Collman, "Man, 53."

of course, was not the intended victim; her father was. Torrez and Lilly's father got into a road rage dispute about a lane change. Nevertheless, Lilly won't be going to kindergarten.[4]

Lots of children accidently kill their brothers and sisters, like the seven-year-old boy in Washington, D.C. who shot and killed his three-year-old sister. He told detectives he thought his sister "would get up like they do on TV. Guns on TV don't do that."[5]

An eight-year-old boy in Arkansas committed suicide with his father's gun while his mother was outside cutting a switch to punish him for bringing home a bad report card.[6]

For years I have kept an Absurdity File that holds the gruesome stories of similar tragedies and accidents, particularly those that involve infants, toddlers, and young children killed with the guns their parents bought to protect them from dangerous persons. Many parents just let guns lie around the house like yesterday's newspaper.[7]

In America, from 1999 through 2013, preschoolers—children aged zero to four—were killed by guns in greater numbers than police officers in the line of duty, with the exception of 2004, when the groups were tied at fifty-eight deaths. Children aged five to nine also outnumber police officers for gun deaths for every year in that period.[8]

Both sides of this national debate have their own stories to tell and their own principles to uphold. Gun aficionados believe gun rights are the *one* right that guarantees all others. Bringing those folk together with those who claim a Constitutional right to domestic tranquility without fear of being shot is a difficult assignment. H. L. Mencken was right: "there is always a well-known solution to every human problem—neat, plausible, and wrong."[9]

Putting an end to America's gun violence is not an either/or, winner-take-all kind of discussion. It requires a both/and solution, a win-win discussion. To get there those who hate guns must be willing to sit down with those whose livelihoods depend on them for food or safety and whose culture has praised guns for generations, while those who have never seen

4. Brose, "Funeral for New Mexico Girl."
5. Alexander, "Boy Who Shot Sister."
6. Cited by Hemenway, *Private Guns–Public Health,* 35–36.
7. Hemenway, *Private Guns-Public Health,* 35–36.
8. Turkel, "Guns Have Killed."
9. Mencken, "The Divine Afflatus."

a gun they didn't like must be willing to listen to the fears of children in our inner cities who hear gunshots before they go to sleep at night and are afraid to go to local playgrounds because that's where kids get shot. We must talk together to find common ground to heal our land.

My friend asked, "Just what do *you* believe about guns anyway?" Perhaps the reader will be surprised to learn my views about guns almost mirror the beliefs of the vast majority of America's gun owners and NRA members. Their opinions were the focus of a national poll taken by Republican pollster Frank Luntz in 2012. I join them in affirming the following:

1. Eighty-two percent support "prohibiting people on the terrorist watch lists from purchasing guns."

2. Sixty-nine percent favor "requiring all gun sellers at gun shows to conduct criminal background checks of the people buying guns." (In 2015, the number grew to 85 percent.)

3. Seventy-eight percent support a requirement that gun owners "alert police if their guns are lost or stolen."

4. Eighty-six percent of all gun owners and NRA members agree with Frank Luntz's core idea that gun rights and gun regulations do not contradict but complement each other: "We can do more to stop criminals from getting guns while also protecting the rights of citizens to freely own them."

5. Sixty-nine percent of NRA members oppose the idea behind the so-called Tiahrt amendment passed by Congress, which prevents law enforcement officials from having full access to gun trace data from the ATF (Bureau of Alcohol, Tobacco, Firearms, and Explosives) and requires the FBI to destroy certain background-check records after just twenty-four hours.[10]

6. Remember, these views are from *the silent majority* of gun owners. It is clear these views stand in stark contrast to the well-publicized views of Wayne La Pierre, Chris Cox, and top managers in the NRA. These elites strictly control everything uttered in the name of the NRA and everything printed in their large gun press. (Waiting for a prescription to be filled at my pharmacy I counted eighteen gun magazines on their shelves.) The most published views about guns are carefully crafted to do two things: sell more guns and protect sales of guns for all buyers

10. Luntz, *National Poll of Gun Owners.*

and sellers. Conciliatory or less strident messages or attempts to find common ground even with their own members are *never* heard by the public. The NRA declares solving gun violence is a simple matter. It requires more guns in more people's hands. You've heard them say it before: More guns = less crime, and "The only thing that will stop a bad guy with a gun is a good guy with a gun." Their solution to America's gun violence is clear and simple. H. L. Menken would add, "and it's wrong."

While I affirm a person's right to keep and bear arms, I reject the idea that the freedom we cherish in America is inexorably linked to gun owner-ship. Guns are made to kill. That is their *raison d'etre;* proven when ninety of us die daily at their barrels. Such carnage persuades me to support bal-anced, sensible regulations on all guns. For that matter, I support sensible regulations on most anything that can cause death and injury to human beings. I'm glad Congress banned lawn darts and puts regulations for safety on swimming pools, automobiles, and medicines. They should put them on guns.

Each time I get on the highway, I'm grateful that federal and state gov-ernments are committed to making and keeping our vehicles and roads as safe as possible. I'm grateful that air bags and seat belts are required. I'm thankful it is illegal to have an open bottle of beer in a moving car. I'm glad brakes, lights, steering mechanisms, tires, and windshield wipers are in-spected every year in Virginia, and that drivers are licensed only after they demonstrate they are physically and mentally competent. Such supervision does not *guarantee* safety, but it has greatly reduced accidents, injuries, and deaths. I hear no talk of what an onerous burden it is for good citizens to take their vehicles to a mechanic once a year. And when self-driving auto-mobiles are ready for market, they will have their own set of regulations, and I say, "Thank God!"

I pray every Sunday with my congregation, "Thy kingdom come, thy will be done on earth as it is in heaven." My Christian faith authorizes me to say, "It is not God's will that 33,000 of us die every year by guns." In the seven and one-half years of war in Iraq 4,500 service men and women were killed, while 220,500 civilians were killed at the barrels of guns on our own streets and in our homes.[11] God is not pleased over that. God does not decree we must live this way. We can and must do something about it.

11. CDC and Department of Defense.

7

There is an African proverb that says, "If you need to go fast, walk alone; if you need to go far, walk with others." We have a long way to go before our nation is as ready to respect both the right of all its citizens to live in "domestic tranquility" (specified in the first sentence of the Constitution of the United States of America) and honor an individual's right to keep and bear arms. When *both constitutional rights* are honored in the halls of Congress, we will be much closer to the kind of country God wills for us. When pro-gun and gun safety people finally have honest dialogue, neither side will get everything it wants, but we *can* get a lot closer than ever before to a safer and saner society. In the process, countless lives will be saved. That is not only the nature of a dialogue, but the nature of a republic. Each of us is more secure when we talk and listen to one another and walk *with* one another.

QUESTIONS

1. What role have guns played in your life? Give two examples.

2. Atwood describes the poll of the "silent majority of gun owners." Do you agree or disagree with the poll results of gun owners and NRA members?

3. Review these statistics from the chapter: "In the seven and one half years of war in Iraq, 4,500 service men and women were killed, while 220,500 civilians were killed at the barrels of guns on our own streets and in our homes." Is this a new perspective for you? Atwood states "God does not decree that we live this way." What role does God play in your understanding of gun violence?

4. Have you ever undergone a background check for any purpose? Did you feel it was overreach or appropriate? .

Assignment: At the grocery or bookstore, browse through one or more of the gun magazines on the shelf and monitor your reactions to the content, ads, and photos.

2

How Did We Get Here?

In 2012 there were 153 separate shootings when mentally disturbed individuals entered houses of worship with high-powered military guns.[1] In response, for the first time our government published guidebooks for schools, colleges, and houses of worship on what to do in such circumstances.[2] Did you ever think we would need those kinds of books in America? In 2015, there were more mass shootings (i.e. four or more persons killed) than days on the calendar. No one will be surprised when there is another and another, and another. As I have noted, ninety persons will die today at the barrel of a gun; ten will be children. Thousands of persons made in God's image were killed last year by guns that, for the most part, were purchased to protect the family. How did we get to this point in America?

Shamefully, the only thing many timid clergy, elected representatives, and elite officers of the NRA are able to do is keep the victim's families *in their thoughts and prayers*. As they pray, thousands of churches are reaching out to the unchurched by offering concealed carry certification classes and celebration Sundays. How did we get to this point in America?

Søren Kierkegaard said, "Life must be lived forward, but it can only be understood backwards." Before we can shrink our astronomical numbers of gun deaths we must understand *how* we got here. It wasn't by chance, nor did it occur in a vacuum. We got here because the American people believe

1. Kiely, "Gun Rhetoric vs. Gun Facts."

2. "Guide for Developing High Quality Emergency Operations Plans For Houses of Worship," FEMA.

violence is efficient and effectual; we depend on it. We trust our guns, both large and small, to keep us safe and provide the security we long for. I saw our trust crisply defined on a bumper sticker: "Peace through superiority in arms." Unfortunately, that idea is nothing new in America: it's been with us a long time.

I grew up in the 1940s with a steady diet of cowboy movies: Roy Rogers, Tom Mix, Johnny Mack Brown, Hopalong Cassidy, and later John Wayne. They were my heroes. I really didn't care for Gene Autry—he sang too much and liked girls. I never missed a *Lone Ranger* broadcast. I read hundreds of comic books and thrilled at the exploits of Captain Marvel, Batman and Robin, and Superman who fought for "truth, justice, and the American way." I thrived on war movies in which each "Kraut" and "Jap" soldier, as we called them then, were always portrayed as both stupid and incredibly mean. That was my socialization. I believed what I saw and internalized two very clear messages: good guys always win, and good guys win with violence. Those messages remain the same.

We do, however, pay a heavy price for wearing the white hats and feeling so much at ease using violence. Since 1979 our gun deaths have never dipped below 32,000 a year.[3] In 2015, 33,000 perished.[4] More American citizens died from guns since 1968 than military personnel on the battlefields of all of America's wars since 1775.[5]

These numbers are obscene, and their effects cannot be fully grasped apart from a hard look at some of our curious national myths. Namely, that God gave us, the American people, a special responsibility in bringing to fruition the Almighty's plans for planet Earth. Our historical documents are crystal clear about that. They claim among other assignments, the task of being "the trustees of the world's progress," "the guardian of the world's righteous peace," and "Christ's light to the nations."[6] These are noble callings indeed, but our national myth also includes that being God's "chosen instrument" *requires* violence.

Such enticing assumptions have not only influenced our national sense of being responsible for the world, but have trickled down into the consciousness of millions of Americans who believe God gave them both

3. Center for Disease Control and Prevention (CDC) Annual Injury Mortality Reports.

4 U. S. Department of Defense.

5. U.S. Department of Defense.

6. Benton, ed., *The Annals of America*, vol. XII, 336–45.

the right and responsibility to own guns so they can protect their families, private property, and their neighbors. Believing we are *an exceptional people* spawns an extraordinary sense of entitlement to use any means necessary to foster our individual and national well-being. Cultivating this sense of entitlement, as we are wont to do, guarantees eventually we will consider ourselves victims of the evil forces that are assaulting us and we must fight fire with fire. Consequently, we will believe the violence we *must* use at times is not deplorable, only necessary. It is not only justified; it is a moral obligation and a duty.

Numerous scholars also remind us that monotheism itself conveys an exclusivity, which is certain to have a violent legacy. The argument goes: "We," the faithful, have on our side the one true God and we stand in opposition to "them," the infidels and renegades.

Believing we were God's agents gave our Anglo-Saxon forebears the chutzpah to tromp through the new world in "ten-league boots," running roughshod over Native American peoples, buttressing our economy on the backs of slaves, and subjugating peoples of other lands in attempts to bring them "civilization" and "salvation." Using this "God-given power" is not only acceptable, but heroic.

Robert Jewett, in his great book, *The Captain America Complex*, writes, "Biblical zeal offers an astounding mystique for violence. It contends that righteous violence can redeem other people, demonstrate one's superiority over rival forces, and even convert the world. This mystique justifies the most appalling atrocities believing that violence is necessary to produce and keep the peace." *It follows that a culture schooled in this tradition of righteous violence will show extremely high levels of violence in both individual and collective behavior.*[7]

Our nation proclaims repeatedly that our goals are not for dominion, but for world peace and security. Nevertheless, right-wing gospel preacher, the Rev. Pat Robertson of the *700 Club,* believes otherwise and speaks for millions of American Christians. Showing disdain for the United Nations, he says, "There will never be world peace until God's house and God's people are given their rightful place of leadership at the top of the world."[8]

A kindred spirit is political analyst William Kristol, who is glad when others call us "an imperial power." He supports a muscular "Pax Americana"

7. Jewett, *The Captain America Complex*, 54–55.

8. "The Rise of the Religious Right in the Republican Party." www.theocracywatch. org.

11

based on "unquestioned U.S. military pre-eminence," and asks, "What's wrong with dominance in the service of sound principles and high ideals?"[9]

We are today the only nation that can realistically be called an empire. We spend 640 billion dollars per year on our military. That is more than the next nine countries of the world combined spend on their militaries. Though our navy has shrunk since the end of the Cold War, it is larger than the next thirteen navies of the world *combined*—eleven of which are our allies and friends.[10]

We may print "In God We Trust" on our currency, but such expenditures are evidence we place a larger trust in the violence that will protect us. We believe in it and rely on it whether it is in the form of advanced military technology or semi-automatic handguns and AK-47s that we stash in our bedside stands or closets. Our weapons themselves control us because over the years, we have seen how flaunting our guns (big and small) has kept us "safe" from enemies, both foreign and domestic.

Gundamentalists along with Robertson and Kristol, want our nation to be dominant in the world. They want the same in their own private worlds because "God gave us dominion over all the earth" (Gen 1:26.) They want to be safe when they go to a bar or the bank, to the office or to church or a concert, or when they take a walk in a national park, or go to a movie. They want their children safe at school, and they feel better if all the teachers are armed so they can control the bad guys.

Carrying loaded weapons has come quite close to being a norm in America. Each of our states issues some form of permit to carry weapons whether openly or concealed (CCWP) even though some of the applicants have never, even once, held a gun in their hand, or had so much as one hour of arms instruction. Some states issue permits to persons with impaired vision while the State of Iowa issues them to citizens who are *totally* blind. In fact, the NRA opposes minimum training and proficiency standards for these permits, calling them "needless mandates."

Biblical scholar Walter Wink says, "Violence is the ethos of our times. It is the spirituality of the modern world. It has been accorded the status of a religion, demanding from its devotees an absolute obedience to death. Violence is successful as a myth precisely because it does not seem to be mythic in the least. Violence simply appears to be the nature of things. It is what works. It is inevitable, the last, and often, the first resort in conflicts. It

---

9. Wallis, "Bush's Theology of Empire," 20–26.

10. Bienaime, "The Russian Navy."

is embraced by people on the left and on the right, by religious liberals and religious conservatives who believe the threat of violence alone can deter aggressors. Violence is thriving as never before in every sector of American popular culture, civil religion, nationalism, and foreign policy. Violence, not Christianity, is the real religion of America."[11]

Violence begets violence is not a rumor, but a sad reality. Trusting one's guns for safety conveys two irreconcilable emotions: one is omnipotence; the other is fear. Strange bedfellows to be sure, but have you noticed the most well-armed nations and individuals with the largest arsenals are the most nervous and fearful of all? They are constantly looking over their shoulders at potential adversaries and wondering if they have enough arms. Haven't you heard that China is *our potential enemy*? "Perfect love casts out fear," the Scriptures say, but it is also true that an inordinate fear of other people destroys one's capacity to love or trust, or even think clearly.

I once met a man in a sandwich shop in Richmond who had a gun strapped to his leg. I ventured, "You must be afraid of somebody?" He replied, "You're damn right, I'm afraid of somebody and I'm going to get him before he gets me." His weapon did not put him at ease.

The NRA frequently counsels "our best and most responsible citizens are those who are armed." Some of them call their guns, "peacemakers" and ask sarcastically, "Can America be 'too safe'?" "Can my home and children be 'too secure'?" Those who are buying the most guns already have large private arsenals.

Walter Wink calls the readiness of gundamentalists to use weapons of war on our city streets, "redemptive violence" . . . an oxymoron to be sure. As if violence against any of God's children could, in fact, *be* redemptive. The Gun Empire is skilled at turning the Bible's injunctions against violence and fear of neighbor upside down as they assert what is evil is actually good and what is good is evil. The psalmist may say, "God hates him that loves violence" (Ps 11:5), but they pretend God didn't really mean that and proclaim instead that God blesses *their* violence because the nobility of *their* cause eclipses any possible revulsion. After all, they are protecting "Judeo-Christian values."

We meet their level of chicanery when we learn how far some committed evangelical Christians are willing to go to witness to their faith. Trijicon, Inc. is a defense contracting firm in Wixom, Michigan, that manufactures gun sights for the US Army and Marines. The effectiveness of their

---

11. Wink, *Engaging the Powers*, 13.

products is due to tritium, a radioactive form of hydrogen, which creates light around the target and helps the shooter to better "service the target" (a euphemism for killing).

ABC News reported the company was etching two biblical texts on its Advanced Combat Optical Gun Sight. Both citations referred to light: The first was John 8:12: "Jesus said, "I am the light of the world; he that follows me shall not walk in darkness, but shall have the light of life." The other was 2 Corinthians 4:6: "For God who commanded the light to shine out of darkness, has shined in our hearts to give the light of the knowledge of the glory of God in the face of Jesus Christ."

The etchers assumed Jesus blesses the gun, the gun sight, and the shooter as he services the target that is one of God's precious children. Such blasphemy is rampant within the circles of gun extremists. Throughout the book I call them gundamentalists. Thankfully, after the Associated Press exposed their "Christian witness" voices of protest were raised and the Pentagon stepped in to stop further etchings.[12]

But the idolatry of guns has spread to the faith community where disciples of Jesus Christ seem to have forgotten God favors life, not death, and that guns do not give life; they take it. The fascination and mystique of guns have untold numbers of people who believe God blesses what the Bible says God despises.

The late Richard Shaull, Professor of Ecumenics at Princeton Theological Seminary, observed the only way idols have to meet the challenge of God is to take the very things God's presence calls into question and make gods out of them, ascribing to them a sacred or divine quality of their own, worshiping them and doing everything possible to get others to do the same. In this way, the order they create is identified with an all-powerful and transcendent good; it is something sacred, and is not to be questioned.[13]

When the earliest Americans came to this land, their model for claiming the new territory was ancient Israel's taking "the promised land" from the Hittites, Amorites, Perrazites, Jebusites, Gibeonites, and all the tribes of Canaan. Their violence was *necessary* because they were claiming the land in God's name. Over the years the value of righteous violence took root in Western culture. During the Crusades, European Christians set out to save the infidels. The Reformation in England then took it up. Puritanism

12. Martinez, Rhee, and Schone, "No More Jesus Rifles."

13. Shaull, *Naming the Idols,* 131.

developed the crusading impulse, visualizing a God of violent justice and righteousness, who called on the redeemed to fight in that never-ending battle between the forces of good and evil.[14]

After 9/11, President George W. Bush declared that America "had a calling from beyond the stars to rid the world of evil." His faith in our redemptive violence goaded us into a needless war with Iraq where our fears dictated our response. We could not wait for a mushroom cloud to appear over New York City. We sowed the wind; today we reap whirlwinds all over the globe. I consider that escalation a peculiar characteristic of violence. Whenever we obey its seductive voice, the bloodshed spreads like a virus throughout the world.[15]

When I first heard the words *redemptive violence* my mind leaped back to the village of Ben Tre, Vietnam, from which the Army Officer radioed back to headquarters, "We had to destroy the village in order to save it." Unfortunate, to be sure, but it was a moral necessity.

Redemptive violence is the theology of gundamentalists (their religious ideology is explained in depth in chapter 4). The weapons of gun extremists become absolutes, i.e., *another* god or idol. These are good folk who have been seduced by an idol masquerading as an Ultimate Good. Their motives are exemplary; they want to liberate, redeem, and deliver our society from the bad guys.

Their badges and bumper stickers proclaim their good intentions: "Guns Save Lives." They are proud to carry their guns in public because they consider them salvific. Weapons save not only the household, but neighbors as well, even though many neighbors resent such magnanimity and consider themselves endangered by the zealot's benevolence. In each real or perceived threat, should their first knee-jerk impulse be to look to a gun for security, they will not be able to hear God's command to love one's neighbor. Instead of pursuing the strong biblical admonitions to avoid the shedding of blood, they obey the caveman's impulse to defend oneself against the neighbor, and, if need be, to kill him. Killing neighbors, including family members, is the unintended, yet inevitable consequence of nurturing fears of others who are different.

To believe violence can be redemptive, and an ultimate good, blame must be placed on *the other* for any real or perceived danger. When two Muslim jihadists in San Bernardino, California killed fourteen persons and

14. Jewett, *The Captain America Complex*, 182–83.
15. Albright, *Memo to the President*, 40.

injured twenty-two, many elected leaders wanted to blame *all* of the world's 1.6 billion Muslims for the terror. The accusations extended to three-year-old Syrian orphans who were banned from entering the United States, as well as other children who had been tortured by ISIS.

The cartoon character Pogo was famous for saying, "We have met the enemy and he is us." Pogo's humble assessment and willingness to see his own contradictions, ambiguities, and sins is a biblically sound approach in conflict situations. On the other hand, those who believe in their own "righteous violence" are convinced evil is always *because* of "them," i.e., our enemies, or "those people who are different." Evil is always the bad guy's fault and the only thing that can stop a bad guy with a weapon is a good guy with a better weapon. We will have "peace through superiority in arms."

Having been intimately involved in gun violence prevention for forty-one years, I have heard almost every slogan and argument to defend guns and gun rights. One of the most popular goes something like this: "I grew up around guns. My father always had a gun in the closet. I got my first .22 when I was in high school. My Dad taught me how to shoot it and I learned to respect guns. I don't fear them, I respect them." To be frank, America's gun deaths are not because we lack *respect* for guns. We have through the ceiling numbers of gun deaths because far too many people *revere* their guns. In short, weapons for millions of Americans have morphed into absolute values and false gods.

In 1990, the Presbyterian Church USA (PCUSA) issued a warning: "The religious community must take seriously *the risk of idolatry* that could result from an unwarranted fascination with guns that overlooks or ignores the social consequences of their misuse."[16] The message was clear. All guns are not idols; nor are all gun owners guilty of idolatry. Nor are all gun owners gun zealots. I, myself, have been a gun owner since 1958. But, millions who claim one of the Abrahamic faiths have added guns to their godhead. They have placed their ultimate trust in firearms and dismissed God's command to love neighbor, stranger, and enemy. They bow before the Second Amendment and reject God's Second Commandment in Exodus 20:4–5: You shall have no other gods before me.

After our most tragic massacres, just what would the Gun Empire have us know? After Charleston, Roanoke, Sandy Hook, Aurora, Tucson, the US Navy Yard, Ft. Hood, Oak Creek, Kansas City, Los Angeles, San Bernardino,

---

16. Presbyterian Church in the United States of America, 202nd General Assembly, 640.

Chicago, Columbine, Virginia Tech, and Orlando? What do they want us to learn after experiencing a massacre every single day in 2015? Just this: "If students, teachers, or citizens had been armed these tragedies (or the extent of them) would never have happened." In short, gundamentalists want us to believe the solution to America's pandemic of gun violence is to have more guns in the hands of more people. As the NRA says, "The only thing that will stop a bad guy with a gun is a good guy with a gun."[17]Although mass shootings represent only 1.5 percent of all those killed with guns, with suicides being the largest category, the horror of mass shootings get far more publicity and create the fear that drives people to gun stores.

The unthinkable and *despicable violence* of terrorists, criminals, rapists, child molesters, and mass shooters can be stopped only with the *redemptive violence* of the "good guys." Like the Lone Ranger of my youth, today's concealed carry good guys will have the magic silver bullet to put an end to violence once and for all. The "straight shooters" and "good guys" will always win. That's what Tom Mix told me seventy years ago and I believed him. Wayne La Pierre and his minions still offer this counsel. This is the essence of violence; the essence of idolatry; it is the essence of gundamentalism . . . the belief that we can shoot our way to peace.

Jim Wallis of *Sojourners* critiques good and bad guy theology. "The world is not full of good people and bad people. Each human being is both good and bad. And when we are bad or isolated or angry or furious or vengeful or politically agitated or confused or lost or deranged or unhinged, and we can easily get a gun, our society is in great danger."[18]

Good guys also make mistakes; good guys have accidents like dozens of arms instructors who accidentally shoot clients attending their self-defense courses every year. And good guys can totally misread chaos. Joe Zamudio of Tucson was armed and in the crowd when Congresswoman Gabby Giffords was shot and six others were killed. Zamudio drew his gun and later confessed he "almost fired at the man" who finally tackled Jared Loughner when he paused to insert a new magazine in his gun.[19]

Consider the New York City Police, who are required to spend many hours on firing ranges to maintain their proficiency. When they shoot at subjects who do not fire back, the average hit ratio is 30 percent. During

17. Motoko, "NRA Envisions."

18. Theocracy Watch, "The Rise of the Religious Right in the Republican Party." http://www.theocracywatch.org.

19. Wallis, "Bush's Theology of Empire," 20–26.

gunfights when the subject fires back, their hit ratio is 18 percent.[20] Would one more good guy with a gun and *with little or no training on the firing range* provide better security? As an aside, let's not forget the NRA consistently opposes *requiring* training for handgun purchasers, calling it a needless mandate. Behind that is the conviction that *big government* has no business telling any citizen what to do with their private property.

Gun violence has changed the character of our country. In my childhood in Detroit, neighbors took walks and sat on their porches at night as children played in the streets. Those are not society's norms today. Children don't play near open windows in many neighborhoods; often they don't even go to playgrounds. Frequently, they fear going to school because other kids bring guns. How could it be otherwise when our Congress and too many clergy think the best thing they can do is keep the families of gun victims in their thoughts and prayers instead of turning heaven and earth in the name of God to stop such madness from happening again?

While verbally scorning violence, our nation has accepted its escalation as inevitable. Like lemmings we submissively adapt and change our norms. We learn to live with the increased tensions violence brings. We psychologically inoculate ourselves against the presence of more powerful guns and the frequency of mass shootings. Violence no longer horrifies us; it only makes us a little more nervous. If you are not tense these days, you're probably not well.

Today, America is *the only nation* in the developed, industrialized world that has huge numbers of gun deaths every day and every year. It's not because people in other cultures similar to our own are more loving or kinder than we. There is another reason and it's a very simple one. Citizens of these countries cannot get their hands on the guns their governments issue to their militaries.

Should they have the same easy access to firearms, they would suffer the same level of injuries and deaths. They would hear gunshots in the night; their children would fear being shot at school; they too would grieve over drive-by shootings and mass killings. Angry, fired workers would "go postal" and kill entire office staffs; there would be road-rage murders on the *autobahn;* they'd spend enormous amounts of money for medical bills of paraplegics and incarceration for the shooters.

We are not meaner or more violent than citizens of other nations. They watch the same violent movies and programs on TV, play the same video

20. Dahl, "Empire State Building Shooting."

games, see the same violence in the news. They, too, have large numbers of the mentally ill who are dangerous. The *only* difference between Americans and the rest of the citizens of the developed world is that *anybody* in the United States can get a powerful gun *at any time and for any reason.* Gundamentalists call that "freedom."

Do you think it strange the citizens of other advanced nations keep insisting they are happy, fulfilled, and *free?* Are they delusional? Is it a miracle their homes and streets *are* safe? America should be so blessed and so free!

QUESTIONS

1. What people or experiences have influenced your view of violence? Have you participated in or been the victim of violence?

2. Has the level of gun violence in America curtailed any activities for you or changed how you or your family lives day-to-day? Do you carry a gun? Why or why not?

3. How do you explain the theory of redemptive violence? Do you see examples of redemptive violence in America working successfully today?

4. If you live in or travel to an open carry state, have you encountered someone carrying a gun in public? What was your initial reaction? Do persons carrying guns in your presence make you feel safe?

5. Do you agree or disagree with Atwood's statement that people in other countries would have just as many gun deaths as we do if they had the same access to guns?

3

Swimming in Guns

According to the FBI, the best guesstimates of the numbers of guns in America are in the neighborhood of 350,000,000.[1] We have every kind of gun you can imagine. We have rifles, shotguns, sawed-off shotguns, machine guns, guns that will launch grenades, and .50 mm rifles that can shoot a round five miles or bring down an airliner, as Barrett Manufacturing Company boasted in an advertisement. We have what the NRA was the first to name "an assault rifle" that can, with the help of an extended magazine, shoot over 100 bullets a minute. We have tons of revolvers, derringers, and pistols of every kind. We have .22 calibers, .38 calibers, .40 calibers, .45 calibers, .380 calibers, .357 calibers, .32 calibers, and .25 calibers. But the Cadillac of calibers is the 9 mm.

Every year, gunfire ends 33,000 lives and another 70,000 people are injured. My state, Virginia, along with fourteen others, reports more gun deaths than deaths from automobile accidents.[2]

Three hundred and fifty million guns make me nervous. I'm uneasy about that many guns because each gun is made to kill. I respect guns . . . always have, but I also have a healthy fear of them. There is a lot of Starbuck in me. Starbuck, you remember, was Captain Ahab's first mate on the whaling ship, the *Pequod*, in Herman Melville's *Moby-Dick*. His ultimate responsibility was to heave a harpoon into the largest creature in the animal

---

1. Ross, "In Gun Control Debate, Imposed Access Control is Best Short-Term Solution."

2. Samuels, "Gun Deaths Versus Car Deaths."

kingdom. A wounded whale could easily crush him and all his men, or in an instant, pull their boat down into the depths of the sea. Starbuck knew the hazards and said, "I will have no man in my boat who is not afraid of the whale." To have a healthy fear of something that can crush you in the twinkling of an eye is not cowardly. It is wise; that is if you want to see tomorrow's sunrise.

Have you noticed many enthusiastic gun owners cannot bear to say they fear guns? They prefer the mantra, "I don't fear guns; I respect them." Well, so do I, but there is a thin line between respect and fear. The psalmist says, "The fear of the Lord is the beginning of wisdom." I believe it wise to keep a respectable distance from the one who holds the power of life and death over you. It is equally wise to be wary of a gun that can take your life. I have seen with my own eyes what guns can do, and I've personally witnessed the heartache they can bring. Guns are made to kill. There are only two exceptions: a starter's pistol for track events that will fire only blanks and a gun that is disabled.

As a grandfather I fear for my grandchildren and great-grandchildren and the society they will inherit because of this glut of firearms. It is not so much there will be X number of guns out there in the future, but rather, there will be X number of guns out there *without any sensible regulations* placed upon them or to keep them out of dangerous hands. Even today we have a gun for every man, woman, and child with hundreds of thousands left over. Only a few regulations exist, even for the owner's safety. We have reached a national saturation point for guns. If firearms died along with their owners we would not have as large a problem. But guns do not die. Their lifespans are measured in decades, generations, even centuries. Thousands of them will be used by the desperate to take their own lives and others who are angry will use them to take the lives of others.

In 2013 US gun manufacturers produced 10.9 million firearms.[3] The following year, 2014, 3,625,268 guns were imported from foreign companies.[4] It won't be long until our country and my grandchildren are trying to live peaceably with *half a billion guns* on our streets and in our homes. Many will be just lying around like yesterday's newspaper or hung up on a wall somewhere. Experience tells us too many things will go wrong.

3. Ingraham, "There Are Now More Guns Than People In the U.S."

4. www.statista.com/statistics/215644/number-of-imported-firearms-into-the-US-by-country.

"I am a responsible gun owner," says Steve Elliott, who confesses he bears some responsibility for the murders at Umpqua Community College in Oregon. He then reflects how after every mass shooting at a college campus, at a movie theatre, in an elementary school, or whenever—someone from the NRA or some other gun rights group, or someone in Congress or running for President, goes on TV and says we can't fund federal studies on gun violence or have universal background checks of gun buyers or do anything that even hints of gun control because it infringes on the rights of responsible gun owners. Such reflections prompted Elliott to disassemble his gun and send the proper paperwork to the state to report it "destroyed."

"My gun is being used to argue against doing anything to even try to reduce gun violence in the nation. That's what being a responsible gun owner means now—I'm responsible. . . . I want to think I'm *not* a party to America's gun violence, but I can't." He proceeds to give the reasons why he *bears a portion of responsibility for our nation's gun violence*: "My grandmother shot and killed herself with a gun, a few years ago my father shot and almost killed himself with one. A family friend lost a teenaged son in an accidental shooting while he and his friends were playing with a gun, and the husband of one of my sister's coworkers was killed in a mass shooting by a guy carrying three of them. And now it's time for responsible gun owners to help end it."[5]

In the following pages I describe some of the reasons why America's overwhelming number of guns, along with its patchwork of absurd laws that protect firearms instead of people, puts our entire nation at risk. Our collective arsenals are growing daily and include literally thousands of models of guns from the famous Russian Kalashnikov Assault Rifle with twenty models, to Crickett guns, made exclusively for small children four to ten years of age, with thirty-six different models the kids can choose from. We are in the midst of an arms race with no foreseeable end, and it will inevitably lead to thousands more unnecessary deaths.

Even though we are armed to the teeth, the American people do not feel safe. Does anyone really disagree with that? With incalculable numbers of unregulated firearms hanging on walls, stored in dressers, bedside stands, gun safes, glove compartments, attics, and garages, as well as in the stockpiles of militias that are always happy to welcome another racist recruit, we live in a nation awash with guns.

5. Elliott, "Why I Destroyed My Handgun."

They are maiming and killing at unprecedented levels. Grandpa and Uncle Bubba died, but the guns they left behind in their wills are being passed down from generation to generation and will be a part of America for decades, even centuries, no matter what laws might pass tomorrow. These old guns still work well and many of them, originally purchased for protection of the family, are being used in 20,000 suicides per year.

No one knows exactly how many firearms are owned by private citizens in the United States. The FBI estimated recently that one in four people owned one or more guns. According to a Gun Industry trade association, each gun owner has an average of eight guns.[6]

As family members and friends die by the very guns purchased for security, we keep producing and buying more. This constitutes a crisis. But, a crisis need not be a death knell. That is, not unless we choose it. When Grandpa has a heart attack and a doctor tells the family the next twenty-four hours will determine whether he lives or dies, *that* is a crisis. It has a verifiable "turning point" that can be either for good or ill.

The Japanese word for crisis: *kiki,* is instructive. It is comprised of two Chinese characters. One means "danger," the other, "opportunity." My prayer is that sooner, rather than later, Americans will see our crisis in the sheer numbers of guns, as an opportunity to put in place realistic, sensible laws that respect two Constitutional rights: the right to keep and bear arms and the right to live with domestic tranquility, free of gun violence. That is *not* an insurmountable task. It is a realistic hope. We do not have to live as we are today, especially if we want a better tomorrow and have the wisdom to respond to God's heartfelt invitation in Isaiah 1:18: "Come, let us reason together." The God whom the psalmist says in Psalm 11:5, "hates the one who loves violence" wants us to accept one another, understand one another, love one another, and live in peaceful communities.

DEFENSIVE GUNS—AMERICA'S SECURITY BLANKET

The Canadian author, journalist, and former soldier A. J. Somerset has given North Americans a good look into the power of the media as well as the NRA in molding gun culture. Somerset is a gun lover, but is "disgusted with what our gun culture has become." His explanation means, of course, he is *not* a gun zealot, but a responsible gun owner who seeks reasonable solutions to our gun pandemic.

6. Osnos, "Making a Killing," 36.

He says, "Spend enough time in front of the tube and you'll come down with *the mean world syndrome,* the conviction that the world is a nasty, dangerous place filled with cruel predators, whose life purpose is to do you harm. Television news that relies on drama, but provides little background or context for the events it reports, is the vector for the mean world parasite. The more sensationalist the stories, the stronger the effect. People who like shocking stories are predisposed to distrust humanity, and the stories they watch feed that predisposition. Keep your eyes on the tube and you'll soon be scared silly."[7]

Machismo, however, makes it difficult for armed citizens to admit fear. Somerset writes, "True Men are not afraid. Fear is an emotional state, and men pride themselves on being rational creatures, devoid of emotion, whatever evidence there is to the contrary. It's unmanly to admit you're afraid to walk to the corner store after dark, past that apartment parking lot where some guy was stabbed two—or was it three?—years ago. To suggest that fear of crime promotes handgun sales, 'is to attack traditional masculinity.' Nevertheless, macho men cling to their defensive guns as children latch onto their security blankets."[8]

Purchasing a handgun automatically conveys two conflicting emotions to the owner. The first is omnipotence and the overpowering feeling, "I am now in control of my life and I have power over the evil intentions of others who may want to harm me or my family." This imagined control is what many gundamentalists call "security" and is the basic reason why men buy handguns. Security and trying to be in control in our out-of-control world is one of humanity's greatest illusions, which will be considered in greater depth in chapter 8.

The other emotion fosters an indefatigable fear of enemies who might want to remove this sense of sovereignty or belief in omnipotence. The belief in the *mean world syndrome* grows into paranoia. At every turn one is beset by fearful images of Muslims, immigrants, gays, socialists, and liberals, all plotting to tear us down and abolish our way of life along with one of the most dreaded fears of all—*big government,* which wants to take away all our guns leaving us *defenseless before the bad guys.*

Someone has rightly said, "there is nothing so dangerous as a bad idea with a gun in hand." Purchasing a defensive gun for personal security is really a bad idea. For the most part, it does not work the way one expects. A

7. Somerset, *Arms,* 205.

8. Ibid., 207.

defensive gun sounds as if it will provide security and safety for its owner, but FBI statistics and numerous research studies show this is pure fantasy. In addition to scientific data, the ineffectiveness of defensive guns to protect us is contrary to what God teaches us about life in Holy Scripture. Feverishly striving for security on this earth is one of humanity's greatest delusions. One of my clergy friends insists, "Security is the world's biggest con game."

Since the seventies American gun deaths have never dipped below 32,000, which has become a standard numerical reference point, although 33,000 were killed last year. It is ironic and sad that more than half of that number are suicides, where people used instruments originally purchased for protection.

In addition, firearm accidents occur daily. Donna Williamson, a civil magistrate in Columbia, South Carolina, because of the nature of her job, applied for and received a concealed carry license. On June 9, 2008, she took her four-year-old granddaughter shopping at Sam's Club and placed her in the shopping cart. When her back was turned, the child got into her grandmother's purse, pulled out her loaded small-caliber handgun and shot herself in the chest. Fortunately, the bullet missed her major organs and the child recovered after surgery. Would that all such accidents had happy endings, but alas.[9]

The magistrate was an intelligent, law-abiding gun owner, but just like the rest of us, was subject to the distractions of everyday life that often lead to serious lapses in judgment. No one plans on accidents, or distractions. She believed her gun would protect her and her family. That's why she bought it, but in the end, its bullet came within centimeters of killing her precious granddaughter. If this were an isolated incident, we would not be discussing a problem that is endemic to America. This is *not* a problem for the rest of the industrialized, developed nations of the world. Can you imagine living in such a place? These people, also firm believers in freedom and democracy, cannot understand why America permits ninety gun deaths every single day. Frankly, I don't understand it either. It's way beyond me as to why we, an otherwise intelligent people, permit it.

What I do know is *we do not have to live this way*. But, at present, reasoned dialogue to reduce our pandemic of gun deaths has not taken hold in America. Nearly 1.7 million kids under the age of eighteen live in homes with firearms that are loaded and unlocked, ostensibly to better

9. Moore et al., "Charges Likely for Grandmother in Sam's Club Shooting."

protect the family.[10] Children, inquisitive by nature, explore their homes. If they discover a gun in a dresser or closet, *even if they have been told not to touch it,* frequently pick it up and pull the trigger, killing or injuring themselves, a playmate, or someone else nearby. For the safety of all concerned, responsible gun owners should, at a minimum, apply a trigger lock when the gun is not in use.

Because of the increasing numbers of guns in our homes, when our kids are invited to play at the neighbor's house, parents, grandparents, caregivers, and babysitters must realize the threat guns pose to our children. Before they go off to play at the neighbors, we *must* ask "Is there a gun in your home?" If the answer is yes, a follow up question is necessary: "Does it have a trigger lock?" One of my colleagues had a twelve-year-old son killed by his best friend. When he went over to his house to play, he showed him his father's new gun. He never came home. My friend offers some advice: "If you think it's hard to ask your neighbor if there is a gun in the house, trust me, picking out your child's casket is harder."

Below are several different genres of guns that help push our numbers of firearms over the 350,000,000 plateau. You can obtain any one you want, and most of them are as easy to get as a quarter pounder at McDonald's.

CHILDREN'S GUNS

Just as Chevrolet's goal is to sell as many Chevy cars and trucks as possible, the gun industry is compelled to sell as many guns as it can. Is there a better way to ensure brand loyalty for future gun sales than to start the buyers off when they are children with a real gun of their own?

The booming market for guns and accessories for women seems to have leveled out, but Keystone Sporting Arms (KSA) in Pennsylvania has found a lucrative niche, marketing and selling its .22 rifles for children between the ages of four and ten. They are custom made for little arms to hold, aim, and fire. Their stocks are painted baby blue for little boys and hot pink for girls. Gun-loving parents and gundamentalists call them "cute," except these kids are holding lethal weapons. Many kids and families can tell their heartrending stories written on death certificates.

They are called "Crickett" and "Chipmunk" rifles, with the cherished slogan that makes children so proud: "My First Rifle." They are available in thirty-six different models with varying barrel and stock designs. The

10. Kraft, "National ASK Day Promotes Children's Gun Safety."

overall length is thirty inches; the weight, approximately three pounds. They can easily be fitted with telescopic sights and other accessories.

Business has boomed since the company's start-up in 1996. According to a 2010 industry report, the company is now the number ten long gun manufacturer in the United States. It started nineteen years ago with four employees and produced four thousand rifles; by 2008 it grew to seventy employees and an output of sixty thousand rifles a year for little boys and girls.

Staying abreast of the market, KSA introduced a single shot .22 hunter pistol in 2009 and a new twenty-gauge, bolt-action shotgun in February 2010. They assure customers that ideas for new guns will continue to evolve. Naturally, they have large hopes that the children who are thrilled with a real gun of their own will turn into lifelong customers as they "put away childish things" and purchase other guns including the big-ticket item: a semi-automatic pistol.

I believe four years of age is much too young for any child to have a gun of their own. Unfortunately, a Virginia State Senate Committee voted down legislation to keep lethal guns away from four-years-olds. They considered it a threat to "impose an arbitrary minimum age at which a person would be allowed to receive firearms training."[11] The same committee advanced bills that would create a lifetime Concealed Carry Weapon Permit (CCWP).

A case in point: on April 30, 2013, inside a rural Kentucky home, a five-year-old boy accidentally shot and killed his two-year-old sister while playing with the .22-caliber single-shot Crickett rifle he received as a gift the year before. (Was it under the Christmas tree?) The children's mother was outside the house when the shooting took place and had no idea the gun was loaded.

The coroner, Gary White, came to the house and heard the child say, "It's a Crickett. It's a little rifle for a kid." White observed, "The little boy was used to shooting the little gun which was kept in a corner, and the family did not realize a shell had been left in it. . . Just one of those crazy accidents." The shooting was ruled "accidental," and no charges were filed.[12]

11. Nolan, "Senate Panel Votes Down Gun Control Bills."

12. Ward, "Five year-old boy accidently shoots, kills 2-year-old sister in Cumberland County."

HANDGUNS FOR THE HANDICAPPED

If one has arthritis or other physical ailments and lacks the strength to pull the trigger of an ordinary firearm, there are alternatives so one can have a gun at one's disposal. One choice is to purchase the Palm Pistol. It is an ergonomically innovative single-shot self-defense firearm chambered in a .38 special that may be held in either hand without regard to orientation of the stock. It is an adaptive aid intended for seniors, the disabled, or others with grip limitations due to weak hand strength, lack of manual dexterity, or phalangeal amputations. The zero bore axis eliminates muzzle rise during firing and directs recoil forces directly into the palm. It can be fired using the thumb or combinations of other fingers.

The industry says "the Palm Pistol features a design which seniors *need* [italics mine] to assist them in their daily living. Using the thumb instead of the index finger for firing significantly reduces muzzle drift, which is one of the principal causes of inaccurate targeting." Sales are restricted to United States citizens and resident aliens as permitted by law.[13]

3-D PRINTER GUNS

Some of the nation's guns are brand new genres of firearms that are close to being available. What is the meaning of "close"? It could be ten years or one. Who knows? But their schematics are on the drawing boards of gun loving entrepreneurs.

In 1988, serious attempts were made to manufacture and sell inexpensive plastic handguns that were undetectable by airport security machines. The CSGV called them "Hijacker Specials." Miraculously, the US Congress, back then, acted to ban these firearms. Perhaps they feared for their lives because the Capitol was "protected" by the same security machines used at airports. The Undetectable Firearms Act (UFA) requires at least 3.7 ounces of steel to be in every firearm manufactured or carried into the country.

A few years ago, when Cody Wilson, a twenty-five-year-old law student in Texas said he was going to print a gun, nobody took him seriously. But then, he actually printed one that fired real bullets. Thereafter, lots of people started printing and firing guns that were made on 3-D printers.[14]

13. www.palmpistol.com.
14. Estes, "3-D Printer Guns Are Only Getting Better and Scarier."

In 2013, Congress reauthorized the UFA, but not before industrialists had actually created plastic guns and distributed blueprints and schematics and printed them on 3-D printers. These miraculous instruments are today widely available and all sorts of people can create unimaginable products, including guns made of plastic *as well as steel,* just by pressing *print.* No, this is not science fiction. Some of these new guns have been printed within the Texas Legislature.[15]

I can barely get my mind around a machine printing a gun. Further, it's beyond my comprehension that supposedly brilliant people are not horrified, but ecstatic, over its potential. Maybe Einstein saw it all coming when he predicted, "The world will have a generation of idiots when technology surpasses our human interaction."[16]It is not that entrepreneurs like Cody Wilson aren't smart; they are incredibly smart, but they are not what the Scriptures call "wise" and apparently they are incapable of recognizing the demonic.

As 3-D printed guns have recently evolved from a kind of science-fictional experiment into a subculture, they faced a monumental problem. Plastic isn't the best material to contain an explosive blast. That was solved by Michael Crumling, a twenty-five-year-old machinist from York, Pennsylvania, who developed a round designed specifically to be fired from 3-D printed guns. His ammunition uses a thicker steel shell with a lead bullet inserted an inch inside, deep enough that the shell can contain the explosion of the round's gunpowder instead of transferring that force to the plastic body or barrel of the gun. Crumling says that allows a home-printed firearm made from even the cheapest materials to be fired again and again without cracking or deformation. While his design isn't easily replicated because the rounds must be individually machined for now, it may represent another step towards durable, practical, printed guns—even semi-automatic ones.[17] It is hard to stuff the genie back into the bottle or the printer, but all of us are asking, "Will the U. S. Congress come down harder on these undetectable plastic weapons and their steel cousins by banning this 3-D gun technology?" To convince Congress to act could be a tough sell. At the 2015 NRA Convention a huge banner was displayed

15. Smith, "Gun Rights Advocates to Build Weapons at Capitol."

16. Mount, "Was Einstein Right?"

17. Greenberg, "The Bullet That Could Make a 3-D Printed Gun a Practical Deadly Weapon."

that obviously was intended more for timid Congresspersons than its own members. The banner read, "If they can ban one, they can ban them all."

BUILDING YOUR OWN AR-15

There are still more ways to get a gun. We cannot forget the guy who is "good with his hands" and boasts, "I can build anything." Can a handyman like that make his own gun? Yes! He can even assemble his own AR-15 assault rifle, considered one of the world's most deadly guns, right in his own workshop. No license is required to self-assemble a firearm, as long as it is not sold to make a profit. (Even if these are "good guys," the temptation to sell them and make a few extra bucks would always be there.) Cody Wilson of 3-D printer fame calls these guns, "ghost guns."

With the growth of 3-D printing, making gun parts has become easier. Now, with Wilson's recent release of a low-cost home milling machine, most any handyman in the neighborhood can anonymously turn out what is called a "stripped receiver," the one essential piece of a gun that enables it to fire. It is also the piece where manufacturers stamp a serial number. So with a self-made receiver with no serial numbers it is completely untraceable by law enforcement. Just what law enforcement needs to fight crime, right?[18]

THE SLIDE FIRE GUN

"Progress is good," said Ogden Nash, "but it went on too long." No industry has made more progress in research and development toward manufacturing more efficient and destructive products than America's gun industry, and it's all legal. Attempts have been made by legislatures, faith communities, and peace groups to temper our human capacity to harm or kill one another, but they are seldom successful. Alas, in the words of Thoreau, we have grown to be more and more "the tools of our tools."[19]

In 1933, as law enforcement battled organized crime, Congress declared machine guns were illegal in the United States. But that was then and this is now. Are you surprised that someone in research and development discovered a loophole in the law that permits a new kind of gun to be

18. Kerr, "Ghost Gunner Lets People Make Untraceable Homemade Guns."

19. Thoreau, *Walden*, 30.

developed, manufactured, and sold? It is called a Slide Fire gun and is, in effect, *a legal machine gun.*

A. J. Somerset *describes* its operation: the Slide Fire stock (of an assault rifle) allows controlled "bump firing" using the recoil of the weapon to rapidly manipulate the trigger. The gun is able to recoil independently of the stock and pistol grip, so that if the shooter pushes forward on the gun's forearm and keeps his trigger finger in position, the cycle of recoil and recovery will repeatedly fire the gun as if it were fully automatic. Since the law defines a machine gun as a weapon that fires repeatedly as long as the trigger is depressed, this design slips through a legal loophole and is considered a semi-automatic gun. Canadian legislators have made it illegal. But we live in the United States, and the gun goes "boom." Of course, it is legal to the delight of every gundamentalist.[20]

TASER AND STUN GUNS

The general public assumes that a stun gun and a Taser are the same. Not so. A stun gun shoots an arc of electricity toward the target. A Taser, while also an electrical apparatus, is more powerful and shoots an electrically charged projectile at the target. Some people describe it as a miniature electric spear gun that can penetrate clothing. Civilians can easily purchase either gun, including the less powerful models of Tasers. Models of the latter, used by law enforcement, deliver a much stronger electrical charge, are effective at longer ranges, and can be shot at higher rates of speed. Civilians can legally own the more advanced Taser models as well, but only with specialized training. Taser guns deliver much more than an electric shock. Just one shot from a Taser can deliver fifty thousand volts of electricity to immobilize an individual.

Tasers can be lethal if used repeatedly on the same person. Mr. Linwood Lambert, Jr., a forty-seven-year-old African American, died in South Boston, Virginia, shortly after three white police officers shot him with Taser guns twenty times within a thirty-minute period. Each of the officers were promoted after this confrontation with Lambert, who was acting irrationally after a cocaine overdose. The incident is finally receiving attention by the Justice Department. Federal guidelines stress that anyone shot repeatedly by stun guns or Tasers get medical attention immediately. Mr. Lambert received none and was heard to ask the officers, "Why are you

---

20. Somerset, *Arms,* xv.

trying to kill me, man?"[21] Amnesty International reports that over a seven-year period in the 2000s, 334 people died in the United States after being shot by police using stun guns; many more have died since then.[22]

Matthew Ajibade was shot only once by a Taser in Savannah, Georgia, on January 1, 2015, by the police and died in his jail cell. It was another example of excessive force by law enforcement. He was handcuffed and his ankles were bound at the time he was shot in a "drive-stun mode" (i.e. where the device is pressed against the body and fired causing great pain). As of November 27, 2015, police nationwide killed forty-eight individuals with Tasers. More than half of those shot suffered from mental illness or had illegal drugs in their system. Fifty-five percent were minorities. But this is the only incident where an officer was indicted. *If a gun is available, it seems there is a strong belief that it should be used.*[23]

At an October 2015, Summit "Subverting the Gospel of Guns" at Andover-Newton Theological Seminary in Boston, Assistant Boston Police Chief Michael Hennessey held up a Taser that was cleverly designed to look like a cellphone. He said, "This is the most popular item for gangs on the streets of Boston; this particular model sells for $13.00."

Disguising a firearm is not a new idea. The Spy Museum in Washington, D.C., displays all manner of guns that are disguised as canes, pens, beepers, etc. John D'Angelo of the ATF says, "As technology progresses and becomes more prevalent, disguised weapons will change to mirror that."[24]

SMART GUNS — SEE CHAPTER 11

IT'S JUST A TOY

For decades, psychologists have written of the long-term harmful effects toy guns and war toys have on children. I agree wholeheartedly and wish the US Congress were as courageous and forward looking as legislators in Sweden and Finland, who banned the sales of toy guns and war toys in their countries. The following paragraphs, however, are not about the risks to children as they learn to be more aggressive by playing with war toys; they

21. Melber, "Man Tased, Shackled, and Driven to Hospital, Dies in Police Custody."

22. Bowerman, "Virginia Man Who Died in Police Custody Tased Repeatedly."

23. Thompson and Berman, "Stun Guns: 'There was just too much use.'"

24. Klimas, "Look Closely: Can You Tell These Cellphones Are Actually Weapons in Disguise?"

are about toy guns and war toys leading to the deaths of scores of children and adults who play with them or use them for dubious purposes in the United States. War toys do not fire, but when toy companies copy their products from real guns down to the last infinite detail, they provoke police to shoot those who are holding or pointing the toys at them.

This is not a new problem. Living in Springfield, Virginia, a Washington, D.C., suburb at the time, I remember a 1988 incident when a District of Columbia college student was killed after he waved and pointed a toy gun at police.[25] That was the year Congress passed laws requiring toy gun manufacturers to place international orange tips in the barrels of toy guns that would distinguish them from real firearms. The NRA and the toy industry teamed up to vigorously fight such legislation. With their friends in Congress they were able to pass amendments to lessen the impact of such a law, in what matters most to them . . . the market. The amendments spelled out exemptions for BB guns, collector replicas, and toys modeled on guns manufactured before 1898.

Would you like to walk with a law enforcement officer who is face-to-face with a child holding a gun that appears to be real and is pointing it menacingly at her or at others on a city street? In those split-seconds when her pulse is racing and she fears for her life, will she wonder if that gun actually is a replica toy gun modeled after a firearm made before 1898?

The NRA and toy company plaintiffs argued that a plastic orange tip would spoil the authentic look *and the market value* of a replica gun. This is but another instance when guns, *even toy guns,* are protected by the Gun Empire, Congress, (and, in this case, the toy industry) while human lives are jeopardized. Can you smell money?

In 2013, the death of a Bay Area boy and the paralysis of a Los Angeles teen—both of whom were shot by law enforcement while carrying replica rifles—were the human faces behind recent state legislation in California that cracked down on the classification and color-coding of toy guns.

In November of 2014, the nation was shocked when a Cleveland policeman shot and killed twelve-year-old Tamir Rice when he mistook his replica toy gun for a real one. In a surveillance video released by the Cleveland Police Department, officers are seen exiting their patrol car and then shooting the boy within two brief seconds.[26] The courts have recently awarded the Rice family six million dollars for this unfortunate event.

25. Kastor, "The Power of Pow: The Debate Rages On."
26. NPR, "Twelve Year-Old Boy Carrying Replica Gun Dies."

Rice's story, unfortunately, is not unique. On August 11, 2014, at a Walmart outside Dayton, Ohio, John Crawford III picked up a pellet rifle that was out of its package and sitting on the shelf. Police rushed into the store in response to a 911 call about a man with a gun. Seconds later, Crawford, twenty-two-years old, was shot and killed by the officers.[27]

State and federal legislation has long sought to curb such shootings by requiring toy gun manufacturers to make their products more clearly distinguishable from real ones. But the effectiveness of such regulations has proven limited, as toys with striking resemblances to real weapons continue to be sold—or police fail to recognize the toy markings when making quick decisions.

Some states, including New York, have recently placed additional regulations on toy guns, where imitation guns are required to have non-removable orange stripes running down both sides of the barrel. But in December 2014, the state Attorney General Eric Schneiderman found that Walmart, Amazon.com, and Kmart were selling toy guns that lacked such markings, and wrote cease-and-desist letters to the companies.[28]

It's revealing for older seniors to reflect on the games we used to play as kids that often featured guns. Cops and robbers and cowboys and Indians were perennial favorites, and, of course, we played war. Another childhood game was stick 'em up. How many times did we sneak up behind a playmate and put a cap gun, or just an index finger in his back, saying, "stick 'em up"?

Today the Commerce Department's Office of Consumer Affairs reports that desperate adults still play stick 'em up. Fifteen percent of robberies involve imitation firearms, or the index finger pointed from within one's pocket that appears to look like a gun. In the past five years police have threatened to use force in 1,100 cases nationwide in which they believed a toy gun was real.[29]

QUESTIONS

1. The FBI estimates that one in four persons own one or more guns, perhaps an average of eight guns. That suggests that three out of four persons do not own guns. In your immediate family—your parents,

27. Gokavi, "Family of Man Shot at Wal-Mart Wants an Answer."
28. Wu, "When Toy Guns Cause Real Harm."
29. Ibid.

siblings, spouse, children—how many guns would you estimate your family owns?

2. Atwood estimates that, at current rates, by 2030 there will be half a billion guns in America. Is there a saturation point for how many guns a society can tolerate? How will climate change and loss of coastal cities interface with this level of an armed population?

3. In this chapter, the story was told of gun owner Steve Elliott, who destroyed his gun because he felt responsible for mass gun violence. Was he responsible? Why or why not?

4. As the varieties of guns evolve with greater firepower should gun regulations evolve as well? Do you have any concerns about the range of guns available now?

5. If you have guns in your home, have you talked to your children about gun safety? Are the comments in this chapter useful for children? Is it a good idea for a play date parent to ask about guns in their home?

4

Gundamentalism

Like a chameleon, America today is changing color. According to US Census Bureau projections, by the year 2018, there will be no ethnic majority among our citizens under eighteen years of age. By the year 2034, no ethic groups will comprise a majority of our population and the super-rich will be living in a different kind of country than the rest of us. As new tribal identities emerge we will be even more divided by economic class.[1]

This is a frightful scenario for many: Caucasians, in particular, fear no longer being in the white majority and unable to lay claim to those accompanying privileges we have unconsciously enjoyed for generations. That is a major reason for much of the unrest and the growth of a new tribe in our country that I call gundamentalism. Although predominantly white, its members are from every race, ethnic background, age, and social class in America. What unites these people is a passionate belief that guns are the answer to their fears and central to their identity and well-being. It is believed that guns will protect them in dangerous situations and from nefarious people and are essential tools for living in peace.

The term *gundamentalism* is not my creation. It was first coined in the late nineties by my valued friend, Rev. Rachel Smith, who served at that time on the board of the Brady Campaign. She is happy to see her coinage resurrected in the context of this book where I describe the beliefs and behaviors of this powerful minority of gun owners who, inch by inch, bit

1. Cooper, "Census Officials, Citing Increasing Diversity, Say U.S. will be a 'Plurality Nation.'"

by bit, and law by law, are promoting "The divine right of guns in America" and are responsible for much of their misuse and bloodshed that is now so commonplace on our city streets.

These passionate believers not only dominate average gun owners, timid legislators in Congress and state assemblies, and faint-hearted clergy who have yet to discover that guns are a religious issue, but they are also leading the American people toward an ominous cliff where we *could* lose our constitutional hope of ever living in "domestic tranquility" with the right to pursue life, liberty, and happiness in a safe community free of gun violence. If we want to keep that hope alive, we must first of all come to grips with what is happening to our communities and democratic institutions because of gundamentalism. Someone has rightly warned us: the lack of awareness is the root of all evil.

The first and only time I saw the word *gundamentalism* in print or used by others in public discourse was when Rachel used it in a Brady publication. However, my editor, Heather Wilson, recently informed me the term has seeped into the American vernacular. She directed me to the Urban Dictionary, which gives anyone who visits their website the right to invent or define any term.

Someone previously defined gundamentalism as: "The worship of guns: a modern religion based on buying, owning, carrying and shooting large numbers of firearms in situations where they are not really necessary."[2]

A gundamentalist is defined by these parts: A) A person who goes beyond the language of the Second Amendment to the US Constitution and takes his or her "unrestricted right to bear arms" as a tenet of religious or quasi-religious faith. B) A haughty gun owner who believes his understanding of the Second Amendment gives him additional rights to harass, slander, defame, and stalk those who disagree with him. C) A gun owner who is willfully ignorant and unwilling to accept differing views of the Second Amendment that come through scientific gun studies and/or court rulings but do not fit his narrative.[3] (I have only tweaked these definitions. Readers will recognize the terms are not included in any authorized English dictionaries.)

The forthrightness of these rough and ready definitions do the public a favor. They cut to the chase and reveal what every American citizen needs to know about gundamentalism and its passionate believers. I am indebted

2. www.urbandictionary.com.
3. Ibid.

to these anonymous individuals, and I trust this book will further expand the public's knowledge of this growing threat to American democracy.

Any belief system that has *"ism"* attached to it inexorably leads to over-indulgence or to a lack of moderation in the expression of one's goals, or the personal behavior of its adherents. Any *"ism"* will steer dedicated proponents to expand their influence in myriads of contexts that are much larger than necessary, or way beyond levels that are even desirable or usable.

This book details such *excess and overreach by this minority* of gun zealots and the larger than life privileges they claim as firm believers in Second Amendment "constitutional rights," and even "divine rights." They are not known for moderation or a readiness to dialogue on how we can reduce 33,000 gun deaths per year; nor are they open to any compromise in their dogma or social behavior. Without embarrassment they profess the solution to gun violence in America is more guns. And what is so troubling about that stance is they consider it totally rational.

Most everything they champion is *larger than necessary, over the top.* Their excesses begin with the insistence that America's freedoms and ultimate values are fully encapsulated and explained in the "divine right to keep and bear arms." They are persuaded the greatness of America is guaranteed as long as we exercise our essential right to keep and bear arms. Our birthright as American citizens itself enables those who "carry" to protect their families and neighbors from harm. Although they consider this an altruistic motive, their ideology, reinforced by heretical understandings of Scripture, is turning our country into an actual shooting gallery.

EXAMPLES OF GUNDAMENTALISM'S OVERREACH:

1. The National Academy of Sciences recently identified the pressing need for up-to-date, accurate information on how many guns there are in the United States, their distribution and types, how many people acquire them, and how they are used.[4]

The NRA and Congress have once again responded by mandating ignorance. Scientific research is to be feared and gundamentalists work very hard to keep the public in the dark about guns and how they are used and misused. Public knowledge about the deaths and injuries guns cause

---

4. Leshner et al., *Priorities for Research to Reduce the Threat of Firearms-Related Violence.*

is a threat to their power. How else can one interpret defunding research on guns by the Center for Disease Control (CDC), the national scientific agency, charged with tabulating all deaths in America from *any* source?

In January 2013, President Obama ordered the CDC once again to study "the causes of gun violence." But, they have not budged. They have done no firearm research since 1996 (i.e., they have not done research or scientific studies on a particular law, policy, or aspect of gun violence to measure its effectiveness in reducing crime or gun deaths with the results made public). Then the NRA accused the agency of promoting gun control (discovering measures that saved lives) and Congress threatened to strip the agency's funding. The CDC's self-imposed ban dried up a much-needed source of funding, which had a chilling effect felt far beyond the agency. Almost no one wanted to pay for gun violence studies, researchers say. Young academics were warned that engaging in research was a good way to kill their careers. Meanwhile, the rare gun study that was published went through linguistic gymnastics to hide significant information. It is an affront to the entire nation for a minority of gun owners to tell a whole community of scientists what aspects of our society they can or cannot study. Nevertheless, these gun zealots believe they possess that kind of authority.[5]

2. A second example of overreach concerns the Florida branch of the National Rifle Association (NRA) that is suing physicians, particularly psychiatrists and psychologists, for asking patients who suffer from depression and/or have suicidal thoughts, if they have a gun in the home. They have also taken pediatricians to court for asking the same question of parents of curious kids. Statistics show most children know where Daddy hides his gun.

The questions themselves did not appear out of the blue. Most physicians know there are twice as many suicides in the country as murders and the most successful method is with a gun. They are also aware ten children and youths die by guns every single day, and most of them were purchased to protect the family. Forty percent of gun owners leave their guns unattended—just lying around the house loaded and unlocked. The NRA, on the other hand, contends asking about a gun in the home is an inappropriate medical question and constitutes political harassment, and is disparaging of guns and gun rights.

5. Frankel, "Why The CDC Still Isn't Researching Gun Violence Despite the Ban Being Lifted Two Years Ago."

The need for such inquiries is made clear when four toddlers in one week shot and killed themselves with guns they found in their homes.[6]

These NRA suits constitute a crisis for those who live with chronic depression and for medical professionals who provide services to them. Such unconscionable obstruction of established medical practices and cessation of funding for gun deaths research are bringing us to the place where so called "gun rights" could, in fact, serve as the determining factor in how doctors can practice medicine in the United States.

Another example of the excesses of gundamentalism is observed when absolute control of the gun market is challenged. By the end of the nineties, several gun manufacturers had been sued and were feeling the financial pinch. One of them was Smith and Wesson and its CEO, Ed Shultz. For "a business survival strategy" as well as to lessen the numbers of gun deaths, Shultz entered into secret negotiations with the Clinton Administration's Secretary of Housing and Urban Development, Andrew Cuomo. The two met over a six weeks period after which Shultz agreed to manufacture a "smart gun" that could be fired only by its owner and to take steps to prevent dealers from selling their products to criminals. What was then the most egregious of these arrangements for the Gun Empire is not specified.

On March 17, 2000, Clinton and Cuomo announced the company would develop a smart gun and take steps to prevent dealers from selling firearms to criminals." Cuomo declared, "We're finally on the way to a safer, more peaceful America." The NRA denounced Smith and Wesson as "the first gun maker to surrender"; released Shultz's telephone number, and encouraged members to complain. He received numerous death threats with one caller saying, "I'm a dead-on shot, Mr. Shultz." Other executives started wearing bullet-proof vests as gun buyers boycotted any and all products from Smith and Wesson. In ten months the company was sold for a fraction of its former worth. Gundamentalists who lead the Gun Empire drive a hard bargain.[7]

Issuing death threats is considered an option for certain zealots when they are frustrated and angry. Even those of us who work for the sole purpose of preventing gun deaths and injuries are well aware of their schemes. One of my female friends who recruited many moms for the Million Mom March in 2000 received more than a few threats upon her life. When she continued her work, the death threats increased and finally were redirected

6. Healy et al., "One Week in April Four Toddlers Shot and Killed Themselves."

7. Osnos, "Making a Killing," 40–41.

on her children's lives. I call that *excessive. What do you call it? . . . "over the top," "cowardly," "un-American"?*

Death threats have also been sent to gun dealers who announced they would sell "smart guns" when they were put on the market. They are a new genre of guns that would surely save lives, but they are anathema to hardcore gundamentalists who want zero changes to the status quo.[8]

Responsible and rational gun owners do not send death threats to those who disagree with them; that is the work of committed gundamentalists. Needless to say, those of us who oppose the excesses of gundamentalism in word and deed, do not respond in kind, nor do we say much about their threats. It is psychologically and spiritually impossible to devote time and energy building safer communities to enhance the dignity of each human life, to threaten to kill those who oppose us. That is not who we are or what we are about.

This unique American "religious cult" that claims God's blessings on guns and gun rights had an enormous growth in power and influence shortly after the dramatic events of 1977, when the erstwhile NRA, devoted to marksmanship, sportsmanship, and a love for the outdoors, was dethroned in a *coup d'état* at the National Convention of the NRA in Cincinnati. Their new selling point, which is still in vogue, became "firepower." The coup's leaders couldn't pass up a magnificent financial opportunity to sell handguns to people who were afraid.

Their new leaders included Wayne La Pierre, who quickly became the mouthpiece for the Gun Industry, which was even then retooling its factories from turning out rifles, shotguns, and sporting guns, to supply frightened Americans with the kinds of firearms they most wanted in an anxious time: efficient handguns. Today the Gun Industry's annual revenue is in the neighborhood of $13.5 billion.[9]

The seventies themselves bring to mind the poisonous atmosphere that reeked with violence: Vietnam, the Cold War, the threat of nuclear annihilation, the Air Force flying 24/7 toward the Soviet Union with nuclear bombs and Poseidon submarines armed with multiple reentry vehicles in all the world's oceans, while home builders designed recreation rooms that could double as bomb shelters. And, closer to home were race riots in our largest cities. The whole nation was anxious and afraid, which meant

8. *Washington Post,* "Straight Shooting."

9. www.newsmax.com/Finance/StreetTalk/gun-stocks-shooting-profits/2015/12/03/ ID/704450/Dec 3, 2015.

the Gun Empire was happy and thriving. It is even happier today selling millions of weapons advertised as "security" and "peacemakers." What the empire lacked, however, was what it most needed . . . The aura of a divine blessing on their industry and on what their guns were made to do, i.e., kill other human beings.

Gundamentalism filled that vacuum by latching onto and extolling "a divine right to keep and bear arms." The first official in the Gun Empire to realize the power inherent in claiming God's blessings on the industry and on people's Divine right to kill, was NRA Executive Warren Cassidy. He implored all Americans to be more deferential to the NRA. Cassidy said: "You would get a far better understanding of the NRA if you approached us as if you were approaching one of the great religions of the world."[10]

Nor did Charlton Heston, of *Ten Commandments* fame, miss his opportunity to venerate cold steel and a beautiful rifle stock. After his first convention speech as NRA President in Philadelphia, he was presented with an antique musket. Thrilled with the gift, he mused, "Sacred stuff resides in that wooden stock and blue steel when ordinary hands can possess such an extraordinary instrument that gives the most common man the most uncommon of freedoms that symbolize the full measure of human dignity and liberty."[11]

If you believe a picture is worth a thousand words, Google "Jesus with a gun" to view dozens of pictures gundamentalists have placed on the Internet. Here you can see images of the one Christians call Savior, offering a confident, ever-so-masculine smile, as he cradles an assault weapon or grasps a Glock 17.

Most Americans, including NRA members and gun owners like myself, are repulsed by this persona, but that very emphasis brings thousands of new converts into this "baffling gun family," which includes a hard-core religious cult with an unwarranted fascination with guns. They want *more* men and women to swell their ranks. Especially they want more men . . . that is *real men* who love their families and want to protect them . . . real, red-blooded, strong men who love Jesus Christ and all he stands for and who, at the same time, revere their firearms. White men, in particular, have found *love for Jesus and firearms* an irresistible combination.

Meanwhile, thousands of fundamentalist Christian churches, most frequently in the Bible Belt, where the most guns are, and not surprisingly

10. Davidson, *Under Fire*, 44.

11. NRA Convention speech, in Philadelphia, 1998.

the most gun deaths, are not only willing but enthusiastic sponsors of "Celebration Sundays" when the congregation gives thanks to God for open and concealed carry and stand your ground laws Congress and their state assemblies have recently passed.

Their clergy, examples to the flock, "pack heat" in the pulpit, where they preach the love of God. They want to be ready to protect "their flock," like the Good Shepherd of John 10 who is willing to lay down his life for the sheep. Gundamentalists find a warm welcome in these churches. They are regarded as places of refuge from *big government,* their permanent enemy that wants to "remove the freedoms for which our soldiers gave their lives and to confiscate their guns."

Many fundamentalist churches and gundamentalists, first cousins in heart and mind, are comfortable talking about Jesus and firearms in the same breath and evangelistic outreach always is a priority. Is there a bigger or better drawing card for evangelizing *real men* than an invitation to attend a free steak dinner with all the trimmings and the chance to win one of twenty-five handguns, long guns, and shotguns? As many as one thousand people attend such events at Lone Oak Baptist Church in Paducah, Kentucky.[12]

One of the event's leaders said, "You have to know the hook that will attract people, and hunting is huge in Kentucky. So we get in there and burp and scratch and talk about the right to bear arms and that stuff." No one needs to take notes over which political candidates want to "take away our Second Amendment rights." That is abundantly clear.

At another smaller Kentucky church, Christian County's Crofton Baptist Church, which has only seventy-five members, several rifles and shotguns were given away and 101 people said they "found Christ" that night.[13]

After the hearty meal, some "born-again gun owners" tell a story or two about their latest hunting ventures before they give their personal testimonies on how Jesus turned their lives around and put them on the right track for eternity. Someone will testify how his faith in God and his trusty gun saved him and his family from certain disaster. Then it is time for what everyone is waiting for: the drawings for the weapons.

I spent two of my teenage years in Murfreesboro, Tennessee, and was intrigued by a Pentecostal Church that offered incentives for newcomers

12. Wolfson, "Ky. Baptists Lure Unchurched to God at Gatherings to Give Away Guns."

13. Ibid.

to attend worship and/or join their fellowship. In those days, the incentive or door prize was a turkey or a baked ham. But, times have changed; today there is a "divine right to keep and bear arms."

Gundamentalists fit right in with religious fundamentalists who hold to a literal and inerrant Scriptural authority that permits no deviation or diversity of thought. Gundamentalists claim as their touchstone the inerrant last half of the Second Amendment to the US Constitution: "the right of the people to keep and bear arms shall not be infringed." The first half of the amendment stressing good regulations for such arms is considered of secondary importance and is seldom acknowledged. The cherry-picking of selected written material that dovetails with one's beliefs is a machination of fundamentalists in every religion and ideology the world over. Notwithstanding, these devoted gun lovers assume their sacred amendment was the work not only of our founding fathers, but of Almighty God who inspired it. Accordingly, they speak of "*God-given* gun rights."

Nor is it uncommon to hear these well-meaning religious people declare God wants all "good people" to be armed so we can stop the evil intentions of "bad people." Guns are, of course, salvific. They save lives. They are certain the violence of us "good guys" is "*redemptive* violence," quite different from the *savage* violence of the "bad guys." Gundamentalists are convinced, "The only way to stop a bad guy with a gun is a good guy with a gun." It has been said, "evil takes root when one person begins to think he is better or wiser or stronger than another." That's also when the lively spirit of militarism and gundamentalism take our minds hostage.

I don't want to give the impression that America's gun craze is limited to ultra-conservative churches in the South. It's a national phenomenon that is seeping into mainline churches where gundamentalists preach their gospel of "security" and "freedom." I know Presbyterian and Methodist Churches in the Midwest that sponsor periodic bazaars or yard sales, offering guns for sale that their members have discovered in attics or garages and no longer want them around. They are gifts to the church and tax deductible. This is a very dangerous practice for both the new owner and for the church, which could be held liable for selling a defective gun.

Nor are gifts of assault weapons limited to church gatherings. Numerous wannabe and incumbent politicians in pro-gun districts are like Tennessee Representative, Andy Holt. Just one day after the worst mass murder in American history, he announced the door prize he will give away at his fund-raiser, billed as a "Hog Fest and Turkey Shoot." Some "lucky" attendee would go home with a brand new AR-15, semi-automatic rifle, similar to the efficient killing machine used in the Orlando nightclub. He also promises to cover the cost of a three-year CCWP for the first five people who contact his office. To be sure, Holt is a gundamentalist at heart and firmly believes there should be no gun-free zones in his state. That was apparently "over the top" for another gundamentalist who, in turn, threatened to shoot him.[14]

America has experienced horrible acts of terrorism from Islamic religious extremists. Jihadists have chosen a few obscure passages from the Koran and used them to justify their hatred of non-Muslims and to claim Allah's blessing on their despicable acts. These acts are also committed against other Muslims of a different tribe, and their victims are far greater than Western peoples. This runs counter to everything Islam stands for. Moreover, it is in opposition to the essence of any of the world's religions.

Just as Muslim Jihadists pollute the teachings of Islam, scores of American gundamentalists who claim fealty to Christianity and Judaism perform the same kinds of biblical eisegesis and reject what Jesus called the most important law (or responsibility) in the world . . . that we love the Lord our God with all our heart, soul, mind, and strength, and our neighbor as ourselves (Matt 22:34–39).

In place of this self-sacrificial, agape love that Jesus Christ exemplified when he laid down his life for his friends, gundamentalists have substituted the much easier task of *defending oneself and one's loved ones against a neighbor, and if the need arises, to kill him or her.*

That is the fundamental heresy of the Gun Empire: regarding self-defense as the ultimate religious value. Jesus' statement that the great commandment *to love God and neighbor as oneself is the most important law in the world* is reduced in importance and replaced by a rather innocuous and perfunctory "religious responsibility" to defend oneself and one's property from harm. This new mantra fits hand in glove with buying more firearms to the delight of the Gun Industry. They overlook completely the psalmist's warning, that God "hates the lover of violence" (Ps 11:5).

Basic to gundamentalism is a non-negotiable conviction that every American not only has a divine right to keep and bear arms, but for their own well-being, should own at least one gun. Better yet, three or four, to be ready at a moment's notice to defend themselves and their families against

---

14. Ebert, "Tennessee Lawmaker Giving Away AR-15 Receives 'Death Threats.'"

Muslims, immigrants, and people of other races who are different and are therefore considered dangerous.

WHAT DO AMERICA'S GUNDAMENTALISTS BELIEVE AND DO?

While the creed of gundamentalism and its non-negotiable dogmas cannot be outlined precisely, through personal experience of trying to reason with them and studying their rhetoric, I can say with confidence the following beliefs, principles, and behaviors are universally endorsed. With one voice and heart they:

1. Nurture deep emotional attachments to instruments that are made to kill.

2. Grow threatened and angry when gun values are questioned and refuse to engage in *honest dialogue* with those who hold differing opinions.

3. Support no preventive measures for gun violence; their only recourse to violence is punishment.

4. Show little or no grief for 33,000 annual gun victims.

5. Oppose vigorously any law to restrict sales of guns even to the most dangerous members of society.

6. Claim an absolute, unrestricted, and unregulated constitutional right to keep and bear arms. (Contrary to Supreme Court rulings.)

7. Declare the purpose of the Second Amendment is to fight government tyranny. (The Constitution defines such as an act of treason.)

8. Claim God's blessings on weapons that are made to kill.

9. Maintain the solution to gun violence is having more guns available.

10. Deny any circumstance when a regulation or restriction for public safety should be placed upon any gun.

11. Believe it accurate to say, "guns do not kill."

12. Believe a heavily armed society is a polite society.

13. Believe more guns in people's hands will reduce crime.

14. Trust guns will preserve America's most cherished values.

15. Believe "gun control" is futile.[15]

Let us be clear. Not all gun owners are gundamentalists. In fact, as noted above, most NRA members and gun owners agree with the core beliefs of 85 percent of the American people that good gun regulations and gun rights are complementary, not contradictory. They are also consistent with the affirmations of the PCUSA and other faith communities in the United States. However, gundamentalists, who hold high office in the NRA, gun manufacturers who pay them handsomely, distributors, some gun dealers, and vocal extremists consider those opinions un-American.

Most gun owners like myself reject the above fifteen articles which are part of "The Creed of Gundamentalism." Most citizens favor reasonable laws that protect both gun rights and public safety and are open to dialogue with others on the place of guns in our society. Gundamentalists, on the other hand, oppose *any* regulation on *any* gun whatsoever, and dishonestly claim a Second Amendment privilege to define "freedom" for all Americans

Gundamentalists oppose background checks at gun shows because they fear *big government* will use them to create a registry of gun owners they can access and be in position to confiscate all of our 350,000,000 guns, leaving our people defenseless before criminals and terrorists.

For the same reason, when law enforcement uses new technologies to trace crime guns back to the original owner, it is believed they are surreptitiously gathering the names of gun owners and placing them on a registry so their guns can easily be commandeered.

I wrote this book because the American people need to know *how* we are being manipulated and exploited by this extreme unbending minority who have never seen a gun they didn't like and show no interest in stopping the killing. I believe it was Jawaharlal Nehru, the first Prime Minister of India after independence, who said, "Evil unchecked, grows; evil that is *tolerated* poisons the whole system." We must demand an end to these excesses that have poisoned our entire democratic system. More than any other group, gundamentalists are claiming the right to dictate what America is going to look like in the years to come. It will happen *unless* we make significant course corrections to fight our pandemic.

Our computers and smart phones give us the capacity for instantaneous communication with everyone on the planet. But what "the other" thinks or feels is obviously not of major concern to gundamentalists. They

15. Atwood, *America and Its Guns,* 20–21.

are asking, why expend the effort to understand "the other" when we are fully capable of protecting ourselves against them? We can shoot first and ask questions later and many are doing exactly that while looking for legal defense in the recent spate of stand-your-ground-laws, which have been adopted by most of our states.

Gundamentalism claims our freedom is best expressed in our ability to buy any gun of choice, but that kind of *freedom* is turning our nation into selfish armed tribes competing for resources and dominance. We all have the ability and opportunity through technology to understand those with whom we differ, but understanding one another is far down our list of priorities. It must be at the top of the list if we expect to live in peace, or even survive. We must relearn our trust in the power of God that can be felt in a welcoming, open hand instead of a clenched fist.

This brief description of gundamentalism is by no means an exhaustive portrayal of those who hold tenaciously to their "divine right to keep and bear arms." It will, however, give those "with eyes to see" a glimpse of the cliff toward which their excesses and bizarre convictions are leading us. If we buy into their myths and slogans, we will prove to the Gun Empire it can continue to feed us lies and misinformation, and we will not protest because we do not want to offend them or the gundamentalists in our congregations.

Those of us who refuse to buy in and yearn for safe neighborhoods, schools, churches, and public parks, must take the time to check the rhetoric of this minority cult for accuracy and we must pay close attention to the scientific facts that reveal a gun in the home, purchased for protection, is "twenty-two times more likely to kill or wound a family member or friend, or be stolen and used in a crime, than it is to stop an intruder." *Simply put: for every time a gun in or around the home was used in self-defense, or in a legally justified shooting, there were four unintentional shootings, seven criminal assaults or homicides, and eleven attempted or completed suicides.*[16] We cannot let facts like that prompt a ho-hum response. We must pay attention. For paying attention is very close to heartfelt prayer.

America's future is at stake. We need to notice where and how gundamentalism and dedicated gundamentalists are taking this nation to places where we dare not go. We need you and your family and friends to slam on the brakes before this nation goes over the cliff.

16. Rowen, "Guns in Homes Pose Greater Risk to Families than Intruders, Data Shows."

QUESTIONS

1. Do you think guns play a spiritual role for some Americans? What spiritual needs are being met by guns? How would you define gundamentalism?

2. Google "Jesus with a gun." How does this compare with your own image of Jesus?

3. Why do gundamentalists oppose any and all measures for gun safety and smart gun technology?

4. Why are the NRA and gun extremists intent on eliminating government-sponsored research into gun violence and gun safety?

5. Not all gun owners are gundamentalists. Why do such a small number of gun zealots have such control over other gun owners and the public? Why are death threats a strategy used by gundamentalists to protect gun rights?

5

Expectations—and Unexpected Consequences

His peers were always asking the master story-teller and playwright Anton Chekhov for advice on how to write more captivating stories and plays. Chekhov's frequent response centered on the small details that enhance one's story. Details give birth to meaning and create expectations, whether one intends them to or not. He advised one playwright, "One must not put a loaded rifle on the stage if no one is thinking of firing it. If you say in the first chapter there is a rifle hanging on a wall, in the second or third chapter it absolutely must go off. If it's not going to be fired, it should not be hanging there."[1]

A gun on the wall creates expectations. Sooner or later, we expect it to fire. That's why it was made. Whenever a gun is nearby, hanging on a wall, stored in a closet or gun-safe, tucked into a purse, glove compartment or desk drawer, or carried openly or concealed in a holster, waistband, bra, or back pocket, expectations abound.

No other consumer product comes out of the box with greater expectations than a gun. Chief among them is "this gun will protect me and my family." "It will keep us safe." "We no longer need fear what dangerous people can do to us."

People's guns fire when they expect them to go off. At least, that's what *usually* happens. They fire when the owner intends them to, but every day

1. Reisenweber, "What's this Business About Chekhov's Gun?"

guns fire unintentionally bringing death to children, friends, and/or family members close by and to the despair of the one whose gun went off unexpectedly. Even man's best friend has pulled the trigger on its owners. In the last five years six Americans have been shot by their dogs from the back seat of their automobiles where the driver laid his gun. Of course, "this number is a floor not a ceiling," says Christopher Ingraham. "If someone gets shot by a dog and doesn't seek medical care, or it doesn't make the local news, nobody's going to know about it. When you have a country with as many dogs and guns as we do this kind of thing is going to happen." But, no gun owner would expect to be shot by his dog from the back seat of his car. In short, it is an unexpected consequence.[2]

In 1936, the sociologist Robert K. Merton founded a new field of research within the social sciences called "unintended consequences" (sometimes referred to as unanticipated or unforeseen consequences" or accidents).

Chemists, scientists, engineers, and industrialists work hard to attain expected results from research or their labors, but there are no guarantees they will obtain them. On occasion, they are surprised when good, unintended results materialize. In 1878, Thomas Edison was working on perfecting the telegraph when he unexpectedly discovered the phonograph. When aspirin was mass-produced as a pain reliever, unexpectedly, researchers discovered it was also an effective anticoagulant that helped prevent heart attacks and strokes.

This relatively new field of research, however, does not focus on occasional pleasant surprises, but rather on the unexpected and unintended results of intentional actions. This field of study is an idiomatic warning that a purposeful intervention in a complex system tends to create unanticipated and often undesirable outcomes. It is something like Murphy's law, or better yet, McGillicuddy's axiom, which decrees, "Murphy was an optimist." The law of unintended consequences itself is commonly used today as a humorous warning against the hubristic belief that human beings can fully control the world around them. I call such a belief life's greatest temptation.[3]

In the 1930s through '50s, the Soil Conservation Service planted kudzu extensively in the South to fight soil erosion. It is a beautiful climbing vine except that it climbs over literally everything, choking out plants and

2. Ingraham, "Dog Shoots Man."
3. Norton, "Unintended Consequences."

tall trees. They did not think it would be a killer. Driving through the South today one can see its disastrous results.

In 2003, Barbara Streisand sued Kenneth Adelman and Pictopia.com for posting a photograph of her home online. Before the lawsuit was filed, only six people had downloaded the file, and two of them were Streisand's attorneys. The lawsuit drew attention to the image, resulting in 420,000 people visiting the site. This became known as "the Streisand effect."[4]

But, no one laughs at the unintended consequences that occur with guns. With the very best of intentions to protect his family, US Marine Colton Jack Luman purchased a Glock handgun and kept a round in the chamber at all times so he would always be *fully* prepared to defend those he loved. This combat veteran of three tours in Iraq accidentally killed his nine-month-old daughter while practicing drawing his gun in their home. The gun fired, striking his daughter in the face as she sat in her high-chair eating fruit. The family was planning a trip to the zoo that afternoon. Twenty-six-year-old Colton Jack Luman pleaded guilty to involuntary manslaughter.

Said the judge, "This is a case on the highest order of sadness. It's a tragic accident and the repercussions are far-reaching beyond this courthouse. He's got his own kind of prison and own kind of hell to go through."[5]

Luman is not alone in his desire to be fully prepared. Expecting even greater safety for his family, as all gundamentalists are, and acting with the best of intentions, he and his loved ones were nevertheless victims of unexpected consequences.

William DeHayes likes to play with guns. That's what he was doing on July 14, 2014, when he invited Carson and Katherine Hoover to his home in Brookfield, Florida. He wanted to show them how he could quick draw like a cowboy and ended up accidentally discharging a round into Katherine Hoover's temple. She was twenty years old and pregnant at the time. Both she and her baby died at the hospital. No charges were filed.

He told the *Daily Beast* he had sworn off guns, but Dehayes could not stay away from them. On March 17, 2016, he had too much to drink and discharged a shotgun into the air while teaching his girlfriend's sixteen-year-old daughter how to shoot.[6] I feel DeHayes has forfeited his right to own a gun.

4. Rogers, "Photo of Streisand home becomes an Internet hit."
5. Bowers, "Chesapeake Marine Guilty of Accidentally Killing Infant Child."
6. Zandrozny, "He killed a Pregnant Mom, but he still gets a gun."

I met a man who boasted he kept his gun fully loaded at all times to protect his family. He says, "An unloaded gun is just like a car in the garage without gas." The truth is thousands of gundamentalists carelessly leave firearms loaded and unlocked all around their houses, hanging on walls, stored in closets, in garages, on shelves, in dresser drawers or stashed away in purses, glove compartments, and trunks of automobiles. Much too frequently they bring unforeseen grief to those who bought them "for security."

Sometimes I wonder if those who expect a gun in the home to keep them and their children safe actually read their newspapers or listen to TV. If they actually read headlines like those below, what adjustments would they make to protect their curious kids from being killed with their weapons? Would such catastrophes prompt them to reason, "It *could* happen to us?" The following are headlines collected randomly in a three-month period.

- "3-Year-Old Kansas City Girl Shot in Abdomen," January 7, 2015, *Kansas City Star*
- "9-Month-Old Boy Fatally Shot by 5-Year-old Brother in 'Horrible, Tragic Accident,'" January 20, 2015, *Omaha World-Herald*
- "Investigations Underway: 5- Year- Old Shot, Teen Killed in Separate Incidents," January 27, 2015, Detroit CBS NEWS
- "Boy, 3, Who Accidently Shot Himself in NW Harris County Has Died," February 28, 2015, HOUSTON KTRK
- "4-year old dies from Self-inflicted Wound," March 1, 2015, HOUSTON KPRC
- "3-Year-old Tenn. Boy Shoots Little Brother in Head," March 4, 2015, Nashville, WKRN

Last spring my regular barber was ill so a young man took her place. As he limped to the chair ahead of me, I asked, "Are you doing OK?" He confessed, "I've had a bad winter." He shot himself with his brand new .45 caliber pistol, breaking a bone in his thigh. He told of putting his finger in the hole where the bullet entered his leg to try and stop the flow of blood and then using his belt as a tourniquet before the EMTs arrived. I asked how it happened. He said he just turned twenty-one years of age and wanted to do all the things he was now entitled to do as a man come of age. He asked his friend, who was "familiar with guns," to check out his .45 and make sure everything was in good working order. He said, "My friend checked it out, but did not tell me he left a round in the chamber. When I took it out of the box, it went off."

If we don't want our guns to go off so frequently and/or with such unexpected devastation, we should not place such high expectations on them to protect us, or give them such prominent places on our walls, or in our psyches. *Particularly* in our psyches—that's where this young man's predicament began. The gun he saw inside the case at the gun store or the picture featured in *Guns and Ammo* was speaking to him. Guns *do* speak, you know. Its message was, "Owning this powerful handgun will make you a man." That is a well-known missive for many young men, and it is an unfortunate, unexpected rite of passage.

D. L. Wilkinson and J. Fagan interviewed sixteen to twenty-four year-old men released from Riker's Island Correctional Facility. One was asked, "How is manhood defined?" The respondent: "Manhood now it's like gun-hood. If you got a gun you are the man [laughing]. Ain't no more manhood, it's gunhood." Gundamentalists would understand.[7] No male growing up in the US can fully circumvent the steady stream of images, stories, and myths that tell him guns are indispensable tools for anyone who wants to be a "real man."

An AR-15 Bushmaster Assault Rifle was the weapon that twenty-year-old Adam Lanza brought into that classroom in Newtown, Connecticut, where he murdered twenty first graders and six adults in less than five minutes. The weapon itself was designed and manufactured by Remington Arms for the military to increase casualties in close combat. It is one of the most lethal weapons ever produced. Even so, Remington Arms markets it to civilians by touting its capacity to "inflict maximum casualties." Advertising copy for the AR-15 includes bestowing outright power on all who would buy it, proclaiming, "Consider your man card reissued," and "Forces of opposition, bow down. You are single-handedly outnumbered."[8]

What is evident in the myths we champion about guns is the expectation they will give the owner strength, power, and dominance over others. If not dominance, for the most vulnerable, they will at least level the playing field. Gun owners expecting to receive that awesome power is precisely what makes them in the final analysis so tragic. The myths that "promise"

7. Wilkinson and Fagan, "The Role of Firearms in the Violence 'Scripts.'" Quote cited by Hemenway, *Private Guns–Public Health*, 112.

8. Barden, "Bernie Sanders is Wrong About Our Gun Lawsuit."

to give us power are in fact figments of our imagination. More often, they bring death and destruction.

It would be instructive to know why Adam Lanza's mother purchased one of the world's most deadly weapons and put it in her gun cabinet so her disadvantaged son could shoot it at the firing range from time to time. I cannot prove it, but I sense she believed by associating with that powerful weapon, Adam would somehow be transformed into a stronger and more confident young man. Guns speak the language of power, but in the final analysis earthly power *never* has the last word. Paul reminds us of that: "Three things will last: faith, hope and love; and the greatest of these is love" 1 Cor 13:13).

Rob Farago didn't buy his first gun until he was fifty years old, but in just a few years he had eighteen more guns. He was transformed from being just a gun owner to a gundamentalist. After he bought his first gun, he says, "I felt grown up. It was like a coming-of-age-thing. I felt like an adult." He speaks glowingly of the visceral pleasure he gets from firing a gun. "There is the moment before, and the moment after. Time slows. It almost stops. It's a Zen thing. You can control time down to the 1/1,000th of a second." In one of his blogs he wrote, "Once you put a gun on, you gain situational awareness."[9]

Most people buy handguns expecting them to provide protection and safety for themselves and their families. Again, no one can fault their good intentions. All the same, the relevance of unintended and unexpected consequences for gun purchases is a haunting reality. Each prospective buyer needs to know *there is no reputable scientific research that shows having a gun in the home will increases one's security. To the contrary, the research cited above shows a gun in the home increases one's risk of harm.*

Owning a lethal gun calls for extraordinary responsibility. Too often firearms are handled casually by people who should know better. This makes a firearm all the more dangerous for owners, their families, colleagues at work, and for the general public. Scores of gun owners are simply too careless to *responsibly* own a firearm. Missouri lawmakers have long supported concealed carry almost anywhere and anytime. The editor of the *Kansas City Star* asked in an editorial if the right extends to the men's room in the state capitol basement? That is where a staffer for Majority Leader Tim Jones left a loaded handgun on top of a toilet paper dispenser.[10]

9. Achenbach, "Always on Alert."

10. *Kansas City Star* editorial, "Flush Arrogant Gun Policy."

I happen to think all gun owners need to know where their weapons are at all times. How about you? Regrettably, even some of the country's most well-regarded officials seem oblivious to the dangers guns present. I can understand misplacing one's glasses or car keys. I do it all the time. But, misplacing a 9mm handgun? How is that possible? On August 6, 2015, Alvin Krongard, former Executive Director of the CIA under George W. Bush, did just that. He was arrested trying to bring a 9mm handgun with five rounds of ammunition past security at Baltimore Washington Airport. He said he just grabbed the wrong bag at home, which contained the weapon. "I didn't even know I was carrying a gun," he said.[11]

In 2014, a record 2,212 firearms were discovered by federal officers in carry-on bags at airports throughout the country. Eighty-three percent of them were loaded.[12]

Someone is certain to pay the price if gun owners forget where their guns are. Twelve-year-old Jacob Larson of Palm Harbor, Florida, would be alive today had his parents paid closer attention to where their gun was. Jacob came across the gun in the family home and shot himself in the head. According to police, his parents had forgotten they even had the gun.[13]

The man of the house in Calcasieu Parish, Louisiana, bought guns to protect his wife and three children, ages one, two, and three. He cleaned them in the living room during the day while his wife and children were gone and did not put them up before he left for work. When the mother returned home about 7:00 p.m. on February 9, 2015, with the three children, the three-year-old girl took one of the loaded guns and killed herself.[14] What was he thinking? Or was he thinking at all?

Robert Merton, the founder of the science of unintended consequences, lists five possible causes for their perverse effects.

1. Ignorance, where it is impossible to anticipate everything, thereby leading to incomplete analysis.

2. Errors in analysis of the problem or following habits that worked in the past but may not apply to the current situation.

3. Immediate interests overriding long-term interests.

11. Lazo and Miller, "Ex-Official with CIA Arrested at BWI."
12. Kelly, "TSA Finds Record Number of Firearms in Carry-on Bags."
13. Herbert, "A Culture Soaked in Blood."
14. *Daily Mail*, "3-year Old Girl Accidently Shot Herself Dead After Finding Father's Gun."

4. Basic values, which may require or prohibit certain actions even if the long-term result might be unfavorable (these long-term consequences may eventually cause changes in basic values).

5. Self-defeating prophecy, so the fear of some consequence drives people to find solutions before the problem occurs, thus the non-occurrence of the problem is not anticipated.

QUESTIONS

1. Give examples of unintended consequences in your life, actions that led to unexpected undesirable outcomes and accidents.

2. Do you personally know anyone killed or injured in a gun accident? What impact did this have on you?

3. Why would gun owners leave loaded weapons accessible to others? Does the worship of guns encourage an unconscious subservience to a gun or an unconscious willingness to be careless?

4. Atwood describes the myth that guns confer manhood and power. Why do some men equate guns with manhood? Why do you think Adam Lanza's mother brought home an AR-15 Bushmaster Assault Rifle?

5. Discuss Merton's five possible causes on the last page on chapter 5.

6

The Inanimate Gun Speaks

Whenever there is a mass shooting or a discussion focuses on the place of guns in our society, gundamentalists rise to the defense of all firearms, asking, "How can you blame an inanimate object for these deaths? Guns don't kill; people kill." They argue guns are somehow peripheral to gun violence. So speaks Dan Quayle, our former Vice President, who, when informed of the massacre at Columbine High School, replied, "That's terrible. I hope they don't blame this on guns."[1] At a massacre, Quayle and his friends don't want us to look at guns, but at what they call "root causes of gun violence."

The Gun Empire has a long list of these root causes. High on the list is mental illness, which is blamed for the majority of deaths in these well-publicized massacres. Actually, most of the mentally ill are more in danger of being harmed than they are of inflicting harm. Only about four percent of interpersonal violence in America is caused by mental illness alone. (There is however, a strong correlation with mental illness and suicide.) Yet, if you were to focus on media coverage surrounding well-publicized massacres, you'd likely come away with the impression that all of the mentally ill are violent, crazed maniacs who are moments away from going postal. This is patently untrue and such notions divert us from a productive discourse about true risk factors for violence—including low socioeconomic status, substance abuse, and a history of arrest.[2]

1. Dees-Thomases, *Looking for a Few Good Moms,* 17.
2. Horwitz, "The Racial Double Standard on Gun Violence."

Gundamentalists itemize additional root causes for the bloodshed. They list violent movies and video games, crime programs on TV, rap and unhealthy music, drugs and gangs, single-parent families, the lack of father figures in the inner city, and a lack of gun safety courses for gun owners. Also high on the list of root causes is "removing God from our classrooms" and "taking the Ten Commandments off courthouse walls." Many of these factors need our serious attention, but if the subject is, in fact, *gun* violence, it seems logical that guns themselves should qualify as at least *one of the root causes*. A friend recently remarked, "The gun is to gun violence, as the mosquito is to malaria. Break the chances of causation and the disease retreats." The Gun Lobby may claim "Guns Don't Kill," but 33,000 death certificates in 2015 signed by physicians and coroners state otherwise.

It's instructive at this point to look at *all* industrialized, developed nations in the entire world for their rates of gun violence. Each nation's rates (except our own) are negligible. Each industrialized country is relatively free of gun violence except our own. It's not because citizens of other nations are smarter or more loving or kind; it is something else. These countries do not permit ordinary citizens to get their hands on guns they issue to their militaries. Glock and Beretta handguns are made in Austria and Italy. They export millions of them to the United States, but Austrian and Italian citizens cannot buy them. Their leaders do not consider them a useful social product. It should be obvious that they have made some wise choices. What is most interesting in these comparisons is both the Austrians and Italians consider themselves *free* peoples. Isn't that ironic? Gundamentalists, however, say they are delusional.

The Gun Empire, wanting to sell more guns, vigorously defends them. They argue "Guns don't kill; people kill." "Firearms are inanimate objects." There *is* a degree of truth to that, but it is slight. America's bustling advertising industry works overtime to sell all manner of goods to every man, woman, and child. Have you noticed, literally everything they are selling is a bona fide inanimate object: A Lexus LS, a special shampoo, the Champagne of Beers, and Viagra itself. They are all inanimate objects, but each carries a compelling message to potential buyers. Of all people, gundamentalists should realize how articulate an inanimate gun really is.

David Ned heard a firearm speak. "Guns talk to you," says Ned, who told of his experiences on National Public Radio's Story-Corps. The manager of Ned's apartment had kids who were kicking his dog. He spoke to her about it. About 10 that night her husband knocked at the door and said, "If you got any problem you need to talk to me about it."

Ned replied, "Are you the manager?" "No," said the man, "My wife is the manager." Ned responded, "I've already talked to your wife." He said, "Well, I'll tell you what, in two weeks, I want you moved and your dog gone." Ned was ticked off.

He told Story Corps, "I walked downstairs, I closed my door and I went to my bedroom and I got my gun. What a gun does, it talks to you. Things that you'd normally say I'm not going to do, or I'll just let it pass, gun talks to you and says, 'You don't have to take that.'" His wife locked the door and told him she didn't want him to go out. Ned stayed home but called the manager of the company and reported the incident. Within a week the property manager was fired.

Soon Ned came home to find his dog had been poisoned and he vowed to "get the guy who did it." Driving down the highway a car passed him and he saw this face and had a flashback of who he was. He chased the man down and snatched open his door and it was the wrong man. Ned confessed, "I know if I would've had the gun, I'd have shot that man. At that point I knew that my anger was so bad, if I don't control this thing, I'm going to hurt somebody or somebody's going to hurt me. So, I'm done. I can't pack no gun no more. And it took that kind of thing to get me right."[3]

When people are angry, distressed, isolated, full of revenge, agitated, or unhinged, and a gun is close by, its owner can hear its voice. Its message is clear and convincing: "I can solve your problem." "As long as I'm around, you are in charge." It makes no audible sound, but the gun's *speech* emboldens one who feels dissed by an employer, neighbor, or lover. At times the gun makes use of the Socratic method: "Are you going to let that guy push you around like that? When are you going to stand up to him and be a man?" Inanimate? I don't think so. Articulate, by all means!

Handguns, in particular, are fluent. One caveat, they have a limited vocabulary. They are conversant in only one stream of thought: being in charge or dominating and controlling others. Firearms do not speak the language of de-escalation. They are incompetent in scaling back a tense situation. They do not know how to speak about reconciliation. They do not encourage patience, or advise their owners to apologize, forgive, seek peace, or be a good neighbor. They are illiterate about the golden rule. They totally dismiss God's command, "Thou shalt not kill," and reject Jesus'

3. NPR, "The Day One Man Decided to Give Up His Gun."

demand that we love our neighbor as ourselves. Compassion and grief and sensitivity before bruised human feelings are not part of the personality of those who regard guns as sacred. The writer of the "Letter to Jeremiah" of the inter-testament period in Baruch 4:36–38 exclaims, "Idols will never save any man from death, never rescue the weak from the strong. They cannot restore a blind man's sight or give relief to the needy. They do not pity the widow or befriend the orphan."

Firearms' eloquent messages are always about settling disputes in the owner's favor. They want him to walk away from any confrontation feeling like "bad, bad Leroy Brown/the baddest man in the whole damn town."

Three of my friends had loved ones savagely murdered by three different, heavily armed persons with mental illness who "heard voices telling them to kill." Would they have obeyed the voices had they not been walking around city streets fondling their guns?

Such people should not have a gun or have access to one. Those who beat their wives and children; stalk an ex-spouse or lover; or those who are a danger to themselves or others should not be able to get a firearm. Period. The 10 percent of Americans with significant anger issues should not be allowed to listen to the intense *urgings* of a firearm because their personal histories are the strongest indicators they will grow violent again and turn on their own family members, friends, or innocent bystanders. One angry customer illustrates the hazard as he complained to his gun dealer, "Why should I have to wait seventy-two hours to pick up this gun, I'm angry now?" The articulate gun was speaking to him. An honest gun dealer would not let him get his hands on another firearm. Alas.

QUESTIONS

1. Have you ever held a gun? Do you understand Atwood's concept that a gun "speaks" to its owner? What other inanimate things speak to you?

2. Why has the phrase "guns don't kill; people kill" been such an effective gundamentalist slogan? Do you agree or disagree with it? Why?

3. This chapter begins to get at the heart of why universal background checks and requiring slightly more steps to get a gun will help save lives. Can you think of examples among your family and friends where the presence and "voice" of a gun could have led to violence that would not would not have occurred otherwise?

4. Depression, anger, mental illness, or distress fall easy prey to the "voice" of a gun. Where would you draw a line on who should have guns and who should not?

7

Straight Talk to a Young Gun Buyer at Liberty University

(Or Anyone Buying a Gun for the First Time)

Dear friend:

As a retired Presbyterian minister and missionary with over a half-century of striving to live out the gospel of Christ, I must say I am very concerned that students at a Christian univeristy are encouraged to buy a handgun. Hear me out. I'm not opposed to guns. I've owned hunting guns for over fifty years. Handguns, on the other hand, are not made for sport, but for protection against others, and if need be, to kill them. The latter is their *ultimate purpose*. That is why they are made. Because of *that* monumental implication, purchasing a handgun must never be a casual decision. Nor can you think of a gun as something abstract: *"Just in case I might need it."*

An instrument that is made to disable or kill another person is not a sterile, antiseptic tool. It is a very messy, gory piece of equipment. To shine it up, and oil and polish it does not hide its very nature or purpose. To speak theoretically about owning a handgun without considering the possibility you might use it to kill another human being, is disingenuous to the extreme. I therefore ask, "Are you ready to kill someone?" As a potential gun owner, what would that mean to you? You must be ready for that eventuality. I heard a handgun instructor say, "If you are not ready to kill, you are more dangerous with the weapon than without it, because it will likely be taken from you and be used to kill you and others around you." Nine out of ten gun instructors will tell you the same thing. You must do some hard thinking about the benefits and risks of owning a weapon before you pay big bucks to the gun dealer.

I heard the president of Liberty University, the Rev. Jerry Falwell, Jr., urge you and other students to get a gun and a concealed carry permit. His call to arms was issued immediately after the tragedy in San Bernardino, California, where Muslim extremists carried out jihad, killing fourteen of their workmates with assault rifles at a Christmas party. It was sad to witness your president, along with scores of Americans, turn xenophobic, and assume *all* 1.6 billion Muslims were terrorists. Falwell advised you to get a gun "so you can take care of any dangerous Muslim who would walk onto the Liberty Campus." At the very least, his advice is ill-advised.

Too many Americans are controlled by their fears and wonder if they could be next on some terrorist's hit list. We fear *those people* who are different from us and consider them dangerous, while we imagine persons just like us are dependable and trustworthy. You need to know *that is simply not true.* That is a deliberate lie, which is having a disastrous effect on you and is tempting you to believe the myths that demonize those whose race, religion, or heritage is not the same as yours. In such fear we turn to guns and violence as our first response to social problems and we target those who are different as the perpetrators. As a prospective gun owner, I urge you to do some honest study and learn who is most likely to do you harm. They are *not* the people you are being led to suspect.

Furthermore, if you were thinking of buying a car, it would be foolish to ignore the latest recommendations from *Consumer Reports* as to the best buys. If you are thinking of buying a gun you need to know some facts about guns that will help you decide which one you should buy, or decide if you *really* want one. It is too big a decision to make without a lot of thought. Your conclusions should be based on solid, objective, scientific facts, not on your subjective fears of the moment. It is a reality that when we are afraid, we often do not make wise decisions. Is a gun likely to make you more secure or put you at greater risk? Let's examine some facts. The evidence is: one in three women and one in four men are victims of physical violence in their lifetime. Who is the person responsible? Answer: *an intimate friend or partner.* Thirty percent of all women killed in the United States, and usually with a gun, are killed by those men who express their love for them (husbands, significant others, exes, and boyfriends).[1]

The FBI informs us that the persons most likely to do us harm are those of our own household, acquaintances, or neighbors. The statistics are clear: 94 percent of African Americans killed by guns are killed by other African Americans and 83 percent of whites are murdered by other whites who usually live in the same neighborhood.[2] A 2011 study by the Harvard School of Public Health concluded there are *no credible studies* that show the benefits of having a gun in the home outweighs the risks. Further, there is no good evidence of a deterrent effect of firearms or that a gun in the home reduces the chances or severity of injury during an altercation or break-in. On the other hand, there is gripping evidence that a gun in the home (or school) is a significant risk factor for intimidation, and especially for the killing of women. A gun is much more likely to be used to threaten friends or loved ones than to protect them against intruders. *Actual self-defense gun use, even in our gun-rich country, is rare.* A study of ten previous years of crime survey data found that of more than 1,100 sexual assaults, in only one did the victim use a gun in self-defense.[3]

Those who *think* a gun will provide security should reflect as well on the methodologies of history's notorious marauders and criminals. As a child I was intrigued by the Viking culture, especially their boats with the square sails and long dragon-necks both fore and aft. I was thrilled to visit the Viking Ship Museum in Oslo, Norway, and see some of those boats that survived the centuries. Even the largest of the craft had the characteristics of a canoe and could carry up to ninety Vikings. These long, maneuverable boats drew very little water, which allowed them to glide up quietly to the shores of sleeping villages where the Norsemen could noiselessly step out to pillage, plunder, or kill. It is no secret today's criminals and marauders use the same tactics as the Vikings of old . . . stealth.

Yes, stuff happens, but solid scientific data tells us there is only an infinitesimal possibility that you will be attacked by a violent individual. But, should some scoundrel be intent on harming you, no matter *where* you are, or *who* you are, he will likely succeed. He will be successful because he

1. "Domestic (Intimate Partner) Violence Fast Facts."

2. Suen, "Fox News Revives 'Black on Black Crime Canard to Dismiss Black Lives Matter.'"

3. Hemenway, "Does Owning a Gun Make You Safer?" Los Angeles Times, Aug. 4, 2015.

will creep up on you "on little cat's feet." There will be no noise, no knock at the door, and neither his presence nor intent will be announced.

If, in the very unlikely event, someone is out to do you harm, you will be blitzed in those seconds when you least expect it. If you have a gun, but are not holding it in your hand *every single moment* while in your home or office, or walking down the street, or bathing your children, fixing dinner, or preaching a sermon, those who would do you harm will attack you when your back is turned, or when you are distracted, or when you go to the bathroom. If at some terrible moment an assailant with a gun, knife, or club *already in hand,* surprises you, you will *not* be able to reach for your weapon and protect yourself, *even if it is close by.*

If you *should* reach for your weapon, which is on the shelf, in the drawer, pocket, purse, or holster, you will be quickly shot or incapacitated. Even a highly trained soldier will *not* be able to react in time to stop an attack, even though the gun is within easy reach. Recall Kris Kyle, the famous Navy Seal sharpshooter who had more sniper kills to his credit than any other person in U.S. military history. He was holding guns *in his hands* when he and a friend were murdered by a fellow Marine with PTSD on February 3, 2013. Total security, for a host of reasons, even for a sharpshooter with guns in his hands, is an illusion.

I listened for over an hour to a young entrepreneur selling a set of DVDs entitled *The Armed American's Complete Concealed Carry Guide to Effective Self- Defense.* He claimed "95 percent of armed Americans are not prepared to survive the reality of a deadly situation and told why [his] eye-popping self-defense truths could help make sure you are ready."

Everything he said pointed to my purchasing a handgun and working my way through his seven chapters of self-defense training. Unintentionally, however, he proved my point that even a well-armed and well-trained soldier is helpless before an attacker who suddenly appears out of the blue. He said, "76 percent of the time the first indication that you are about to be attacked is the attack itself." I don't know where he got the figure of 76 percent, but that statistic, used *to sell his DVDs,* proves my point. If one makes even the slightest move to reach for a weapon, while under a surprise attack, he will be quickly shot.

Donna Dees-Thomases, the founder of the Million Mom March, tells of growing up in New Orleans where her father owned a pharmacy in an economically depressed area. He had difficulty hiring other pharmacists to come and work for him because of the store's location, so the family moved to nearby Metairie in hopes of living and working in a safer place. The smaller community, however, was no safe haven. Though her dad had never been held up in New Orleans, he was robbed at gunpoint many times in Metairie. A customer asked him why he didn't buy a gun for protection. He replied, "Because I want to live to see the next holdup."[4]

We all know of dangerous places where predators and unsavory characters hang out. The best way to live another day is to studiously avoid such places and to take sensible precautions in one's own safe places. At a minimum that would mean *avoiding dark alleys and unlit streets;* installing alarm systems, locks, and good lights in and around one's home; getting a dog that barks; not opening doors to strangers, etc. Those are simply precautions as there are no guarantees for safety or security. That is, not in this world.

The reason so many Americans are buying handguns is because of the media's gripping coverage of mass shootings, which scare the daylights out of us and dominate our thoughts. The blood and gore of *three to four hundred* Americans killed in these mass shootings is what manipulates the news from coast to coast for days on end, while *the murders of ten thousand* Americans per year are acknowledged, if at all, on the back pages of our newspapers or on a brief TV clip. The media's most captivating reports do not describe the *average* street scene where you live. It's not sensational enough for TV. Collectively, deaths from mass shootings (defined as four or more persons) amount to only *1.5 percent* of all gun fatalities in the US.[5]

Americans listen intently to hype and hysteria and ignore statistics that tell us there is only an infinitesimal chance you will need to protect yourself from a madman, let alone a mass murderer. Of course, that does not mean you tempt fate by walking through Central Park at night, or leave your front door unlocked.

The Rev. Falwell, Jr. and others pushing for guns on college campuses have not *carefully* thought through all the implications of arming your student body. I raise only one: the booze and the beer are flowing at the big party, off campus, of course, and two of the guys are drunk. They get into an argument and punches are thrown. The one who loses the scuffle is embarrassed and goes to his room where his gun is in the third drawer of his dresser. A disaster is getting ready to happen. If you think that is not possible at a "Christian university," you are delusional.

4. Dees-Thomases, *Looking for a Few Good Moms,* xvii.
5. Osnos, "Making a Killing," 37.

Not only should a potential gun owner know some of these facts about who is our greatest threat, one needs to do some spiritual introspection as well on what one believes about *God;* about life in general; one's life in particular; and the value of the human life one must be ready to end, *should that be necessary.*

Prospective gun owners, especially youth, need to do some soul-searching. One needs time to reflect on what one has learned about life and other people from kindergarten days through high school and college. Before you pay several hundred or a thousand dollars to buy a gun, think about the first time your parents or teachers taught you about the love of Jesus; and when you memorized the Golden Rule and the Bible's injunction to love God and one's neighbor as oneself, and even one's enemies. This recital may sound like a third grade Sunday school lesson, but in reality, these teachings are the core values you have followed your whole life long.

In days past WWJD? or WWJHMD? were badges worn at Liberty University when its founder, Rev. Jerry Falwell, Sr. was President. For those unfamiliar with the code, the letters stand for "What Would Jesus Do?" and "What Would Jesus Have Me Do?" Because Liberty prides itself as a Christian community where students develop deep personal relationships with Jesus Christ, it is not out of line to ask Rev. Falwell, Jr. what firearm he, in the name of the Good Shepherd himself, would recommend? Would it be the small caliber pistol Falwell carries in his back pocket; or the sophisticated Glock 17 semi-automatic; or the powerful .45 caliber; or an AK-47 assault rifle accompanied by a thirty to fifty round magazine for even greater security against a Muslim who might walk on campus? There are lots of choices.

But the kind of weapon is not the only question a potential handgun buyer needs to consider. Purchasing a weapon also means deciding what kind of ammunition one would use. Ammo is what gives the gun its stopping power. As with guns themselves, there are many choices about ammunition. Choosing a particular kind of ammo is necessary but the decision itself is not for the squeamish. As stated above, "Owning a gun that can kill is messy stuff." The discussion that follows may seem stark to some, but we are talking about *stopping someone in his tracks* who may want to harm you. Ammunition is what does the stopping.

One choice is a lead bullet. It is also the most economical. Lead rounds, however, have a tendency to flatten out or fold over before they spread out in the body. Consequently, they have less stopping power than other kinds of ammo. WWJD? Would the Savior suggest another genre of bullet? For example, a copper hollow point bullet that would provide more stopping power because on impact the projectile splits into a cone of several piercing "needles," sending them far throughout the body? As a new gun owner, the question is admittedly unpleasant, but you are purchasing a *lethal* weapon and it is *essential* for you to consider this matter each and every time you buy ammunition. What level of stopping power do I want in my ammo? That's simply a euphemistic way of asking what damage I want my ammo to inflict? WWJHMD?

But, if you do buy a gun, you will want to know how to shoot it accurately. Shooting accurately requires a lot of time at the firing range. The NRA reminds us, "Accurate shooting requires practice." To shoot accurately is why law enforcement personnel are required to spend countless hours honing one's shooting skills. Whether one plays the piano, or basketball, or purchases a gun for protection, practice makes perfect. One must not only develop the talent to shoot accurately, one must *maintain* that skill.

And, as you practice shooting, you must decide "What part of the human body you should aim for?" WWJHMD? You have three choices: A) Aim for the knee to disable an attacker, but not kill him (although the possibility exists one might hit an artery); B) Shoot for the head, which is the most fatal area for a bullet to strike, but also the most difficult to hit; C) Aim for the torso, which is a much easier target.

President Falwell's NRA friends frequently cite the work of one of their favorites: Lt. Colonel Dave Grossman, former Army Ranger, psychology professor at West Point and a frequent speaker at their clinics. Grossman tells us in all US wars prior to Vietnam, our infantrymen, as well as the militaries of other countries, which were fighting at close range had terrible hit ratios. They discovered a human revulsion to shoot at the bodies of other human beings. Things changed for the US military during the Vietnam War when instructors at boot camp replaced the old bull's eye targets with human body silhouettes. This simple innovation vastly improved their kill ratios because soldiers grew accustomed to shooting at the human body.[6]

Liberty University maintains three firing ranges. If President Falwell and the Board of Trustees want their students to buy guns so they can stop dangerous people who might intrude on their campus, perhaps they should do away with all bull's eye targets on their ranges and replace them with

---

6. Grossman, *On Killing,* xviii.

human silhouettes so these young leaders of the church of tomorrow can grow more comfortable shooting at people? WWJHMD?

Grossman quotes Bill Jordan, law-enforcement expert, and career US border patrol officer who says: "[There is] a natural disinclination to pull the trigger . . . when your weapon is pointed at a human. To overcome this resistance one can *will* oneself to think of your opponent as a mere target and not as a human being. Further, if you pick a spot on the target, you can remove the human element from your thinking. If this works for you, try to continue this thought in allowing yourself no remorse. Our enemies are outlaws who have no place in world society. Their removal is completely justified, and should be accomplished dispassionately and without regret."[7] Should you have trouble following those instructions, you could always ask President Falwell or the chaplain to pray for you, even as you ponder, WWJHMD?

ALL GUN OWNERS SHOULD CRITICALLY EXAMINE THE GUN LOBBY'S STATISTICS

The elite leaders of the NRA and gundamentalists will try to present evidence to demonstrate how efficacious it is to own a gun, and they have *their very own facts* to prove it. Let's give them their due: to be sure, armed individuals every year do, in fact, stop *some* crimes and even attempted murders by shooting and/or killing an attacker. Other crimes are stopped when armed individuals point their guns at an attacker. The gun lobby demands that the media publicize such accounts. They make excellent copy and demonstrate people can protect themselves. These episodes, however, are anecdotal; they are few and far between; and they are not the norm, *no matter how persuasive they seem to those who are living in fear and those who are determined to sell you a gun.*

In the monthly column of the *American Rifleman*, entitled, "The Armed Citizen" the NRA prints the details of supposed successful first-hand incidences where gun owners have stopped an attack or a crime. The Gun Industry wants us to believe these events are, *in fact,* the norm. Here, we get to the numbers. Their editors state: "6,850 times a day, every 13 seconds, law abiding people use their guns to defend themselves and their families against criminals, or 2.5 million times a year." In other places they say, "Studies indicate firearms are used more than 2 million times a year

7. Ibid., 258.

for personal protection, and that the presence of a firearm, without a shot being fired, prevents crime in many instances."[8]

There are dozens of studies of gun deaths conducted by researchers, epidemiologists, the FBI, National Institute of Health, and the CDC, but *each of them is categorically rejected by the NRA and the Gun Empire.* Why is that? Is it because these established American bodies are undependable? Is it because they have the odor of *big government* about them and, therefore, are not believable? Or does the Gun Empire need bigger numbers to sell more guns? The CDC and the FBI's research reveals that 100,000–125,000 persons are shot or killed by guns every year, and that includes approximately one thousand persons shot by law enforcement.[9]

The "studies" which the *American Rifleman* cites are from the work of Dr. Gary Kleck, Professor of Criminology and Criminal Justice at Florida State University. They provide the much heftier, bulked up numbers the NRA and the Gun Industry count on to impress prospective buyers. Gun dealers have used Kleck's bogus statistics for decades. If you sell guns for a living, and want to convince a customer he needs to buy your product, would you be more likely to quote the CDC and FBI's more modest numbers or Kleck's 2.5 million defensive gun uses per year?

I deliberately put quotes around the word "studies" by Kleck because his work is not worthy of being considered factual for a host of reasons, not the least of which is Kleck's numbers are *mathematically impossible.* In light of reliable data from hospital records, national crime victimization surveys (NCVS), gun violence archives, and police records, it is deceitful to claim such a number.

According to data found in Gun Violence Archives (GVA), the most comprehensive and systematic effort to catalog every publicly available defensive gun use (DGU) report—there were fewer than 1,600 DGU in 2014. Pro-gun advocates have been forced to argue that the reason researchers can barely find .064 percent of the 2.5 million DGU a year claimed by Kleck is because virtually nobody reports defensive gun use to the police.

The only thing known is what the data shows: namely, there is a reliable floor for defensive gun use estimates at around 1,600 a year. In addition, according to the most recent data on DGU, we have reliable evidence showing that owning a firearm does *not* give individuals any significant

---

8. Frum, "Do Guns Make Us Safer?" And "The Armed Citizen," 10.

9. Jacobsen, "Do 100,000 People Get Shot Every Year in the US?"

advantage in a criminal confrontation, and they are no less likely to lose property or be injured by using a gun in self-defense.[10]

Repeat: There are no reputable *scientific studies* that show having a defensive gun increases security.

QUESTIONS

1. Do you think gundamentlists readily accept the possibility of killing someone?

2. The letter briefly alludes to research into the low "kill" rates of Americans in battle since the Revolutionary War. Throughout most of our history, many soldiers simply could not make themselves shoot to kill human beings. What are some of the psychological costs of being willing to kill other persons?

3. Atwood stresses that "There are no reputable scientific studies that show having a defensive gun increases security." Have you or someone close to you been attacked violently? What impact would gun ownership have had on that attack?

4. The letter clarifies how gun violence really occurs in America: primarily among people who are family and friends, among those closest to us and of our own race and nationality. With that reality, why do gundamentalists focus so much on fear of the "other, the stranger"?

5. Is it off-base to ask WWJD about gun choices, ammunition, body silhouette targets? Is that a fair question to ask a young Christian who is considering buying a gun? Why or why not?

Assignment: Reach out to any young person you know who might consider buying a gun. Share some of the issues in this chapter with them.

10. Defilappis and Hughes, "Gunfight or Flee."

8

Life's Greatest Temptation—
Feeling in Control

A recent cartoon portrayed a father sitting on a couch with his son. He is explaining the facts of life: "Here's the deal," he says. "Your mother and I call the shots when you're young, you will call the shots when we are old, and everything in between is a non-stop battle for control." We may speak disparagingly of those who are control freaks, but trying to control others is a time-honored tradition for all of us. It is a temptation we cannot fully avoid or overcome. As we witness more acts of senseless violence, we covet assurances that we can be in control of our own lives and situations. Gundamentalists will say, "That's why I bought a gun!"

In 1821, President John Quincy Adams warned our still-new nation about "searching the world over for monsters to destroy" so that we might control the destinies of other nations and peoples. His warning was tempered by the realization that even if we *could* become the dictator of the world, our beautiful national spirit would, of necessity, have to change from that of "liberty to that of force."[1]

"Searching the world (or the city) for monsters to destroy" is equally the temptation of militarists, gang leaders, and all too many gundamentalists. Their belief systems are essentially the same, differing only in proportionality: seeking always to have enough weapons to control all enemies

---

1. Mount Holyoke School of Education, "Warning Against the Search for Monsters to Destroy."

both foreign and domestic. Living with the illusion that our weapons give us license to control the behavior of other nations is a craving for the United States and all powerful countries. It is also an enormous temptation for those who consider buying a handgun to defend the family or the neighborhood.

The temptation itself may be based on the most altruistic motives, but in reality, it is a harbinger of disastrous unintended consequences. The risk of having a gun close by is graphically portrayed in HBO's documentary, *Requiem for the Dead: American Spring, 2014.* The film puts a human face on the 8,000 Americans who died by guns in those few spring months. It shows touching family pictures, laughing children, happy brides and grooms, and proud parents and grandparents. The majority of the 8,000 died not at the hands of violent criminals or strangers who invaded their space, but by impulsive acts of spouses, family members, and friends through accidents, suicides, and murders.

This is the open-ended catastrophe of a country swimming in guns and looking to firearms for solutions to personal problems. We look to them to provide security and protection, but they end up taking the very lives we most want to protect. History records too many unintended consequences. Well-intentioned citizens, who are arming themselves are in fact destabilizing the peace and order they most desire.

I call the hubristic belief that we can actually be in control of our own lives, let alone control other's behavior, life's greatest temptation. It's a seductive pull to want to be "a defender of the innocent," or "a protector of the neighborhood," or "one of the good guys" whom Wayne La Pierre describes as those with a CCWP. He says, "They are the most trustworthy Americans."[2]

There is an insidious belief in America that only the righteous violence of "us good guys" can save the rest from the despicable violence of "the bad guys." The late theologian Walter Wink called this heresy "the real religion of America."[3] A gun may only be a thing, *but it is a thing with a spirit that hungers to be in control.* It is a life-force that captures its owner's thought process, turning his/her values about love and neighborliness upside down. The spirit of that gun does not rest until the owner himself starts believing that which is made to kill is now one's ultimate value providing "life," "security," and "inner peace." Isn't that the work of a god?

2. Violence Policy Center, "License to Kill."
3. Wink, *Engaging the Powers*, 13.

In *America and Its Guns: A Theological Expose*, I refer to firearms morphing into false gods or idols (i.e., incrementally growing into another absolute which competes against Almighty God for one's obedience). The Abrahamic faiths declare the Creator God is the world's *only* absolute. As in "You shall have no other gods before me" (Exod 20:2) or "in front of me"; "alongside me"; "in my place"; "instead of me"; "against my face" or "at my expense."[4] For those who profess faith in the one and only Creator, to concede there is another absolute (an oxymoron in itself), is idolatry. Idolatry is present whenever people revere the Second Amendment and reject the Second Commandment.

Wayne La Pierre, Executive Director of the NRA, regards a gun as absolute protection. One week after the Newtown, Connecticut, massacre of twenty first graders, he proclaimed, "The *only* way to stop a monster from killing our kids is to be personally invested in *a plan of absolute protection where the good guy with a gun can stop a bad guy with a gun.*"[5]

To subscribe to the NRA's religious fantasies that guns are worthy absolutes is to join a mystical fraternity of those who depend on and are devoted to their guns. Because the human spirit is fickle, it is easy to vacillate between trusting God *and* trusting one's firearm. In reality, both can make an identical profession of faith: "The Lord [or my gun of choice] is the stronghold of my life; of whom shall I be afraid? When evildoers assail me to devour my flesh—my adversaries and foes—they shall stumble and fall. Though an army encamp against me, my heart shall not fear; though war rise up against me, yet I will be confident" (Ps 27: 1–3). Such is the subtlety and threat of gundamentalism. It slips up on you and can take you prisoner.

H. E. Mertens writes, "Each of us believes in, wagers on, and trusts in a god or a deity, i.e. an all-orientating and all-dominating prime value, something or someone whereby all else ultimately matters, and to which or to whom all the rest of life is related. Tell me which prime value dominates your thoughts, your actions, your life in fact (perhaps unconsciously), and I will tell you what is the concrete name of your god and what is the color of your real religion, even if sociologically you belong to another."[6]

As guns evolve into idols, many owners evolve into an agent of destiny and control. One starts believing she can become the *absolute protector* of one's family. I read somewhere of a young American girl having a deep

4. Miller, *The Ten Commandments*, 20.

5. Speech at the Willard Hotel, Washington, D.C., December 21, 2012.

6. Cited in Burggraeve, *Desirable God*, 38.

conversation with her aunt who was visiting from India. She revealed all of her detailed plans for the future. The aunt says to her American niece, "Ah, my dear–to believe that you can control everything in your life! How absurdly American!" Believing we can control our surroundings has been on a pedestal before. Francis Bacon (1571–1626) claimed through scientific technology nature can be "dissected" and "forced out of her natural state and squeezed and molded" so that "she takes orders from man and works under his authority." Rene Descartes, arguing in his famous *Discourse on Method* (1637) said, "through knowledge of nature and human craft we can "render ourselves the masters and possessors of nature."[7]

It's bewildering to watch those who, in the footsteps of Bacon and Descartes, feel they can build a luxurious home on a flood plain or on top of the San Andreas Fault and others refuse to leave their beach home in the face of a Category V hurricane, believing they can weather any storm.

In the primeval story of Genesis 3, Adam and Eve rejected God's instructions for living in that beautiful garden. They disdained taking orders; they made plans to give orders. They scorned dependence, wanting independence. Yearning to be in charge, they rejected the boundaries God prescribed for them. You know people like that. The English poet, William Ernest Henley was one. He tried valiantly to be in command of his own life. Hear him boast in his most famous poem, which he composed as a twelve-year-old after his leg was amputated:

> Out of the night that covers me,
> Black as the pit from pole to pole,
> I thank whatever gods may be
> For my unconquerable soul.
> It matters not how straight the gate,
> How charged with punishments the scroll,
> I am the master of my fate;
> I am the captain of my soul.[8]
>
> —"Invictus"

He *was* "an unconquerable soul" . . . until his cherished little daughter took sick and died. Her death convinced Henley he was not in charge; he was neither the master of his fate, nor the captain of his soul. His boasting was a figment of his imagination.

7. Merchant, *Radical Ecology,* 46–47.

8. Found in public domain at https://www.amazoncom/William-Ernest-Henley-Classic-Reprint/dp/B008WX4BJs.

However much the culture admires the confident and determined individual, no one can claim the power to control nature or other human beings, let alone the power of evil. Nothing made by human hands or conceived in the human mind can provide the security we all would like to have. Security is at best a superstition.

To illustrate how misleading "security" can be, listen to my friend, Robert Close: "I went for my morning jog in a public park and an oak tree fell on me." He survived with some broken bones and a skittish spirit, which lasted for some time. He was but an inch or two away from being crushed before breakfast.

Things like floods, tornadoes, shark attacks, or automobile accidents take place in the blink of an eye. No one is immune from unexpected hazards and surprises. Life itself is risky for all God's creatures great and small. To be human is to live in a world where life is constantly coming apart at the seams, and we must make adjustments and rebuild it over and over again. Circumstances change the entire contexts of our lives. Life's surprises repeatedly redefine our relationships with family, neighbors, and strangers. Hosts of things can go wrong. When a gun is present in the midst of trouble and pain, it often *appears* to be the answer. Trust me, it's not!

Following a spate of mass shootings in June 2015, John Morlino wrote a letter to the editor of the *Washington Post*: "Our psychological well-being, like our physical health, is subject to change *at any time*. While some of those changes may be minor, others are far more serious and can be accompanied by grave consequences. Being anointed a 'responsible gun-owner' after passing a background check is akin to receiving a decent grade on a mid-term exam. It might be comforting at the time, but it does not predict future behavior."[9] Another friend sums it all up: *"Life happens."*

Marriages made in heaven can quickly go on the rocks. Little spats can turn into arguments; and arguments into domestic violence; and domestic violence into murder. Children for whom we have longed, may be born physically or mentally challenged, and stretch our sanity and faith to the breaking point. In teen years, or even before, our kids may join gangs or get hooked on drugs and we often respond with unbridled fury. Those who are pictures of health become invalids; the most well-adjusted grow depressed and impulsively take their own lives with the bedside gun purchased for protection. After an unforeseen divorce, scores are besieged with anger and kill their ex-spouse and children in murder-suicides. It happens all the time

9. Morlino, "Guns make the Difference."

and with increased frequency today because so many articulate guns are just lying around talking to us, as if the violence they counsel is sage advice.

We buy life, home, fire, and automobile insurance to help us and/or our survivors respond financially to events, both expected and unexpected. After a calamity, the insurance we collect helps put our lives back together again. No one, however, can purchase insurance to *protect us from* life's disasters. They are simply part of the human situation, which no one can predict, rein in, or control. It would be such a comfort if we could purchase protection *from* catastrophes, but, alas, it is unavailable. Notwithstanding, we hear the soothing, confident voice of the gun dealer: "I sell protection. I sell security. I sell safety. Come, step into my parlor."

FOR GOOD DEFENSE, CONSIDER PEPPER SPRAY

The NRA's ever-present claim is, "The *only* thing that will stop a bad guy with a gun is a good guy with a gun." But, "it ain't necessarily so." Science tells us, having a gun around puts all the family at greater risk.

On the other hand, there *are* scientific studies that prove bear spray is more effective in stopping a charging bear than a gun. We don't meet charging bears within our city limits, but what will deter an angry grizzly will stop a human being in his tracks. Mark Matheny has been on a personal crusade ever since pepper spray saved his life in 1992. He was on a long-bow hunting trip outside of Yellowstone Park when he had a horrifying encounter with a three-hundred-pound mama grizzly bear. He was badly mauled, which left him scarred both physically and emotionally. His hunting partner finally drove away the bear with pepper spray. This led him to start his own company, UDAP, now one of the biggest bear spray companies in the country.

Matheny has evidence that bear spray works better than a gun to stop a bear. Unlike using a gun, aiming is not as big a factor when one is trying to hit a vital spot while terrified of the charging animal. If bullets don't hit a precise spot, the attack can intensify. Bear spray on the other hand stops the bear in its tracks by impairing its sight, breathing, and sense of smell even as it is expelled in the bear's direction.

Bear researchers have shown that firearms were less effective in protecting individuals against bear attacks than many had previously believed, including the researchers themselves. Among their conclusions were 1) "firearm bearers suffered the same injury rates in close encounters with bears whether they used their firearms or not," and 2) "bear spray [has] a better success rate under a variety of situations . . . than firearms."[10]

In 2008, Smith coauthored a similar study looking specifically at the effectiveness of pepper spray in bear encounters in Alaska. He analyzed 600 Alaskan bear- human encounters from 1985 to 2006, of which 71 involved pepper spray and aggressive bears—mostly grizzlies. In all of the incidents involving spray, there were only 3 injuries, and none of them fatal—a 98 percent success rate.

Bear spray, or its human counterpart, personal defense pepper spray, is equally as effective on human beings, according to Matheny. "You may only get one shot with a gun. With the spray you've got an awful sound and a fog being released out of the canister, which will disable an assailant. The effect is like getting ice picks in your eyes—the assailant would immediately drop everything and start rubbing his eyes which would make the pain even worse. It will totally disable a person with a gun for 30–45 minutes, with no long-term lasting effects. And the great thing is that personal defense pepper spray is legal with some restrictions in all 50 states and users could be trained to use it in a very short period of time. The canisters can fire a stream of spray up to 30 feet—or more than across the average U.S. classroom."[11]

My friend Arnold Brooks, who first told me of the effectiveness of bear spray in self-defense, poses a provocative question: "If a 2:00 a.m. "intruder" in your home turns out to be your college student coming home for a surprise visit, you may wish you had a can of pepper spray rather than a Glock handgun."

That exact scenario played out last New Year's Eve 2015, in St. Cloud, Florida. A woman woke up just before midnight and fired a shot at a person she thought had broken into her home and was approaching her bedroom. The person was not an intruder. It was her twenty-seven-year-old daughter, who died a few minutes later at the local hospital.[12]

10. Smith and Herrero, "Efficacy of Firearms for Bear Deterrence in Alaska."

11. *Field and Stream* public paper, "Use Pepper Spray Instead of Guns to Stop a Charging Grizzly."

12. Almasy and Newsome, "Florida Mother Shoots Daughter She Thought Was Intruder."

QUESTIONS

1. Can you name fears in your own life where you seek to be "in control"?

2. Why does the author stress wanting to be in control is a huge temptation, especially in regard to guns? Do you agree? Why or why not?

3. The proven most violence-prone situations include marriage and family conflict, economic stress, health and mental health disintegration and other anger-related dysfunction. Reflect on alternative ways of facing out-of-control realities without resort to guns.

4. Atwood states, "A gun may be only a thing, but it is a thing with a spirit that hungers to be in control. It is a life-force that captures its owner's thought process, turning his/her values about love and neighborliness upside down." To what extent is everyone vulnerable to the control temptation offered by guns? Are you or someone close to you vulnerable to it?

5. Gundamentalism makes guns into an idol. Reflect on your own source of security and ultimate trust.

9

A Vicious Circle

The Ethos of Gun Violence

MORE VIOLENCE
33,000 killed by guns every year
Mass shootings almost daily
Terrorism
TV- Movies- Video Games

**UNEXPECTED DEATHS,
INJURIES, AND ACCIDENTS**
Guns bought for protection are 22 times
more likely to be used against family
members, friends, or in a suicide, or
stolen and used in a crime, than to stop
an intruder.

WE BLAME "THOSE PEOPLE"
Muslims –Immigrants
The Mentally Ill
Other races, religions, classes while
persons like ourselves are the most
likely to do us harm.

**WE BUY A GUN & EXPECT
PROTECTION**
"We have a level playing field."
"No longer are we defenseless."
"We take control of our lives."

**FEARS CLOUD OUR
THINKING**
"They are so dangerous."
"No one is safe."
"We may be on their hit- list "

CAVE-MAN INSTINCTS SURFACE
"Do Guns *really* save lives?"
"Would a gun keep us safe?"
"We *should* control our lives and homes."
"Police can't protect everybody."

Preston Striebig ©

81

Americans are accustomed to living in the vicious circle of fear, guns, more fear and more guns; we complain occasionally about it, but do nothing substantive to break its endless cycle. We are used to it. That is not to say we don't regret it every now and then. We do. We wish it would go away forever, but instead of purposeful action, scores of clergy and political leaders address the brutality of gun deaths by keeping the families of those whose loved ones were shot and killed, in their thoughts and prayers.

After a shooting, someone will say, "We must tell our representatives to stop this madness." Predictably, a nearby gundamentalist will respond, "This is not the time for *politics*; we must respect those who are grieving and pray for them." Are they listening to the apostle who urged us in Romans 12:12 to be "constant in prayer"?

Perhaps after the sit in at the House of Representatives, led by John Lewis, such empty, hypocritical calls to prayer and ubiquitous moments of silence will be seen for what they really are: attempts to let cowardly legislators and timid clergy off the hook for doing nothing about a pandemic.

Rabbi Abraham Heschel peels back the layers of duplicity with his affirmation: "Prayer is meaningless unless it is subversive, unless it seeks to overthrow and to ruin the pyramids of callousness, hatred, opportunism, and falsehood."[1]

Mass shootings may be on the increase, but, as said above, they represent only a tiny percentage of gun fatalities. Even so, "If it bleeds, it leads" (an expression often heard in newsrooms). The networks, hungry for drama and the sensational, present these killings with all their frightening and gory details for several days, even weeks, at a time. This is to the utter delight of gun manufacturers and those who own stock in their companies. The ongoing story turns into free advertising for the gun industry as fear grips those who fantasize they could well be the next victim and they better get a firearm without delay. Many years ago William R. Ruger, CEO of Sturm Ruger and Company, was prescient as he boasted: "We have a little money making machine here. All we have to do is keep introducing the correct new products."[2]

On the other hand, the media's coverage for the vast majority of gun murders (in the neighborhood of ten thousand) is somewhere between non-existent and hidden away on the back pages of our newspapers.

1. Waskow, "Continuing Heschel in Our Lives."
2. Diaz, Powerpoint Presentation.

Suicides, murders, and accidents have become commonplace and merit little press coverage.

One can make a solid case that the Military Industrial Complex and the gun industry are the sole beneficiaries of the violence portrayed on television 365/24/7. Not only the news, but the network's programming is the equivalent of one continuous *free* non-stop commercial that promotes fear of "the other" and extols the "blessing" of owning a gun. In the distance I can hear the gun manufacturers: "Is this a great country, or what? We can even use the human instinct for self-preservation to hoodwink fearful people into believing the *next* mass shooting *might* be in their neighborhood and they need a gun, *or another gun,* for protection!"

Massad Ayoob, a journalist for the magazine *Shooting Industry,* advises gun shop dealers to *"Use fear to sell more guns on impulse*: Customers come to you every day out of fear. Fear of what they read in the newspaper. Fear of what they watch on the 11 o'clock news. Fear of the terrible acts of violence they see on the street. Your job, in no uncertain terms, is to sell them confidence in the form of steel and lead. An impulse of fear has sent that customer to your shop, so you want a quality product in stock to satisfy the customer's needs and complete the impulse purchase."[3]

Getting hold of a gun is not difficult in America. We have more gun dealers than McDonald's, Starbucks, and supermarkets combined.[4] Thousands of young people, particularly those at-risk, know two things: who has the drugs and who has the guns. When a youth wants to be cool, tough, or needs some quick money; or wants to protect himself from a bully; or when in a fit of anger, wants to shoot someone, he can pick up an illegal gun through a straw purchaser, go to a gun show, or pick up a firearm over the Internet. In the inner city, one can rent a gun for a day, week, or longer.

Fear not only sells guns, it sells *more* guns, both big and small, to those who already possess large arsenals. One of my favorite cartoons portrays a mighty king surrounded by his generals. They are standing at the base of a high wall, grieving over the recent death of Humpty Dumpty whose remains are splattered all over the ground. The king speaks: "Yes, I know 'All the king's horses and all the king's men cannot put Humpty Dumpty together again.' But, his death shows why I need 50,000 more horses and 100,000 more men."

---

3. Ayoob, "Trend Crimes and the Gun Dealer," 18.
4. Zatat, Narjas, "More Gunshops", Indy 100.

Like the king in the cartoon, strong nations and well-armed individuals are fearful they might not have enough weapons to keep them safe. They need "just a little bit more." The gnawing suspicion that we *might not have quite enough* morphs swiftly into *we have a desperate need for more.* I met a gundamentalist who boasted he had a gun in every room of his house. I didn't press him if that included his bathrooms. I have discovered through the years that purchasing just a few more guns does not assuage one's fears; it increases them all the more.

Ironically, after every gun massacre, as the nation mourns the loss of life, gun sales actually go up. Gundamentalists are encouraged to buy more weapons "while they still can." The gun press will likely speak of the United Nation's plans to strip our citizens of their Second Amendment rights, register all civilian firearms, and ultimately confiscate all guns all around the world.

No matter that the Charter of the UN expressly forbids any of its member states to be involved in the internal affairs of *any* of its members. Their capacity to turn disinformation into an art form works very well for their purposes. It terrifies their political base about *big government's* intentions, sells more guns, and brings in more donations to the organizations that thrive only because they can manufacture fear.

Let's consider the oft-used words, "Buy them while you still can." I think the words themselves *may contain a subtle psychological hint* that even a few of the most ardent gundamentalists realize down deep in their hearts, *some* restrictions *should* be placed on lethal weapons. Even their repeated pleas for unrestricted gun rights before the American public, may be a subconscious prayer: "Won't somebody out there stop us?" In their heart of hearts they must be aware that 33,000 gun deaths every year are unacceptable and freedom and democracy must have a deeper meaning than buying more powerful guns.

Meanwhile, the NRA proposes we break the vicious cycle of violence by putting more guns into the hands of good guys. *Everybody* should be armed. The *despicable violence* of the bad guys can be stopped only with the *righteous violence* of the good guys. Martin Luther King captures our conundrum in his famous quote, "Injustice anywhere is a threat to justice everywhere," but when the prophet spoke out against the war in Vietnam he was also thinking of violence.[5] It matters not *where* the violence takes place, its seductive evil spirit leaps far beyond the geographical locale where it

5. King, speaking at the University of Minnesota, April 27, 1967.

first occurred. It is the ethos in which we live. We read about it in our newspapers; listen to it on our car radios; see it on TV. It pops up regularly on our smart phones, computers, and networks as breaking news. We feel it in our depths and often are tempted to fear for our lives.

As I write this paragraph not only Paris, but Europe, the US, Canada and the entire developed world is traumatized by terrorist attacks in Paris, the City of Light. One hundred and thirty people were murdered. We are wedged in by fear. Philadelphia Mayor Michael Nutter reminds us, "There is really no level of distinction between the violence that goes on, on the streets of America on a daily basis and the episodic acts of international terrorism that also take place—primarily in cities."[6]

After authorities revealed three of the Paris attackers came ashore in Greece and made their way to Paris, a xenophobic panic gripped America to the point that majorities suggested we renounce God's command to love our neighbors and show hospitality to strangers, particularly as it relates to 1.6 billion Muslims. Congress, without considering the long-term implications of our paranoia, denounced any and all Syrians, even those tortured by ISIS, and sought to ban all refugees, including three-year-old orphans, from entering the country. Some raised the possibility of placing all refugees from the Middle East in concentration camps just as we did Japanese-Americans at the beginning of World War II. One thing is clear: our fears are once again pushing us over the edge into hating those who are different and the most devastating, unintended, and far-reaching consequences continue to be found in what our hatred is doing to our own souls.[7]

I've been told that 365 times, one for every day of the year, the Bible counsels us not to give in to "cave-man fears of the other." We are exhorted not to place our trust in princes or chariots or arms, but in Almighty God who can help us, teach us, and empower us to love "the other" who shares the same human dreams and weeps the same salty tears. The Apostle Paul reminds us in his counsel to his young friend, Timothy, "God did not give us a spirit of cowardice, but rather a spirit of power and of love and of self-discipline" (2 Tim 1: 7).

During the Republican presidential debates in the spring of 2016, when the more bellicose candidates were trying to ratchet up fears of Muslims, Police Commissioner of New York City, Bill Bratton, injected a moment of sanity into the discussion by announcing he, personally, knew

---

6 King, "Pray for the District, Too."

7. CNN, "American Deaths in Terrorism vs. Gun Violence in One Graph."

the whereabouts of 900 organized, heavily armed Muslims in New York City. "They are serving on the NYPD." Mayor de Blasio chimed in: there are "peace-loving, law-abiding Muslim Americans in neighborhoods all over New York City who should be respected like all other members of our community."[8]

Only the truth can rescue us, and the truth comes clothed in facts. If we could push our pause buttons to give our fears a rest and pay closer attention to facts, it would allay our angst and calm us down. We should be asking first of all: how great a threat is Muslim terrorism to Americans? From 2001 to 2013, 350 US citizens were killed in terrorist acts *overseas* and 3,380 persons died in all terrorist incidents *inside* the US (including the attacks of 9/11 and the Boston Marathon bombing). Adding the 14 killed in San Bernadino and 50 murdered in the Pulse Night Club in Orlando, the total number of Americans killed in terrorist acts within the US since the turn of the century is 3,444. In the same period of time, 406,496 people died by firearms on US soil (2013 is the most recent year CDC data for deaths by firearms is available). Put those numbers in juxtaposition: 406,496 deaths from our guns vs. 3,444 deaths from the most violent terrorist organizations in the world: the Taliban, Al-Qaeda, and ISIS. What keeps us from taking action on our greatest threat?[9]

I sense a tiny bit of concern among those legislators who are in the pocket of the NRA for the astronomical numbers of Americans killed by guns, but I discern a palpable fear in their ranks that a rational law or two regulating the indiscriminate sale of guns to dangerous individuals, including terrorists, *might* get some traction in Congress. What is wrong with us?

FEAR OF THOSE WHO ARE DIFFERENT SELLS GUNS

I'm told former President Richard Nixon once said, "Fear is easier to believe than love. They won't tell you that in Sunday school, but it is the truth." Many of today's young people, especially in our inner cities, have given up on love, justice, hope for tomorrow, equality, and living to a ripe old age. To gain respect, some youth feel they must get hold of a pistol or semi-automatic handgun. The truth is these guns have been speaking to their subconscious for months or years.

8. New York City Mayor's Office, "Ted Cruz's Call for Muslim Patrols Angers N.Y. Police."

9. Jones and Bower, CNN.

Like the Chevrolet dealer who wants to sell more cars and trucks, gun manufacturers and their collaborators at the NRA want to sell more guns. They know fearful people buy the most firearms, and the Gun Empire knows how to exploit those fears. It must have been an unguarded moment when Wayne La Pierre, the high priest of anxiety, opened the door just a crack, so we could peer in to learn of their deceitful marketing strategies. La Pierre said, "The only thing we have to fear is the absence of fear."[10]

Don't confuse his words with those of President Franklin D. Roosevelt, who at the beginning of World War II said, "The only thing we have to fear is fear itself." He sought to *minimize* the nation's fears over the war. La Pierre and his partners work hard to *maximize* America's fears, particularly about "the browning of America," that threatens the status quo.

The Gun Empire creates angst and spawns phobias as it warns us of the dangers posed by four kinds of people: 1) Those who are simply mean and/ or evil; 2) Persons of color who live in our inner cities; 3) Immigrants who gather at our Southern borders to wade across the Rio Grande and "take over our country"; 4) Terrorist cells who worship in America's mosques where they are trained to kill Americans.

The violence these gundamentalists predict is abstract, staged, dramatized, and *unrelated to* our daily experiences of violence, which are not neat, clean, and unambiguous in character. In short, selling more guns is primarily the interests of a minority of American men who are most removed from the violence of the streets and live in rural, suburban, white middle-class neighborhoods.

They are held captive by their fears of "those people" who are different and, therefore, are considered dangerous, but the facts are substantially different. Most murders are committed by family members, friends, and acquaintances who carry keys to our homes. The culprits are not criminals, terrorists, or persons of another race or religion. People just like us commit the crimes. If America's gun dealers told the truth about who are the greatest threats to life and limb, they couldn't make a living.

In spite of these indisputable facts, vast numbers of well-meaning Americans continue to go along with hateful hype that demonizes those whose race, religion, or heritage is different. A case in point: In November 2014, La Pierre wrote a letter to NRA members—fittingly entitled "Is Chaos at our Door?" "[The] world that surrounds us is growing more dangerous all the time," he warned. "Whether it's enemy state actors, foreign terrorists,

10 La Pierre, YouTube, September 19, 2013.

Mexican drug cartels, or domestic criminals, the threats Americans face are massive—and growing." He invoked massive terrorist attacks like those in Mumbai in 2008 or Kenya in 2013, hordes of armed and violent gangs that "are embedded coast to coast" and an influx of illegal immigrants with criminal backgrounds. La Pierre complained that the government had detained and then "intentionally released 36,000 illegal aliens" with criminal records. "Where all these released criminals went," he wrote, "no one knows. But you can bet on this: They're among us, embedded throughout our society. For all you know, you pass them in your car on your way to work." His argument can be boiled down to this: Americans are on the verge of—or already sinking into—a state of anarchy, where it is each man for himself. In that state, "the government can't—or *won't*—protect you . . . Only *you* can protect you," he warns.[11]

La Pierre speaks right to the hearts of fearful, powerful *people* who hide behind the flag and voice the shibboleths of "Constitution," "freedom," and "gun rights," so they can resist any changes to Prosperity Island, our lovely refuge that is surrounded by a raging sea of poverty. Their trumped up fears about the future and the loss of privileges that come with being white, have become so much a part of their tribal identity that they are reluctant to entertain any questions about their validity; let alone take a chance on love by extending an open hand and heart to those who are different.

Unlike La Pierre, I learned years ago in my high school civics class to be proud of the diversity that is America. I count it a blessing to live in a melting pot nation comprised of many peoples, races, and cultures. *E Pluribus Unum*—out of many, *one*—should be repeated with pride, not fear. One has further incentive to believe in the blessings of diversity when one meets it so frequently in the Bible. "Red and yellow, black and white, we are precious in God's sight. God loves all the children of the world."

One of my favorite memories is of a little boy who visited our home when my wife was pastor of Garden Memorial Presbyterian Church in Washington, D.C.'s inner city. Roxana invited several children for dinner. This little guy was brand new to the group and was just feeling his way along, getting used to new people, two of whom were white. After he ate his spaghetti, he followed Roxana into the kitchen. As she washed some dishes he said, "I think I love you, but I'm not sure. I don't know you very well yet." God speed the day when our human family can gather around

---

11. Quoted in DeBrabander, "How Gun Rights Harm the Rule of Law."

dinner tables and really get to know those who are different. Only then can we decide if we are going to love them.

FEAR AND LOVE

What if there were a requirement for every gun dealer to display a sign over the front door that read, "Those most likely to harm you are your family members and friends?" FBI Uniform Crime Reports have been proving that year after year. Our greatest threats are not from strangers, foreigners, terrorists, immigrants, or criminals; the most dangerous persons in our midst are people *just like us*. They often have a key to our house. That is the plain unvarnished truth. But, that is a very difficult truth for most people to comprehend. It is counter-intuitive and goes against everything we have been taught since childhood. The Gun Industry cannot sell the numbers of guns they want to sell by telling customers their own family, friends, and neighbors are the most likely to harm them. Even though it is unquestionably true, it simply is *not* believable. Those who are seized by fears, need an enemy to blame for all their problems.

A little known protest song in the sixties, whose author is unknown, speaks to their need. The last verse reads:

> Gotta have an enemy
> To keep alive the flame.
> Gotta have an enemy
> To carry all the blame.
> Gotta have an enemy
> To show we're not the same—
> An enemy, an enemy, an enemy!

Face to face with national statistics that black people kill other black people 94 percent of the time, and white people kill other white people 83 percent of the time, we still fear those who are different. That is the reason the Gun Empire produces scary video clips of a tough-looking African-American man breaking into a home where a beautiful blonde is sound asleep in her bed. That is a blatant racist caricature with no basis in fact. Yes, such a thing *is* possible, and it has happened before, but it is *most* unlikely and highly improbable, just as improbable that you will be the victim of a terrorist attack. Nevertheless, such deliberate disinformation playing upon racist fears sells millions of guns. If that racially prejudiced scene does not scare Caucasians into buying more firearms, you may hear the gun dealer hark back to that iconic movie, *The Terminator*, where Arnold Schwarzenegger utters his famous line—"I'll be baaaaack."

As fearful scenes are maximized and guns are portrayed as solving human problems with non-stop frequency on our evening entertainment on TV, fearful people start *thinking* guns will quiet *their fears*. In the primeval swamp, our forebears made bigger and better clubs to defend their own. Today, we simply ratchet up the firepower of our weapons.

One of the most thought-provoking statements I have ever read is from Alexander Solzhenitsyn's acceptance speech for the Nobel Prize for Literature in 1970. His words direct us to an *indisputable connection between violence and lies that always accompany it*. His words reveal why the NRA, the Gun Empire, and gundamentalists are so successful in spreading lies and misinformation. We should let Solzhenitsyn's words steep in our minds like a fine tea: If we did, just perhaps, we would not be so gullible. *"Let us not forget that violence does not live alone and is not capable of living alone: it is necessarily interwoven with falsehood. Violence finds its only refuge in falsehood, and falsehood its only support in violence. Any man who once acclaims violence as his method must inexorably choose falsehood as his principle."*[12]

Older readers will remember Sergeant Joe Friday on the radio. They can quote his most famous line: "The facts, ma'am; nothing but the facts!" Essentially, *the facts are that a gun in the home is twenty-two times more likely to kill a member of the family or an acquaintance, be used in a suicide, or be stolen and used in a crime than it is to stop an intruder.*[13]

The Bible deals with facts or if you prefer, spiritual realities. It has something to say about fear. As we noted, 365 times, once for every day of the year, it counsels us not to give in to our fears. I particularly like Paul's advice to his young friend, Timothy: "God did not give us a spirit of cowardice, but rather a spirit of power and of love, and of self-discipline" (2 Tim 1:7). And John sums it up succinctly, "There is no fear in love; perfect love casts out fear" (1 John 4: 18).

12. Solzhenitsyn, Acceptance Speech for Nobel Prize for Literature.
13. Rowen, "Guns in Home Pose Greater Risk."

QUESTIONS

1. Who is "the other" in your life? As a category of persons whom do you fear?

2. Atwood states that from 9/11/2001 to the Orlando nightclub murders, 3,444 Americans were killed by terrorist acts. In the same time, 406,496 Americans were killed by Americans with guns. He asks, "What keeps us from taking action on our greatest threat?" What is your answer?

3. Why does the purchase of guns tend to lead to a perceived need for even more guns? Reflect on ways that the gun and ammunition industry use fear as a marketing device.

4. Atwood suggests that gundamentalists, deep down, *perhaps* unconsciously, know that gun regulation is needed. Do you agree or disagree? How is the NRA and gun industry able to suppress that awareness?

5. It is a fact that we are far more likely to be killed by a friend or family member than by an intruder. Starting from that reality, what types of gun regulations are needed?

10

The Human and Economic Costs of Gun Violence in America

The NRA used to say frequently, but not so much lately, "An armed so-ciety is a polite society." If that were true, decades ago we would have already been recognized as the most polite country in the world. But as more families buy guns to defend themselves against neighbors, we must confess politeness has eluded us. Even Congress seems to have forfeited civility. More significantly, firearm homicides are twenty times higher in the U.S. than the combined rates of twenty-two countries that are our peers in wealth and population. The following statistics are "simply more facts with the blood washed off."[1]

- Guns claim on average one life every sixteen minutes in the United States.

- More Americans die in gun homicides and suicides every six months than have died in the last twenty-five years in every terrorist attack and in fighting the wars in Afghanistan and Iraq combined.

- More Americans have died from guns in the United States since 1968 than on the battlefields of all the wars in American history since 1775.

- American children are fourteen times more likely to die from guns as the children in all other developed countries combined.

1. Nelson and Zarracina, "A Shocking Statistic About Gun Deaths in the US."

- Thirty-one percent of all mass shootings in the world are in the United States.[2]

Suicides don't receive a lot of press. Consequently, most of us are unaware that far more people take their own lives with a gun than are murdered by one. More Americans in all age groups kill themselves with guns than with all other means combined, including hanging, poisoning, overdose, jumping, or cutting. Though guns are not the most common method by which people *attempt* suicide, they are the most lethal. Drug overdose, the most widely used method in suicide attempts, is fatal in less than three percent of cases. Eighty-five percent of suicide attempts with a firearm end in death. They are an irreversible solution to what is often a passing crisis. Suicidal individuals who use other means have time to reconsider their actions or to summon help. With a firearm, once the trigger is pulled, there's usually no turning back.[3]

Because it is a right to have a handgun in the home does not mean it is a good idea. Deciding whether to own a gun should entail a careful balancing of potential benefits and risks. One of the risks for gun ownership, for which the empirical evidence is strongest, is that of a completed suicide, which is the tenth leading cause of death in the US.[4]

Taking one's life is a heartbreak that cuts across all age, racial, economic, social, and ethnic boundaries. For those who succeed in killing themselves, their lives are over and the pain is gone forever. Not so for their loved ones who remain. They are bequeathed a lifetime of asking, "Why?" I have experienced such pain as I tried to figure out the reasons friends and a member of my extended family took their own lives, when, on the surface of things, they had everything to live for.

My pastor in my college days was Dr. William Martin, Jr., of the First Presbyterian Church in Tallahassee, Florida. He helped me wrestle through my call to pursue the ministry, just as he influenced at least ten other young men and women to enter a church vocation. I went to church one Sunday morning expecting to hear him preach a sermon on the topic "Facing Life Steadily." Instead, the church was locked and a wreath was on the front door with the devastating message: "'Dub' Martin died early this morning." He killed himself with a shotgun. I was shattered, as were thousands of

2. Langford, "Stop the Paralysis."
3. Chan, "Guns and Suicides."
4. American Foundation for Suicide Prevention.

students and faculty at Florida State University, not to mention his wife and two children. How could that happen to one who was a tower of strength and a source of inspiration for so many?

Aphrodite Matsakis wrote her book to give understanding and hope to the wives of over 100,000 Vietnam War veterans who committed suicide, almost doubling those who died in combat (58,220).[5] She says suicide casts a blanket of fear and guilt over entire families and is particularly evident in little boys who loved and trusted their fathers. "They often get the idea that self-destruction is a viable solution to the problems of living, or they learn that life itself is not worth living."[6]

Every year on average 42,773 persons take their own lives by various means and for every success, there are 25 other attempts, though many of the latter are half-hearted efforts and cries for help. Suicides cost the US economy $44 billion. Half-hearted attempts at suicides often lead to serious injuries, ongoing trauma to families and friends, and economic loss. One can continue to live after overdosing, cutting, or jumping, etc., but if a gun is used, it is usually "successful." Experts tell us the actual number of those who take their own lives is higher because many suicides are recorded as accidents, even murder, and some officials will not list suicide as the cause of death unless there is a suicide note. Their reasoning is that suicide is a deliberately chosen act. I have no solution to their dilemma, but it would be even more accurate if we could say it was an "unintended consequence" of owning a gun.[7]

In 1999, several epidemiologists studied whether ownership of a handgun increases or decreases the risk of violent death. Their conclusions were: the purchase of a handgun is associated with a substantial increase in the risk of suicide by firearm *and by any other method*. One epidemiologist writes, "The increase in the risk of suicide by firearm is apparent within a week after the purchase of a handgun and persists for at least six years."[8]

In chapter 4, I point to the excesses of gundamentalists who are suing Florida's psychiatrists for asking depressed patients or members of their families if there is a gun in the home. Physicians have long recognized the importance of keeping guns away from those suffering with depression.

5. James, "Suicide Rate Spikes in Vietnam Vets."
6. Matsakis, *Vietnam Wives*, 256.
7. American Foundation for Suicide Prevention.
8. Wintemute et al., "Mortality Among Recent Purchasers of Handguns," 1583.

I maintain in several places throughout this book that guns *talk* to their owners, but when depression is severe, they shout, "Death is the answer."

Gun owners and their families are much more likely to kill themselves than non-gun owners. This is not because gun owners are more suicidal, but because a gun *is available.* The gun is *there* carrying its own set of expectations and recurrent messages. About one third of American families own guns and such easy access raises the suicide risk for everyone: gun owner, spouse, and children alike.[9]

A case in point: in Morrilon, Arkansas, in 1998, a third grader shot and killed himself while his mother was outside cutting a switch to whip him because he brought home a bad report card. Christopher Parks, eight years old, climbed onto a dresser to get the gun that was hanging from a nail on the wall, then shot himself in the head.[10]

Among industrialized nations, the overall suicide rate in the United States falls roughly in the middle. However, the suicide rate for children five to fourteen years of age is twice the average of those in other developed countries because of our firearms related suicide rate, which is ten times that of the average of other nations.[11]

SUICIDE BY COP

A relatively new phenomenon in the study of suicide is suicide by cop, when people want to die but do not want to kill themselves. To accomplish their death wish, they position themselves where a police officer is forced to shoot them. An example: Police in Pittston, Luzerne County, Pennsylvania, reported the shooting death of Robert Patrick Quinn, seventy-seven years old on August 11, 2015. It was ruled "suicide via police officer." Acquaintances, his roommate, and ex-wife reveal he had been complaining of constant pain and had suicidal thoughts for at least a decade. His ex-wife revealed recent statements he made about being shot by police.

Quinn was waving a realistic-looking pellet gun while sitting on a motorized scooter. Officers reported asking Quinn fifteen to twenty times to drop his weapon and opened fire only after he pointed the gun at one of them.[12]

9. Chan, *Guns and Suicide*, 1.

10. Hemenway, *Private Guns-Public Health,* 35–36.

11. Ibid., 37.

12. Lee, "Luzern County D. A. Man Killed by Suicide by Cop."

Suicide-by-cop incidents are extremely dangerous for police officers because they never know if the individual will try to kill them too. Some suicidal individuals will point an empty gun at the police because they know they will shoot in self-defense. Others will have a loaded gun and will want to kill as many police officers as possible before they die.

Most police officers who are involved in these shootings suffer emotional difficulties afterwards, including PTSD. Some who die from suicide by cop leave notes explaining their reasons for taking their actions and apologize to the officers.

This kind of suicide occurs more frequently than most people would imagine. In a study published in the *Annals of Emergency Medicine*, researchers analyzed data from the Los Angeles County Sheriff's Department and found suicide by cop was surprisingly common and the number of incidents were rising; between 1987 through 1997, 11 percent of officer-involved shootings were suicide by cop incidents. Other findings were:

- 98 percent were male
- 39 percent had a history of domestic violence
- Many individuals abused alcohol and/or drugs
- Many individuals had a prior history of suicide attempts
- 17 percent used a toy or replica gun
- About 50 percent of the weapons used were loaded[13]

Anyone who has even the slightest thought about dying from suicide by cop, or by taking one's own life in any fashion, should get treatment immediately. Depression is the number one cause of suicide.

More than three-quarters of all suicide victims are not in psychiatric treatment at the time of their death, and half do not appear to have had any prior treatment. There is a common belief that those who take their own lives have made plans to do so over a long period of time, but research reveals most suicides are impulsive acts when an individual is confronting a severe but temporary crisis.[14]

13. Caruso, "'Suicide by Cop' Suicide Prevention, Awareness, and Support."
14. Rich, Young, and Fowler, San Diego Suicide Study: "Young vs. Old Subjects."

A major impact on such impulsivity could be produced by interventions that reduce impulsivity and that render impulsive acts less lethal. Protection could be obtained by restricting one's firearms.[15]

Once again, Gary Kleck is the *one* "researcher" whose findings differ from those of his peers. He writes, "general gun ownership levels appear to have no net effect on total suicide rates." His "research" once more gives the Gun Empire encouragement to try and keep doctors from linking depression and suicide with the presence of a gun.[16] According to a multitude of scholars, epidemiologists, and those who do research on guns and gun deaths, Kleck's conclusions about guns and suicide are contrary to all available evidence.[17] Nevertheless, do you understand why the NRA loves to quote Gary Kleck?

MURDER-SUICIDE

More men kill their intimate partners than women. But domestic disputes and deep anger are not limited to men as the following reveals: Darryl Hamilton, fifty years old, a major league outfielder for five teams over thirteen major league seasons, was found dead at his home in Pearland, Texas, after a murder-suicide. According to a report from Pearland police, Hamilton suffered multiple gunshot wounds from his wife during a dispute at the home in suburban Houston. That spouse, Monica Jordan, forty-four years old, was found dead in another part of the home, apparently by self-inflicted gunshot wounds. Hamilton and Jordan's fourteen-month-old child was also in the house unharmed, according to the police, and was turned over to protective services.[18]

Those who engage in such brutal behavior are not people from another planet. They are people just like us. Nor can we expect social leaders and law enforcement officials to be more in control of their emotions than other members of society. That is far from realistic. Cops are people just like us and often have to live in their own private hells, susceptible to impulsive actions. That was the case in Harrison, New York, when two teenage sisters were killed by their father, a retired police officer, in a murder-suicide. Fifty-two-year-old Glen Hochman served in the White Plains Police Department

15. Lipschitz, "1995 Suicide Prevention in Young Adults (age 8–30)."

16. Kleck, *Targeting Guns*, 384.

17. Ibid., 39.

18. Lourim, "Darryl Hamilton, Killed in Apparent Murder-Suicide."

for twenty-two years before retiring one month earlier in January. He shot and killed the girls, Alissa Hochman, eighteen years old, and sister Deanna, thirteen, as they slept on Saturday and then took his own life. His wife and their eldest daughter were not at home at the time of the killings. Harrison Police Chief Anthony Marracini said the killings were premeditated, but impossible to understand. "I'm not sure that anybody can even understand how a person kills his children, that's something that's not comprehensible to me." [19]

This is a grizzly subject but it must be addressed. Murder-suicides are rare but there has been a recent spike in familicide cases all across the country. Since 1988, the homicide-suicide rate among couples fifty-five and older in Florida has increased about tenfold, according to Donna Cohen, a professor of psychiatry and behavioral sciences at the University of South Florida's Department of Aging and Mental Health. Though statistics for the entire country are unavailable, Cohen believes the Florida numbers are representative of other states. She estimates nearly twenty older Americans die each week in homicide-suicides. But those who murder a single member or several members of one's family, friends, lovers, and then kill themselves are from all age groups, races, and both sexes.[20]

When they do happen, murder-suicides are always heart-rending and chilling. They force us to ask, "Why do we let these horrible things happen with such regularity in America? Why do we insist on being unique in the family of developed nations? Being Number one in the developed world in murders, murder-suicides, and mass killings should not be the way we show the world what America is all about.

Jacquelyn Campbell of Johns Hopkins University explains most people who commit murder-suicide are non-Hispanic white males who kill their mates or former mates (91 percent) with a gun. Prior domestic violence is by far the number-one risk factor in these cases, but a criminal history is not a major influence. Other risk factors may predict more severe domestic violence cases, such as a stepchild in the home or estrangement. In the aftermath of a family murder followed by a suicide, communities, police, researchers, and others search for explanations. In difficult financial times, it is natural to look for economic influences, especially when the killer has recently lost a job or has enormous financial problems. Participants found

19. Langford, "Family, Friends, Bid Final Farewell to Harrison Sisters Killed by Father in Murder-Suicide." CBS News, Feb. 27, 2015.

20. Cosgrove, "Murder-Suicide in Elderly Rise."

that unemployment was a significant risk factor for murder-suicide but *only when combined with a history of domestic violence.* In other words, it was not a risk factor, in and of itself, but was something that tipped the scales following previous abuse.[21]

David Adams, researcher in domestic violence cases from the University of Pennsylvania, offers his perspectives based on years of research. In 92 percent of the murder suicides he examined, a gun was involved and the best predictor of domestic violence was past behavior. He compared high rates of intimate partner homicide in the United States with the considerably lower rates in other wealthy countries, noting America has the most permissive gun laws of any industrialized nation. He made similar comparisons among US states that have restrictive versus permissive gun laws and lower versus higher homicide and suicide rates.

He gives three reasons why guns are used more frequently in murder suicides: 1) They are more efficient than other weapons; 2) They can be used impulsively; 3) They can be used to terrorize and threaten. Adams asked those who killed with guns if they would have used another weapon if a gun were not available; most said no. Significantly, he adds, "The most common type of killer was a possessively jealous type. Many of the men who commit murder-suicide, as well as those who kill their children, also seem to fit that profile." He adds, "A jealous substance abuser with a gun poses a particularly deadly combination of factors; one that was present in about 40 percent of the killers I interviewed."[22]

Whenever a discussion arises about murder or murder-suicide, gundamentalists come quickly to the defense of guns, saying, "If it were not a gun, then the perpetrator would have used one of a dozen other means to kill." The weapon usually suggested is a baseball bat. Once again, we confront a common myth that is repeated endlessly by these extremists. To meet such misinformation the reader is directed to The Infoplease website that records all weapons used in all murders and suicides across the United States. The last year for which records are available was 2012. Guns were the instruments used 69.4 percent of the time. Baseball bats or other blunt objects were used 4 percent of the time. See the website for other statistics.[23]

21. Auchter, "Men Who Murder Their Families: What the Research Tells Us."

22. Ibid.

23. www.infoplease.com

THE TRAUMA THAT KEEPS ON GIVING — PTSD

When I was a boy, my mother bought me a soldier suit during World War II. I loved to wear the khaki pants and dark brown jacket with a strap draped over my shoulder just like the soldiers. They were my heroes. One of my idols was Sandy Trout, a six-foot-four family friend and boyfriend of my sister, Harriet. Sandy was a foot-soldier in some of the heaviest fighting in Europe and was wounded severely in the Battle of the Bulge. When he returned home from the battlefield, he had a limp and walked with a cane. I was at first awe-struck with Sandy but soon grew disillusioned. He was still his same jovial self in ordinary conversations, but refused to talk about his experiences on the battlefield and that's what I wanted to hear about more than anything else.

Having met and read about casualties of our wars since then, I understand his reluctance to speak about the Battle of the Bulge, where 19,000 American soldiers lost their lives. Some 47,500 were wounded, and 23,000 were captured or missing in action. Memories of those bloody scenes were too painful and the scars too deep for him to revisit. From what I know now about psychological trauma, it is clear Sandy had Post Traumatic Stress Disorder (PTSD).

PTSD, the malady associated with wars that can be traced back to antiquity, was called soldier's heart during America's Civil War; it was termed shellshock in the First World War, and battle fatigue during the Second. It became operational exhaustion in Korea, and PTSD only after the Vietnam War, when the American Psychiatric Association added the term to its list of recognized mental disorders. By whatever name its effect is the same.[24]

The condition itself is a mental disorder that may occur in people who experience or witness intense violence, serious accidents, or life-threatening situations. Involvement in these terrors can make people feel hopeless, fearful, and horror-struck. In America today, PTSD is not an isolated case or two, but an epidemic. A wide variety of symptoms are common among those who are experiencing posttraumatic stress disorder:

- Feeling upset by things that remind one of what happened

- Having nightmares, vivid memories, or flashbacks of the event that make one feel like it's happening all over again

- Feeling emotionally cut off from others

24. Thompson, "Unlocking the Secrets of PTSD."

- Feeling numb or losing interest in things one used to care about
- Feeling constantly on guard
- Feeling irritated or having angry outbursts
- Having difficulty sleeping
- Having trouble concentrating
- Being jumpy or easily startled
- Have conflict with authority figures (bosses, doctors, government)

The problem is exacerbated not only by experiencing the symptoms above, but by how individuals react to them and make life even more difficult and dangerous. Those with PTSD

- Frequently avoid places or things that remind one of what happened
- Consistently drink or use drugs to numb one's feelings
- Consider harming oneself or others
- Start working all the time to occupy one's mind
- Pull away from other people and become isolated[25]

More than half of the 2.6 million Americans who fought in Iraq and Afghanistan struggle with physical or mental health problems stemming from their service, feel disconnected from civilian life, and believe the government is failing to meet the needs of veterans, 41 percent of whom experience continuing mental and emotional problems. Half of our soldiers know a fellow service member who has attempted or committed suicide, and more than one million of them suffer from relationship problems and experience outbursts of anger—two key indicators of post-traumatic stress.[26]

Many of these veterans who return home leave their minds and emotions in a war zone. Suffering from PTSD, dealing with significant anger issues, and having difficulty maintaining relationships with spouses and children, they move into civilian neighborhoods, bringing with them the trauma experienced half a world away. Fighting depression and suicide, those who were accustomed to living with guns at their sides in war zones, feel they need them to protect themselves and their families. Too frequently

25. US Department of Veterans Affairs/PTSD, "Make the Connection."
26. Chandrasekaren, "A Legacy of Pain and Pride."

these guns take not only their own lives, but the lives of their wives and children in murder-suicides.

PTSD: NOT JUST FOR SOLDIERS

Sorrowfully, PTSD is not only for soldiers and/or soldier's families. PTSD symptoms are present in those who have experienced the trauma of a mugging, robbery attempt, home invasion, being near a shooting, or shot at, and/or shot at and hit. School counselors in the inner city tell us PTSD is often present in a child who listens to gunshots in her neighborhood before going to sleep at night.

One of my good friends, Kenneth Barnes, devotes much of his time encouraging youth who live in volatile inner city neighborhoods. They may escape getting shot or killed, but they cannot escape the toxic atmosphere thousands of guns create in their community. It has the feel of hopelessness and the finality of a war zone. Kenny recounts one visit to a middle school in Washington, D.C., located in a high crime area. He had instant rapport with the youth because his seventeen-year-old son was killed by a violent young man who escaped from a half-way house. As the entire student body gathered in a crowded gymnasium, he asked the youth to stand if they knew someone who was killed by a gun. *The entire student body stood up.*

I am convinced each of these young people has some measure of PTSD. Particularly, the members of a seventh grade class who were looking out the windows onto the playground below and saw one of their classmates gunned down right before their eyes. Whatever innocence they had was taken away in that instant. They will never really be the same. Where does a youngster get the motivation to do his math homework after witnessing that? He is too busy trying to survive to be interested in school work or in a perfect attendance pin. He can never get that scene out of his mind. PTSD is not just for soldiers, it is for kids and adults who live 24/7 with guns, gun shots and gun deaths, particularly in urban America.

Gun violence has a snowball effect that can be scientifically measured in education, health, incarceration rates, family instability, and social capital. Anxiety levels and cognitive functioning worsens among school children following a violent crime within half a mile of their home.[27]

The Brookings study shows how individuals who witness violence are at greater risk for a variety of mental health issues: PTSD, depression,

27. Reeves and Holmes, "Guns and Race."

poor academic performance, substance abuse, risky sexual behavior, delinquency, and violent behavior. These costs weigh heavily on the shoulders of young black Americans and make it very difficult for them to escape the clutches of poverty and violence.

Between 180,000 to 190,000 persons are directly injured by firearm violence every year. According to research done by Sandro Galea, Dean of the Boston University School of Public Health, 60,000 of those individuals, suffer long-term depression or PTSD that lasts for years. Dr. Garen Wintemute, MD, of the University of California, Davis, adds that firearm injuries are unique and more debilitating than injuries from other violent causes.[28] If there are no revisions for our gun policies in America, one need not be clairvoyant to see that as more guns become household items, they will be used in more murders, suicides, and accidents. We will continue to bury 33,000 persons every year, while one third of all persons who are shot (over 100,000) will be plagued with PTSD for years to come, and some, *forever*. This is too high a price to pay!

Whenever there is a mass killing, those who are killed get the headlines, but family members and friends left behind are *the real, long-term victims*. Like a pebble dropped into a quiet pond, the ripples expand to the farthest shore. They reach dozens, hundreds, and thousands of persons associated with that one life. The deceased had a mother, father, brother, sister, sons, daughters, cousins, aunts, uncles, and grandparents who loved him/her. They had friends and business colleagues, and some of them bowled together every Thursday night. Their lives will never be the same for one of their friends has been *shot to death*. His or her death leaves a hole that can never be filled even by a multitude of relationships. Each was a valued member of a neighborhood, but is now gone. If that person belonged to a church the congregation and the choir knows where she sat. Her Sunday school class is not the same anymore. They remember her.

Who knows how many people are grieving? If he belonged to or coached a Little League baseball team, or summer league basketball camp, or played in the band, or read to the visually impaired, or was part of a book club or bridge club, hundreds of persons are robbed of his presence. They miss the one whose life was snuffed out; they think about how he died. If that person was a Brownie Scout, or Boy or Girl Scout, there are dozens of kids and parents who cannot forget one of their number was *murdered*. It is not supposed to be that way. Office staffs and workmates are reminded

---

28. NPR Science Friday, "Is Gun Violence a Public Health Issue?"

daily of the violence that took away one of their own. Ninety people die every day die by guns, and the ripples of these deaths expand to thousands of different shores. And there's one more ripple: when the one killed was the breadwinner.

ECONOMIC COSTS

For every person killed, injured, or threatened by a gun, there are enormous economic consequences for individuals, families, schools, hospitals, government agencies, work places, stores, and entire neighborhoods. Researchers in 2000 documented gun violence cost the American people $100 billion a year.[29] Sixteen years later that colossal figure has more than doubled to $229 billion.[30] That is a preposterous number, and it is accurate!

Should it sound unbelievable, consider only one segment of the overhead: security personnel. Start with city, county, state, and national police forces. You see them every day. Perhaps you have been stopped by them. Continue on to millions more who provide a small measure of security for public and government buildings, schools, hospitals, ports, airports, train stations, subways, banks, hotels, stores, gated communities, and athletic events. We even hire security personnel at my retirement community. They are ubiquitous. While the security business itself is thriving and the factories that manufacture scanners and a host of other devices reap large profits, the American taxpayer foots an enormous bill for living in a society where gun violence is so common it determines what all public and private budgets will look like.

In spite of all that, expenditures for security personnel is far down the list of economic costs for the nation. What is at the top? When asked, many reply, "medical expenses." That's an intelligent choice with one third of all Americans knowing someone who has been shot. Most of those shot in the inner city do not have medical insurance and must be treated in emergency rooms at city hospitals. One guess as to who pays *that* bill. And what of those who are unable to walk out of the emergency room, but must spend the rest of their lives in wheel chairs and live as paraplegics? That cost is one million dollars per person per year. Even so, medical costs are not the big-ticket item either.

29. Cook and Ludwig, *Gun Violence*, 11.
30. Follman, "The True Cost of Gun Violence in America," 3–4.

In 2009, the city of Chicago conducted a study to learn the annual cost of gun violence to the municipality. The answer was $2.5 billion or $2,500 per Chicago household. That's one city. Consider the math for the country![31]

The big-ticket item for the country is reserved for court costs and incarceration.

America's burgeoning prison population has soared over the past quarter century. We have only 5 percent of the world's population, but we have 25 percent of the world's prison inmates. China, four times larger, has half the number of prisoners. In 1982, one in seventy-seven adults were in the correctional or judicial system in one form or another, totaling 2.2 million people. In two decades, an explosive growth of prisoners and others associated with the correctional system swelled its population to more than 7.3 million, or one in every thirty-one US adults.[32] Who pays the bill for the construction of these facilities that are so expensive to build and maintain? Only one guess. An African-American friend remarked, "Our people are moving from underfunded schools to overcrowded prisons." It's not a co-incidence that prisons have become private enterprise, and depressed areas of the country curry favor with such businesses to locate in their county where they have become dungeons of injustice. Thankfully, both political parties are at last in agreement that we need a complete overhaul of this broken system that is a tragic waste of human potential.

I have neither the space nor the expertise to unpack the total economic cost of gun violence to America. Explaining it to your satisfaction is beyond my ability, but I know one simple fact: it is inexcusable and obscene. Our lawmakers, who frequently like to grandstand and bemoan the unnecessary spending in our federal and state budgets, should take a long look at the absurd and totally unnecessary costs of gun violence. The passage of only a few reasonable laws would not impinge upon anyone's gun rights and would make these exorbitant costs plummet.

31. "Report: Chicago Gun Violence Costs 2.5 billion a Year."

32. Pew Charitable Trust: A Public Safety Performance Project, "One in 31 U. S. Adults are Behind Bars, On Parole, or On Probation."

QUESTIONS

1. Have you known anyone who killed themselves with a gun? What was the impact on you, on their family and friends?

2. Atwood states: "Just because it is a right to have a handgun in a house does not mean that it is a good idea." Do you agree or disagree? Why?

3. The ninety Americans who die by guns every day create long-term emotional and economic damage for families and society. Why are we willing to accept these burdens as normal? Is this normal?

4. PTSD is a problem not only for war veterans and even children and youth who have experienced violent trauma in their lives. How can our country best approach and heal PTSD? How could strong gun laws help?

Assignment: Do you have a friend who suffers from depression? Reach out to them or their family to discern if they have easy access to a gun and if they are aware of the danger of that access.

11

Can Guns Be Made Safer?

The answer to this chapter's title is, of course. That is, if manufacturers had a mind to do it. President Obama reminded us, "If we can make a medicine bottle a child cannot open, we can make a gun a small child cannot fire."[1] Actually, so-called "safe guns" were manufactured before. In the 1880s, when so many children were killing themselves, Smith and Wesson produced a childproof handgun that required a lever to be depressed when the trigger was pulled. The company boasted at the time, no ordinary child under eight years of age could possibly fire it. They sold a half-million of them, but for some reason, stopped production. Why do they refuse to make a safer gun today? For some reason child safety is not a concern for the gun industry.

Most arms manufacturers today include a standard safety mechanism on their products, although the popular Glock semi-automatic handgun does not have an external safety. They are not required to do that, but most gun owners would not buy a firearm that did not come equipped with a safety mechanism. Notwithstanding, the Gun Empire, the NRA, and gun-damentalists are not interested in having discussions on what measures can be taken to make guns safer, though we know that four children *will unintentionally* come upon them on a daily basis. This raises the question, if we *know that is a certainty,* can the deaths of toddlers be considered *purely accidental?*

---

1. "Remarks by the President on Common Sense Gun Safety Reform."

The Consumer Protection Act of 1972 helps maintain the status quo of guns, which kill hundreds of adults and children every year *by accident.* By this act of Congress, the Consumer Protection Commission (or any other federal agency) is barred from examining the quality *or safety* of any gun or any piece of ammunition. To keep children's toys safe, Congress insists that teddy bears, dolls, and *toy guns* pass four sets of strict safety regulations (toxicity, flammability, loose parts, and rough edges) but guns, that is, *real* ones, are exempt from any examination for safety reasons, even the safety of the shooter.

Because no requirements exist for the *safety* of their products, many of which would add just a few cents to the cost, some money-grabbing manufacturers have turned out thousands of *junk guns* made of inferior steel and coming out of the box without a standard safety mechanism. Millions of these low-grade firearms are literally everywhere although no respectable gun lover would have one because it is an accident getting ready to happen. If dropped from a table or shelf, it will drop fire. I once read a review in a gun publication of one such junk gun "This gun is not accurate beyond nostril range." After reading this commentary, I asked a gun lover how in good conscience a gun dealer could sell a second-rate firearm like that. His reply: "Poor people need guns too."

Many safety issues for guns could be resolved with very little expense for manufacturers. As a consequence, fewer people would die. One simple measure would be to install a device similar to what is standard in disposable cameras that reveal how many exposures remain on the film. Knowing how many bullets remain in the magazine and/or firing chamber would undoubtedly save lives and cost only a pittance to install.

Another modification for safety would be to set a stronger trigger pull at the factory. This would make it more difficult for an infant or toddler to fire the weapon. If such procedures were in place today, Manal Abdelaziz, Jr., might still be alive. The three-year-old boy was with his father in the family's convenience store in Lumberton, North Carolina, when he spotted a gun lying on a shelf and picked it up, accidentally shooting and killing himself. His dad was but five feet away and "had taken his eyes off the child for just a moment." It's criminal to leave a gun lying around like that. I contend it is also a criminal offense for manufacturers to refuse to incorporate even minor changes to firearms that would save the lives of curious children.[2]

2. Kaplan, "N. C. three-year-old finds gun in dad's store. He shoots himself dead."

Another measure that would save lives is a magazine safety. The simple removal of a magazine would prevent a pistol from being fired, even if there was still a cartridge in the firing chamber. Inexperienced users may not realize or remember that removing an ammunition clip does not completely unload the weapon if a cartridge has already been fed into the firing chamber. In a 1999 study of 259 pistol models, only 14 percent had a magazine safety. Patents as early as 1903 recognized the importance of both magazine safeties and loading chamber indicators in preventing injury. Why would the gun industry be totally opposed to reviving such safety measures today?[3]

There are more measures for gun safety that could be incorporated over time, but one of the most effective measures for gun safety would be a national understanding that our unacceptable levels of gun deaths every year constitutes a public health issue. Such awareness would permit changes to be made to guns just as we make changes in automobiles or to our roads, which make both of them safer. The public health approach does not place blame or try to remove the product from the market; it simply focuses on scientific measures to make the product itself safer. The public health approach is not moralistic, just pragmatic.

However, to admit we *have* a public health problem would probably mean the gun industry would be forced to concede the inanimate gun does, in fact, kill people. Those in other high-income countries often make fun of what they see as our bizarre priorities. The Canadians describe themselves as "unarmed Americans with health insurance." The British say they live in a country where health care is a right, but carrying a semi-automatic weapon is a privilege. One of our British cousins, puzzled like most Europeans and citizens of developed countries throughout the world, over how easy it is for anybody to get a gun, exclaimed, America is the only country in the world that chooses to turn a cigarette lover into a persona non grata but enables a terrorist to buy an assault weapon. A Society that is armed to the teeth, albeit with clear lungs, may be a worthy aim, but that is open to debate.

In Conyers, Georgia, in 1998, there was an incident in Wal-Mart that involved some shopping carts that resulted in a customer being shot in the face. It was recounted tongue-in-cheek, by a British reporter: "the point of the tale of trolley rage is not that America is especially dangerous . . .Nor

---

3. Vernick et al. "'I Didn't Know the Gun Was Loaded': An Examination of Two Safety Devices That Can Reduce the Risk of Unintentional Firearm Injuries."

should we conclude that guns are dangerous . . . The moral of the story is obviously that which is most dangerous in Georgia are shopping trolleys, and that the authorities should consider banning them. They were the source of the argument between these men, and unlike pistols, revolvers, machine guns, Armalite rifles and rocket launchers, there is no constitutional protection for the right to bear shopping trolleys."[4]

Because nothing is done to make guns safer, we will grieve over more accidents and unnecessary deaths with firearms. It is not surprising to learn that in twenty one of our states and the District of Columbia, more Americans are dying by guns than by traffic accidents. This was true only for Alaska, Maryland, and the District of Columbia three years ago. Eighteen more states can now claim such a dubious distinction. US deaths per one hundred thousand people from motor vehicle accidents are 10.3. Deaths by gun violence are at 14.6.[5]

Lower death rates by traffic accidents did not suddenly appear out of thin air; they have dropped by more than half since the 1960s because of a national commitment to automobile and road safety. The decline in death rates can be attributed to several factors, which include improved technology, smarter regulations, and improved medical care, but most importantly, federal and state public servants are ever vigilant to assimilate new technology to make not only our cars, but also our roads, safer. I appreciate the rumble strips on highways if I unintentionally leave my lane, and on rainy nights I'm especially grateful for lane markers that glow in the dark.

I have witnessed a steady stream of safety measures for automobiles since I started driving in the fifties when Congress mandated padded dashboards. Seat belts were required in the early sixties. The seventies saw anti-lock brakes. The eighties saw a rise in anti-drunken driving advocacy. In the nineties, new automobiles came off assembly lines with air bags. More recently, blind spot technology alerts the driver of a passing vehicle, cameras indicate it is safe to drive in reverse, and warning sounds advise the driver if he wanders out of his lane. Soon all models will have automatic braking systems that will avoid many collisions.

These innovations were not incorporated without a struggle. The automobile industry fought many of these safety upgrades tooth and nail, protesting the great expense that would be passed on to consumers. Today,

---

4. Esler, "Logic Which Makes Guns Safe But Shopping Trolleys Lethal."
5. Ingraham and Johnson, "CDC Study: Gun Deaths Catch Up To Car Deaths."

the industry touts them as major selling points. Our vehicles are safer than ever before.

On the other hand, the American gun market has undertaken many intentional changes over the years. For decades it was focused on providing recreational firearms for hunters and sports shooters to kill deer and pheasants, and to punch holes in paper for target shooters. Since the NRA *coup d'état* in Cincinnati in 1977, the firearms market has been fixed on guns that are designed primarily to kill people more efficiently.[6]

The former NRA's mantra was summed up in three words: "skill, accuracy, and marksmanship." The emphasis of today's Gun Industry was explained back in 1993, by the NRA's former Executive Director for General Operations, Gary Anderson. He said the gun market is dominated by the Rambo Factor, i.e. large caliber arms that can be fired rapidly. The three words that describe the industry's emphasis today are "power, speed, and firepower."[7]

The most popular guns today can shoot more rapidly and with more destructive power than any previous models and though they have more power, they are also lighter, easier to carry, and more comfortable to hold and fire, which is a big attraction for women. They can be safely tucked away in a holster or in one's bosom. Nevertheless, there is something new on the horizon in gun circles that could have a dramatic impact on gun safety. Smart guns.

SMART GUNS

In a world where even elementary school children are skilled in the use of smart phones, tablets, computers, and a host of electronic technologies, no one should be surprised over attempts to develop a smart gun that will fire only at the command of its owner.

Several companies are devoting large sums of money to be the first to market these firearms. Armatix, a German company, is negotiating with Congress so they can put a "personalized smart gun" on the market in the United States. Their gun, the iP1, can be synced with an intelligent watch, which is worn on the shooter's wrist. The authorized owner inputs a five-digit code into the watch, which activates the gun. Without the code and the proximity of the watch the gun cannot be fired. The firearm detects the

6. Diaz, *Making a Killing,* 83

7. Anderson, quoted by Diaz in Powerpoint presentation.

nearness of the watch so that even if the gun were stolen after the code has been keyed in, it could not be fired.[8]

In addition, the Mossberg Corporation of Daytona Beach for ten years has been working on smart gun technology. They have the credentials of a well-known shotgun manufacturer. Similar to the iP1, Mossberg's smart gun uses a ring to communicate with the firearm, so that only accredited persons can fire it.

Countless gundamentalists, however, are afraid of this new technology and are diametrically opposed to its development. To try to smooth the way for countless gun lovers to accept this evolution in firearms, Mossberg says, "We're gun people, so we know when you pick up a gun you want to shoot it. You don't want to swipe your finger. You don't want to talk to it. In an emergency situation, you want to pick it up and use it."[9]

The NRA, speaking for their generous benefactors the gun manufacturers, has denounced the smart gun and all attempts to make changes in firearms so they are safer. The greater fear for the gun industry, however, is that the largest buyer of handguns nationwide, *big government,* might mandate smart gun purchases. The Gun Empire is especially nervous about a 2002 New Jersey law that specifies three years after smart guns are available anywhere in the United States, only smart guns can be sold in New Jersey. It is likely other states would follow suit. Gun dealers, manufacturers, and the NRA are nervous over what may come next.

A small number of mom and pop gun stores announced they would begin selling the Armatix iP1 models when they are available. Their plans, however, have been put on hold, not only because of nasty comments made about them, but because of death threats from gundamentalists who don't want anyone messing with their guns. They like them just the way they are. Would a smart gun take away the mystery and mystique of the firearm? I doubt it. It is only a matter of time before smart guns will be on the market. The great industrialist, Alfred Sloan, has predicted the future: "the changes in new models should be so novel and attractive as to create dissatisfaction with the old models." The question remains: Would smart guns save lives? Of course, they would. No doubt about it.

8. Mauch, "My Gun, Your Choice."
9. Pane, "James Bond Meets Samuel Colt; Seeking to Build a Safer Gun."

QUESTIONS

1. Why does the NRA oppose all efforts to make guns safer or the development of smart guns?

2. Did you know that in 1977 the NRA leadership, committed to hunting, sports shooting, and marksmanship was replaced in a *coup d'état* by industry advocates who prioritized the sale of handguns and assault weapons? Why and how is the NRA able to oppose gun safety steps that are supported by the vast majority of its own members?

3. Atwood proposes treating gun violence as a public health epidemic. Many medical groups agree. How could this change the national discussion and action on gun safety?

4. Should Congress continue to provide unique immunity for the gun and ammunition industry from consumers? Why or why not?

5. What other steps, mandated or voluntary, can increase gun safety?

12

Where the Guns Are and How Dangerous People Get Them

When I lead seminars and conferences across the country, I frequently give participants "A Citizen's Test" of twenty questions, which cover much of the multi-faceted scope of guns and gun violence. We discuss the questions, share the correct answers, providing everyone with sources and reliable data they can re-use to raise awareness among their friends about gundamentalism and how it is turning our country into one big shooting gallery.

Regardless where the test is given, the most wide-ranging answers come from two questions. What section of the country has the most guns? The multiple choices are: A. The West. B. The South. C. The Northeast. D. The Midwest. The other question is what section of the country has the most gun deaths? The choices are again: A. The West. B. The South. C. The Northeast. D. The Midwest. The correct answers for both questions are B. The South.

Each time I give the test many assume most gun deaths are in the Northeast. Why this is so frequently checked remains a mystery because the Northeast has some of the strongest gun laws and lowest levels of gun deaths in the country. Perhaps it is because many crime shows have New York City as their backdrop, but that is only conjecture. When I ask why they checked the Northeast people often reply, "population density."

The reason most gun deaths occur in the South is a very simple one. *That's where the most guns are due to very weak gun laws and a dearth of regulations.* Are you surprised? When Willie Sutton, the notorious bank robber, was asked why he robbed banks, he replied, "That's where the money is." For Sutton, it was just logic. Logic also helps us understand most gun murders, injuries, suicides, and accidents occur where the most guns are. In a similar vein, it is common knowledge heavy smokers have a higher degree of lung and other cancers than non-smokers or those who smoke moderately. It is logical and there are ample statistics that prove the more tobacco is used, the greater the incidence of cancer. Correspondingly, there are statistics that show most gun deaths occur where the most guns are easily accessible. If they are nearby, they *will be used*, intentionally or unintentionally.[1]

Many youths who belong to gangs in our larger cities carry guns, almost always illegally. The adolescents most likely to carry are those who engage in other high-risk, dangerous, and often illegal behaviors. Says David Hemenway, Harvard epidemiologist, "these are the very adolescents we do not want to carry guns." The main reason they give for carrying is for protection or self-defense. The fact that many immature, high-risk individuals carry guns creates a need for others to do likewise. Ergo, we meet another vicious circle.

Among Hemenway's typical findings is his survey of inner city seventh and tenth graders in Boston and Milwaukee in the mid-1990s. Seventeen percent of these youth reported carrying a concealed weapon, including 23 percent of seventh grade males. Almost one in four of these students claimed to have carried a gun by age thirteen.

How do these kids feel about that? They were asked, "Would you prefer to live in a society where there were more guns, the same number, or fewer guns?" Eighty-seven percent wanted fewer guns, and only 2 percent wanted more. Similarly, they were asked, "Would you prefer to live in a society where it was easy, very difficult, or impossible for teens to get guns?" Seventy-six percent wanted it to be impossible, 19 percent wanted very difficult, and 5 percent said "easy."[2]

HOW DANGEROUS PEOPLE GET GUNS

Every crime gun in America begins with a legal purchase. The *major* source of crime guns in the United States for gang members, at-risk youth,

1. To download the test go to www.PresbyPeaceFellowship.org/Toolkit.
2. Hemenway, *Private Guns- Public Health,* 116.

members of drug cartels, and other dangerous individuals can be traced to the activities of *just five percent of all legal gun dealers.* Over 57 percent of guns seized at crime scenes are traced to this tiny sliver of *licensed, yet deceitful sellers.* It is difficult to comprehend that this insignificant number of gun dealers can be the cause of so much murder and crime, but those are the facts. These dishonest businessmen and women care more about dollars in their pockets than protecting human lives. They knowingly sell their products to straw purchasers or to those who resell them to those who could not pass a background check. This is known as gun trafficking.[3]

A case in point: "Dad is dead." That's the text message Janet Delana got from her daughter Colby on the day she shot and killed her father, Janet's husband of thirty-nine years. Janet said, "Colby suffers from schizophrenia and depression; *she should never have had a gun.*"

One month earlier, Colby bought a gun at a local dealer. Her parents quickly took it away and tried to make sure she couldn't get another. They called the dealer to alert them of Colby's illness and warned them she might come back.

Janet begged them not to sell her daughter another gun, but they did anyway. Two days after Janet called, they sold Colby a gun again and pocketed the profits. An hour later, Colby shot and killed her father.[4] The Brady Center has filed a lawsuit for Janet against the dealer to help her get justice and save other families from going through what she has endured. The dealer is arguing that a gun lobby law gives them a "get out of court free" card, claiming that even if other people or companies could be held liable for doing what they did, they're immune. The dealer is referring to the Protection of Lawful Commerce Act of 2005, signed by President George W. Bush. *The law denies victims of gun violence the right to sue manufacturers, distributors, or dealers for negligent, reckless, or irresponsible conduct.* No other industry in America enjoys such blanket immunity and protection.

Most gun dealers are honest and obey federal and state laws. Unfortunately, for the general public, but fortunately for the benefit of 5 percent of rogue gun dealers, they have the unqualified support of the US Congress, which passes dozens of laws that make it easier for the gun industry to sell more guns to dangerous individuals, yet harder for law enforcement to curtail any of those sales.

3. Grimaldi and Horwitz, "Industry Pressure Hides Gun Traces; Protects Dealers from Public Scrutiny."

4. Stern, "Mom Files Suit Against Gun Dealer Over Sale to Mentally Ill Daughter."

Moreover, in those rare occasions when the ATF closes down a licensed dealer for gross infractions of the law, the owner can sell the business to a family member or a trusted employee and through change of legal ownership continue to operate the business in the same way and reap the same large profits.[5] The American people were warned about these kinds of shenanigans, but they did not pay close attention. Prior to the presidential election in 2000, the NRA declared publicly, "If George W. Bush is elected President, the NRA will have an office in the White House."[6] President Bush and his Republican friends in the Congress delivered big time for the Gun Empire and the laws passed in those eight years have perpetuated murder and chaos throughout the country.

The 5 percent of corrupt gun dealers contribute to crime not only through straw purchases and gun trafficking, but by refusing to take regular inventories of their stock; storing their weapons in unlocked cases; or hiring employees who have criminal records themselves and are willing to look the other way to make a sale when a customer fails a background check; or they literally pass guns out the back door. An average of eighty guns disappear from gun shops every day.[7]

To avoid a citation from the ATF when one of his guns is discovered at a crime scene, all a corrupt dealer has to say is: "Oh, that gun must have been stolen. I have no idea how it disappeared." In October 2002, the entire D.C. metropolitan area was tormented by a sniper who killed ten persons and wounded three others in Southern Maryland, the District of Columbia, and Northern Virginia. The sniper and his nephew paralyzed the entire region with an AR-15 Bushmaster assault rifle, which traveled all the way across country after disappearing from Bull's Eye Shooter's Supply of Tacoma, Washington. It was one of 238 guns the store lost over a three-year period. I wonder what they said when apprised *the gun they lost* killed ten people almost 3,000 miles away.

Every year approximately a half-million guns disappear from homes, cars, gun shops, and directly from manufacturers and the military. Eighty percent of guns stolen are from gun owner's homes. Even law enforcement agencies lose lots of firearms every year. More than seven thousand firearms

---

5. Pompilio, "States With Weak Firearms Laws Led in Crime Gun Exports."
6. Borger, "Gun Lobby Claims it would 'work out of President Bush's office.'"
7. Witkin, "Handgun Stealing Made Real Easy."

are stolen from cars and thirty thousand from licensed gun shops. Police officers say 10 to 32 percent of these stolen guns are used in crimes.[8]

AMERICA'S UNLICENSED GUN SELLERS

Two large sources of crime guns in America are the Internet and 5,000 gun and knife shows in all 50 states. At these venues, private sellers are not required to perform a background check before selling a firearm. The result is that too many guns fall into the hands of dangerous people. An estimated 40 percent of all firearms sold in the United Sates are from *unlicensed sellers,* a term often defined as *those who are not in the business* of *selling guns for a living.*[9] Large percentages of Americans, including most gun owners, mistakenly *think* background checks apply to all sales at all gun shows. That is what *ought to be,* not what is.

For an ordinary citizen, to sell one's firearms at a gun show and at present, over the Internet, is no different from selling them in one's backyard or living room. That's why some gundamentalists ask derisively, "What gun show loophole? There is no loophole." They are technically correct, but terrorists, criminals, and those intent on doing harm, know how to skirt the intent of the law and pick up a gun. Eric Harris knew about gun shows. He said to his friend, Dylan Klebold, "If we can save up about $200 real quick we can go to the next gun show and find a private dealer and buy ourselves some bad-ass AB-10 machine pistols."[10] That's what they did shortly before heading to the Columbine High School cafeteria where they mowed down fifteen fellow students.

Having been critically injured in the Virginia Tech massacre and after a long period of rehabilitation, one of my friends, Colin Goddard, went undercover and filmed several purchases of assault weapons at gun shows in several states. You can watch these sales on YouTube. Another friend, Omar Samaha, whose sister, Reena, was a victim at Virginia Tech, was filmed by ABC News filling up the trunk of his car with guns he purchased in less than an hour in the parking lot of a Richmond, Virginia, gun show. Not once were Goddard or Samaha required to produce any identification to buy their killing machines. According to state, local, and federal law enforcement reports, criminals, criminal gangs, so-called militias, and even

8. Ibid.

9. http.www.smartgunlaws.org/gun-laws/policy-areas-background-checks.

10. "Columbine Shooter Eric Harris' Journals and Writings."

terrorists regularly secure guns at gun shows that they could not otherwise secure lawfully.

It's quite an experience attending a gun show. There are literally miles of guns all shined up, oiled, and attractively displayed. If you are interested in such things, for a few dollars, you can buy a guidebook on how to make a bomb. Just look for a stand decorated with a big red Nazi flag that sells several kinds of Nazi paraphernalia.

What has caught the attention of Americans of late and put the discussion of guns, gun laws, and gun shows on the front burner is the number of mass shootings carried out by radical extremists from the Middle East who claim allegiance to ISIS or Al Qaeda. These dynamics have backed the Gun Empire and the NRA into a corner from which they cannot easily escape. For years state and national legislators have been warned about terrorists buying guns over the Internet and at gun shows. Only a few took those warnings seriously. There was no political will to do anything to curtail the sale of any gun, which is regarded as a sacred right; that is, until now, when people from the Middle East are doing more of the mass shootings.

We are living in a culture that nourishes a naïve understanding that access to guns in America and the threat of terrorism can be controlled by putting them into two separate and unrelated worlds. In the last few years those worlds have blurred and gun violence and terrorism are intimately connected. The weapon of choice for any mass shooter is an assault weapon. It can be purchased in America as easily as one can purchase a quarter pounder with cheese at McDonald's. The very mention of a mass shooting somewhere increases our nation's fears ten-fold. But should the shooter have a connection with the Middle East, our fears increase exponentially.

When we discuss our usual murders, suicides, and gun accidents, which comprise 98 to 99 percent of the total number of gun deaths, we, as a people, are rather calm, cool, and collected. The dialogue seems abstract and theoretical. We show little emotion when talking about 33,000 yearly gun deaths. On the other hand, when informed of a mentally ill young man slaughtering twenty first graders and six teachers with an assault weapon in Newtown, we are hardly composed. We cannot hold back the anger or the tears. Although these horrible incidents comprise only 1.5 percent of our yearly gun deaths, the drama and the gore consume us. We are outraged over mass shootings, but even so, new gun sales spike and many guns fall into the hands of terrorists.

In a two-hour video, Adam Gadahn, an American-born spokesman for Al Qaeda, cited America as an example where Muslims in the West have tools at their disposal for a holy war against "the enemies of Islam." "America is absolutely awash with easily obtainable firearms," said Gadahn, a.k.a. Azzam al-Amriki. "You can go down to a gun show at the local convention center and come away with a fully automatic assault rifle without a background check and most likely without having to show an identification card. So what are you waiting for?" he asked.[11]

ISIS, the Islamic State, has openly called on lone-wolf attackers to take their war to the streets of America, and it has become a full-blown national-security hazard. One who answered their call and took advantage of America's *laissez-faire* gun policies was Omar Mateen, of Orlando, Florida, a self-directed terrorist who twice was placed on an FBI watch list. He bought his AR-15 Bushmaster Assault weapon and a handgun from a lawful dealer and used them to kill fifty persons and injure fifty-three at the Pulse Nightclub in Orlando, the worst mass shooting in US history.

After the terrorist attack in Orlando, Senator Dianne Feinstein proposed an Anti-Terrorism Law on Guns, which the Senate rejected. If it had been in place, authorities would have had opportunity to stop Mateen, as well as terrorists in the future from getting their hands on these military weapons. The NRA is opposed to such legislation because some aspiring gun owner somewhere may have been placed on the list *by mistake* and could not exercise his/her right to buy a gun. Feinstein's proposal lacks due process provisions to remove such a mistake, says the NRA.

Since 9/11, the United States has responded aggressively, *in some places,* to the danger of terrorism, taking extraordinary measures, invading two countries, launching military operations in many others, and spending more than $800 billion on homeland security. We have accepted unprecedented expansions of government powers and invasions of our privacy to prevent such attacks, but we have done *nothing* to stop the sale of powerful weapons and explosives to dangerous people the FBI puts on a No-Fly list because of their suspected ties to terrorism.[12] The Government Accountability Office (GAO) tracked those who cannot board an airplane from

11. Foxnews.com, "Al Qaeda Urges American Muslims to Buy Guns for Terror Attacks."

12. Zakaria, "Change Your Gun Laws, America."

2004–2014, and discovered that 2,032 persons on the No-Fly List have purchased guns legally.[13]

TV's public service announcements and signs in airports, train stations, subways, and buses, warn us to be vigilant about terrorism. "If you see something, say something," urge the signs. If our leaders tell us to *say something*, why won't they *act when we tell them what we have seen?* I've seen a lot; I've heard a lot; read a lot; and I've said a lot to state and national legislators about nefarious people with alleged ties to terrorism, who are buying guns at gun shows with no questions asked. My congressman, Robert Goodlatte, Chair of the House Judiciary Committee, who cherishes his A rating from the NRA, is much more alarmed that *someone, somewhere,* may have been *mistakenly* placed on the No-Fly List. He cannot get his mind off such a catastrophe taking place and is insisting on better due process. In the meantime anyone can buy an AK-47.

TURNING OFF THE FAUCET

When the faucet is running and the bathtub is overflowing, it is not very smart to start mopping up the floor without first turning off the faucet. In America, we have thousands of illegal guns pouring from the faucets of illegal gun trafficking. Because of the inaction of Congress, the spigot is always open, not with a trickle, but at flood stage. Nevertheless, there is a growing consensus in America that too many of God's precious children are being sacrificed to the idol of gun rights. Thirty-three thousand deaths every year is far too many. The faucet for illegal guns needs to be turned off.

I'm fully convinced someday in the near future it *will be* turned off. It is inevitable; not only because more and more people are being shot, but because it is morally right. Moreover, not even the NRA wants terrorists buying guns, especially if they have Middle Eastern names.

We do not have to live this way. Responsible citizens do not need military assault weapons that can fire one hundred rounds a minute; we don't need guns with silencers; we don't need grenade launchers; we don't need any more junk guns that are unsafe even for shooters. Responsible citizens do not need a .50 mm rifle that can bring down an airliner. What the vast majority of American people need are responsible gun reforms that will

---

13. Ingraham, "From 2004 to 2014, Over 2,000 Terror Suspects Legally Purchased Guns in the US."

save human lives and at the same time not infringe upon Second Amendment rights.

President Obama was not only eloquent but prescient at the memorial service for the nine victims of the Charleston massacre: "Let's be clear," he said, "At *some* point, we as a country will have to reckon with the fact that this type of mass violence does not happen in other advanced countries. It doesn't happen in other places with this kind of frequency and *it is in our power to do something about it.*"[14]

We could go a long way toward fixing America's problem of gun violence if gun owners themselves would speak up and vote for representatives who want to fix our problem by protecting people instead of additional gun sales. As for those public officials who receive checks from the NRA, Republican pollster Frank Luntz reminds us, "There are too many taking an absolutist position when they don't have to because they are scared into doing it."[15]

14. President Barack Obama, speech at the memorial service for the victims of the Charleston, South Carolina, massacre, June 18, 2015.

15. Dionne, "Making Gun Safety (Politically) Safe."

QUESTIONS

1. Discuss the levels of difficulty in transporting guns from one state to another.

2. Law enforcement reports that the majority of guns used in crimes can be traced to 5 percent of licensed gun dealers. How is Congress able to keep the Bureau of Alcohol, Tobacco, Firearms and Explosives weak and ineffective in addressing gun crimes?

3. As of this writing, Congress has failed to exclude those persons from purchasing guns or explosives whom the FBI's has put on the No-Fly List because of "suspected terrorist activity." What are their reasons?

4. Gun shows, attended by thousands of unlicensed sellers and sales over the Internet, account for 40 percent of guns used in violence. Many of these shows pay rent to be held in facilities owned by local governments. Cities receive income from promoting the sale of guns without background checks while their police departments plea for universal background checks. What is going on?

5. Should we require universal background checks for all guns sold at gun shows and for all online purchases, just as we do for licensed gun stores? Why or why not?

Assignment: Visit a gun show in your area.

13

The Big Red Herring and the Apocalypse
The Second Amendment

I call the Second Amendment America's most effective red-herring, i.e.
something used to divert attention from the basic issue. It is the nation's
most efficient distraction that keeps us from concentrating on our gun
pandemic that buries 33,000 people per year. When a politician shouts, "I
am pro-Second Amendment," gundamentalists are galvanized once again
to fight the ghosts of *big government* that wants to take away all their guns.

Conversely, when concerned citizens gather for a rational discussion
on what can be done to prevent so many deaths, someone in the crowd
is likely to ask, "But, what about the Second Amendment?" This usually
means people must first confront the fears of those who *think* even *talking about gun deaths* will start a brouhaha in the church or the book club,
and their 501(c)3 tax exempt status might be endangered. Don't think for
a moment gundamentalists have not noticed the timidity with which gun
violence is approached, even today.

In truth, I don't know anyone who is trying to repeal the Second
Amendment. I myself have used its provisions to own guns for over fifty
years. None of my colleagues, including those whose loved ones were killed
by guns, want to outlaw them. They are not in favor of confiscation, nor
do they consider such a remote possibility. We are fighting for sensible

regulations that will keep firearms out of the hands of dangerous people. We accept the Second Amendment. We have to; it is the law of the land.

Some may not like the law of gravity, but only a fool would deny its existence. I have been working in the gun violence prevention movement to keep people alive. It will probably surprise some gun enthusiasts, but the amendment itself supports my work. At least, that is the way my colleagues and I read it: "A *well-regulated militia being necessary for the security of a free state,* the right of the people to keep and bear arms shall not be infringed."

While I believe the Supreme Court's decision in 2008 (*Heller v. District of Columbia*) that overturned 200 years of judicial history was misguided in interpreting the Second Amendment as an individual right to bear arms as opposed to a collective right, the court said clearly, "it is *an individual right with reasonable restrictions and it does not infringe upon gun rights.*" As a good citizen I must accept that. It's the law of the land.

Justice Antonin Scalia, writing for the five-four majority of the Supreme Court, explains their decision: "This individual right *is not an unlimited or unrestricted right.* It does not cast doubt on longstanding prohibitions on the possession of firearms by felons and the mentally ill, or laws forbidding the carrying of firearms in sensitive places such as schools and government buildings, or laws imposing conditions and qualifications on the commercial sale of arms. . . . Like most rights, the Second Amendment right is not unlimited. It is not a right to keep and carry any weapon whatsoever in any manner whatsoever and for whatever purpose: For example, concealed weapons prohibitions have been upheld under the Amendment or state analogues."[1]

No one can accuse Scalia of pandering to the left, but his summation of *Heller v. District of Columbia* did not endear him to gundamentalists or those on the extreme right. They wanted a lot more; namely, they wanted the court to declare the Second Amendment was *an unlimited individual right.*

No matter. An unlimited right to keep and bear arms is exactly what the gun lobby and gundamentalists claim in *every* argument they make before state or national legislators. They tout it so forcefully that many legislators are cowed into agreeing with them, even though the Supreme Court decision contradicts their speeches. Their deceitful interpretation of the Second Amendment is maintained each time they cash a generous check from the NRA. Notwithstanding, in years to come there will likely be

---

1. *Heller v. District of Columbia,* 2008.

many more challenges to the Court on the meaning of these twenty-seven words, but until then, the Second Amendment is an individual right *with limitations*.

THE SECOND AMENDMENT
AND THE COMING APOCALYPSE

Where devotion to the Second Amendment becomes a present danger is when the NRA uses these twenty-seven words as a paranoid excuse for individuals to stockpile weapons for a coming battle with the federal government. (Anything at all to sell guns.) Gundamentalists work overtime to convince their underlings that one day there is going to be a gunfight with *tyrannical big government,* and they need to purchase more guns "while they still can" to get ready for the conflagration.

The gun press perpetually reminds its subscribers of the despicable plans of dictatorial leaders like Barack *Hussein* Obama-D, Diane Feinstein-D, Charles Schumer-D, and Nancy Pelosi-D, who champion causes like health care for all citizens and the effort to stop global warming and are waiting in the wings for the right moment when they will sound the alarm and send "jack-booted thugs" out to confiscate America's guns. Among America's hard-core believers in this coming apocalyptic battle are anti-government "patriot groups" that have sprung up since Barack Obama's second presidential election. The Southern Poverty Law Center documented 1,360 such groups in 2012, marking an 813 percent rise in hate groups since 2008.[2]

Of course, they are gundamentalists. What else would they be? These "patriots" belittle the idea that our forebears wrote the Second Amendment for anything less than self-defense against our elected government *when it becomes tyrannical.* (What tyrannical, in fact, means, remains undefined and is left to the discretion of each individual.) I find it interesting that in the 1700s a bunch of rag-tag colonists, many of whom were fighting barefoot and struggling to stay alive against the world's greatest power at the time, would postulate constitutional authority for beleaguered citizens to take up arms to fight against the colonies themselves that were struggling to be free from English control.

Although the definition of tyranny is left up to individual extremists to define, several times a year gun zealots call for some uprising or

2. www.usatoday.com, March 5, 2013.

insurrection. The latest of which I am aware is the Bundy Brothers occupation of a national wildlife refuge in eastern Oregon where they proclaimed their willingness to kill or be killed in the fight against *big government* that "has been usurping private lands out West." Thankfully the incident was resolved by law enforcement that showed both courage and cool heads.

In the most significant act of domestic terrorism in America, Timothy McVeigh blew up the Federal Building in Oklahoma City, killing 168 persons and injuring 600. He was angry over the FBI's siege of a heavily armed Waco, Texas compound belonging to the religious group, the Branch Davidians. McVeigh shared his views regarding governmental tyranny with a student reporter in 1993: "The government is afraid of the guns people have because they have to have control of the people at all times. Once you take away the guns, you can do anything to the people. You give them an inch and they take a mile. I believe we are slowly turning into a socialist government. The government is continually growing bigger and more powerful and the people need to prepare to defend themselves against government control."[3]

Apparently, true insurrectionists feel obliged to stockpile assault weapons, silencers, grenade launchers, .50 caliber rifles, and other arms for the coming war against the US Marines. Yet, it is worthwhile noting, in describing their cause insurrectionists do not mention the Constitution. In several places it speaks about armed resistance against our democratically elected government and calls it treason.[4]

"Nations live on myths," says military historian Allan R. Millett, "and none is more precious than the notion of the people with arms springing to the defense of their homeland." To many Second Amendment activists that concept is not baseless fantasy; they insist armed civilians can effectively protect their homeland and the "freedoms" they imply. They are convinced they can hold out against a division of Marines backed up by a C-130 gunship.[5] Typical of such foolhardy encouragement is the rhetoric from Wayne La Pierre. "The twentieth century provides no example of a determined populace with access to small arms having been defeated by a modem army. The Russians lost in Afghanistan, the United States lost in Vietnam, and the French lost in Indo-China. In each case, it was the poorly

3. Wikipedia.org/wiki/TimothyMcVeigh.

4. Article IV, Section 4; US Constitution.

5. Dunlap, "Revolt of the Masses and the Insurrectionary Theory of the Second Amendment," 643.

armed populace that beat the 'modern' army. . . . Modern nations like Algeria, Angola, Ireland, Israel, Mozambique, and Zimbabwe only exist because guerrilla warfare can triumph over modem armies."[6]

The *Tennessee Law Review* handily debunks his make-believe. "To the student of military affairs, trying to link the cited conflicts with a Second Amendment discussion is all but meaningless. Waging guerrilla war is a complicated endeavor involving much more than mere access to arms. The outcome of such conflicts often depends upon political and social factors. Moreover, a civilian who simply possesses arms is not necessarily a combatant of any kind. Thus, relating access to small arms to competency to wage war requires assumptions wholly apart from the purview of the Second Amendment. La Pierre also daydreams about China, Cuba, and Nicaragua, where the established leaders, Chiang Kai-shek, Battista, and Somoza lost." Colonel Charles Dunlap, Jr. adds that these insurgencies were hardly a guerrilla struggle—both sides fought with tanks, artillery, aircraft, and hundreds of thousands of troops.[7]

Adding fuel to their fire is David Kopel, a leading gun rights theorist, Associate Political Analyst of the conservative Cato Institute, and a member of the Board of the NRA, who calls guns "the tools of political dissent" and argues that gun owners have no obligation to obey or respect *any* law, even though it is made through our established democratic process, if they happen to disagree with it. An article of faith for such gundamentalists is that "people have a right to take whatever measures are necessary, *including force*, to abolish oppressive government; armed resistance to government is legitimate and appropriate."[8]

Another gundamentalist, Larry Pratt, whose organization, Gun Owners of America, claims 750,000 members, recently opined, "the election of a Democrat in the November (2016) election would mean there would have to be a *'resort to the bullet box'* in order to reassert proper constitutional balance." Just one day following his threat, twenty-five–year-old Dionisio Garza killed one person and injured six others during a shooting rampage at a Houston, Texas car wash. He embraced anti-government conspiracy

6. Dunlap, "Revolt of the Masses and the Insurrectionary Theory of the Second Amendment," 656.

7. Ibid., 643.

8. Horwitz and Anderson, *Guns, Democracy, and the Insurrectionist Idea*, 169.

theories and was a big fan of Donald Trump.[9] Perhaps with Trump's election, Pratt can put his bullet box back on the shelf for another four years.

Most Americans, including gun owners, pay little attention to such inflammatory, nonsensical language. They allow it to flow over them like water off a duck's back. *Nevertheless,* those words enflame the fears and anger of gundamentalists, like Garza, who in turn can threaten the stability of every community in America, as they flaunt their weapons and take out their anger on innocent civilians in public places or engage in mass murder. Pratt, Kopel, La Pierre, and others have First Amendment rights for free speech, but by their inexcusable bombastic language, they are guilty of inciting riots. The inflammatory hate speech of radio talk-show hosts as well, have played a significant part in the rise of armed militias in the United States mentioned above, which are "getting ready to fight." That may *sound* alarmist, but it is a reality. We *must* pay close attention.[10]

When Sarah Palin advised her followers, "Don't Retreat, Reload," and placed crosshairs on Gabby Gifford's Congressional District, she was talking the language of gundamentalism and insurrectionism. While it cannot be proven, Jared Lee Loughner, Gifford's shooter, *may* have acted on Palin's rhetoric and those provocative cross-hairs. Psychologists tell us this kind of tough talk stimulates a violent response in angry and unstable people. Words matter.

Shamefully, in order to avoid arguments with hard-core gundamentalists, the media *seldom* challenges their fanatical views. Meanwhile, the gun lobby knows they can hoodwink many Americans with almost any harebrained idea about guns as long as they introduce their schemes with those magical words about "freedom" and "rights" that, in essence, are code words for keeping things the way they are. Those of us who value rational thought must raise our voices against their extremism. Otherwise, America will become the country Palin, La Pierre, Pratt, and Kopel want it to be . . . "where those with the guns make all the rules and freedom will always ride with a gun by our side."[11]

In the very first sentence of the Preamble to the US Constitution, our forebears put into plain English the reasons why they were writing the document in the first place. "We the people of the United States of America in order to form a more perfect union, *establish justice, ensure domestic*

9. Horwitz, *Huffington Post,* June 6, 2016.

10. Potok, in interview on the Diane Rehm Show.

11. La Pierre, NRA Speech, March 11, 2009. YouTube.

tranquility, provide for the common defense, *promote the general welfare,* [emphasis mine] and secure the blessings of liberty to ourselves and our posterity, do ordain and establish this Constitution for The United States of America."

Two of the six reasons they gave for writing the Constitution were to establish a secure, peaceful society in which each citizen could enjoy the blessings of liberty. At present, our courts dismiss the full impact of the Preamble to the US Constitution. They classify it as "aspirational desires." People of faith should be asking, "What's wrong with aspirational desires?" To paraphrase a biblical word: "Where there is no aspiration (i.e., vision) the people perish" (Prov 29:18).

All people deserve to live free from the fear that we or our loved ones will be gunned down when we attend places of worship, see a movie, go to school, or celebrate love and life in whatever setting we choose. Unfortunately, that is not the country we live in today. The reason is that anybody and his brother or sister can get any kind of gun they want, no questions asked.

After the massacre at Emanuel AME Church in Charleston, South Carolina, the columnist E. J. Dionne wrote an op-ed for the *Washington Post* entitled, "The Right to Be Free from Guns." In it he called for a revolution in popular attitudes that would *finally* put the rights of non-gun-owners at the center of the discussion. He cites, the pollster Guy Molyneux: "Those of us who want to live, shop, go to school, and worship in gun-free spaces also have rights. In what way is 'freedom' advanced by telling the owner of a bar or restaurant they cannot ban handguns in their own place of business, as many states now do? Today it is the NRA that is the enemy of freedom, by seeking to impose its values on everyone else."[12]

The Book of Ecclesiastes is famous for that passage that speaks of a "time and place for everything under the sun." I believe a gunshot in the woods during hunting season is appropriate; a gunshot in one's home or classroom, on a playground, in a house of worship, a shopping mall, a theatre, or nightclub is inappropriate, unacceptable, and obscene. It denies every single American his/her constitutional rights for domestic tranquility and opportunities for life, liberty, and the pursuit of happiness.

12. Dionne, "The Right to Be Free From Guns."

QUESTIONS

1. What role does the Second Amendment play in your life?

2. Can you think of other American rights that have some form of limitation or that must be balanced with competing rights?

3. How do you think the Founding Fathers meant for the Second Amendment to be used?

4. Do you think the two constitutional rights to keep and bear arms and to live in domestic tranquility are mutually exclusive, or can these rights complement one another?

5. Gundamentalism uses the rhetoric of violent overthrow of government as a marketing tool for the sale of guns and ammunition. Could this amount to treason?

<u>Assignment</u>: Visit www.billofrightsinstitute.org.

14

The Founding Fathers and "Unintended Consequences"

Our founding fathers were incredibly wise, but they were not omniscient. They had big blind spots. They could not foretell the future any more than we can. Neither were they paragons of virtue. If they ran for public office today, they would have to hustle to be reelected. Even when they wrote our Constitution and fought for our liberty, they denied that very liberty to thousands of their neighbors. Many of our Founding Fathers listed hundreds of human beings on their ledgers as personal property.

George Washington, Benjamin Franklin, Thomas Jefferson, James Madison, and Patrick Henry were all slave-owners. Jefferson proposed that in the census slaves be counted as three-fifths of a human being. Patrick Henry, famous for saying "give me liberty" did not ask for liberty for his slaves, and tried to shift the culpability for being a slave owner onto his Christian faith. He came close to saying, *God made me do it.* Said Henry, "It is not a little surprising that Christianity should encourage a practice so totally repugnant to the first impressions of right and wrong."[1]

Our forebears marched to the beat of a different drummer. Some of their ideas were exemplary; others deserve scorn. As people of their own day and time, they embraced some bizarre concepts. When ill, they expected doctors to bleed them back to health; they considered dueling a gentlemanly act. I've never heard that any of them voiced disapproval

1. Pavao, "Slavery and the Founding Fathers."

over the inhuman treatment of those considered to be witches; nor did they protest the custom of taking children to public hangings. They believed women should not vote and child labor was good for the economy. Being only human, our founding fathers made some bad moral choices.

I wish I could have been a fly on the wall when they put pen to paper to write the Bill of Rights and the Second Amendment. Their oft-inspiring words are encumbered because they could not see into the future, or even imagine our twenty-first-century world. The documents themselves were written in ink with a bird's feather. They had no clue their descendants in 200 years would watch television and own lap-top computers.

When they returned home at night they made their way in the dark on horseback. They could not imagine that in a short span their descendants would return home driving a horseless carriage at 70 miles per hour. They arrived at a house heated by a wood or coal stove, and after using their chamber pots, they climbed into feather beds. They could not imagine a flush toilet, or central heating and/or an air-conditioned bedroom and a sleep number, king-sized mattress. Neither could they comprehend flying home at the end of their legislative session at 650 miles per hour. They were simply fallible creatures oblivious to the coming new technologies of the nineteenth, twentieth, and twenty-first centuries.

We should honor them and respect their good deeds and the wisdom of their words, but we should not give their writings the weight of infallibility. There have been some wonderful consequences to some of their words; others, on the other hand, have had tragic and perverse unintended consequences.

When our forebears wrote, "A well-regulated militia being necessary for the security of a free state, the right of the people to keep and bear arms shall not be infringed," just what arms were they referring to? Obviously, they had in mind the flintlock muzzle-loader rifle and pistol used by the Continental Army. Could they possibly have been thinking of anything else?

Jeffery Levin of the *Los Angeles Times* writes about all the effort required to fire such a weapon: "gunpowder and the shot, which came in little greased pouches, had to be poured into the barrel of the weapon. Powder first, then the shot. Both were then rammed tight into the muzzle with a ramrod. That done, the little greased paper that held the powder and shot got rammed in the muzzle too, just to hold everything in place. Then a small amount of powder had to be put into a little pan outside the barrel.

The gunman then aimed—no sights, mind you, he just looked down the barrel—and pulled the trigger. This caused the flint mechanism to send a spark through a hole in the barrel, which set off the gunpowder."

A gifted militiaman, could perform all these actions in about thirty seconds. Average soldiers needed a minute. One shot in sixty seconds. Hence, we read Levin's conclusion as to what our forebears originally meant when they penned the Second Amendment:

> I believe the framers intended that the right of every American cit-
> izen to bear flintlock muskets and pistols should not be infringed.
> I believe that American citizens today without fingerprinting,
> without a license, without a background check—ought to be able
> to own as many flintlock muskets and pistols as they want. If they
> want to fill up their garages with them, that should be nobody's
> business but their own. If they want to load them up on their pick-
> up trucks and drive around public streets with them, the Constitu-
> tion says they can. No U. S. Government has the right to take away
> a man or woman's flintlock musket or pistol.

Levin continues, "I think even gun control fanatics will be with me on this. And here's why. If some musket-owning American who is one neuron short of a synapse takes it into his head to start firing at innocent people at best he's only going to get off a single shot. By the time it would take him to reload, right-minded American citizens who don't believe that firing your gun at whoever you want is a constitutionally protected right will be all over him like a cheap suit. And that, I believe, is exactly what the founding fathers intended."[2]

Somewhere there is a cartoon that depicts the Founding Fathers sitting around the table where they had just finished writing the Constitution. One asks, "Now, should we add something to the effect about how wise we are and that nothing we've written should ever be changed?"

Our progress in firearm technology enables not only a well-trained militiaman, but an average civilian or teenager who is mad as hell at his boss or teacher, to shoot 100 rounds a minute at them and their friends at a Christmas party. Ignore for a moment how effective that gun might be on a battlefield, and then ask yourself, is such a weapon what we need in a crowded apartment complex in New York City or a college dormitory in Texas? In other words, is the "right" to own such a gun an "unexpected benefit" or a "perverse result" of the Second Amendment?

2. Levin, "In Defense of the Right to Bear Flintlock Muskets."

What follows are derivatives of the right to keep and bear arms. Do they match the intents of our forebears when they wrote the Second Amendment into the Bill of Rights? Are they "unexpected benefits" or "perverse results"?

1. Scores of Americans understand the Second Amendment as the most important twenty-seven words of the entire Constitution. They call it "The one right that guarantees all the others."

2. At America's 5,000 gun shows unlicensed sellers offer any gun of choice to anyone with no questions asked and no identification required. It is strictly cash and carry.

3. In most states, a purchaser of an AK-47 or an AR 15, two of the most powerful guns in America, is not required to have any training in its use.

4. The Consumer Protection Act of 1972 prohibits the Consumer Protection Agency or any other from examining the quality or safety of any gun or any piece of ammunition.

5. Claiming stand-your-ground laws, thousands of citizens feel empowered because they do not need to retreat from anyone if they *feel* threatened.

6. The House of Representatives (July 2015) voted to remove federal funding for all scientific research on gun fatalities in the United States.

7. In tracing certain crime guns, the FBI must destroy within twenty-four hours *certain records* of completed gun sales and background checks.

8. In spite of 90 gun deaths every day and 33,000 a year, gundamentalists shout, "Guns Save Lives."

9. From 1968 to the present, 1.5 million civilians died by gun violence, which is more than all battlefield deaths of US military personnel in all of our wars since 1775.[3]

10. The United States registers births, deaths, marriages, divorces, cars, trucks, boats, trailers, bicycles, houses, lands, livestock, dogs, and cats. Everything except guns.

11. More than half of America's gun deaths are by suicide.

3. Department of Defense and US Statistical Abstract.

12. The NRA has sued doctors in the state of Florida to bar them from asking a depressed patient, an abused child, or their family, if a gun is in the house.

13. Eighty-seven percent of all gun deaths in the entire developed world occur in the US.[4] Gun violence costs the US economy $229 billion per year.[5]

14. The Tiahrt Amendment of 2003 denies the ATF authority to disclose crime gun trace data to the public and exempts gun dealers from conducting an annual inventory to address the tens of thousands of guns that disappear annually from gun shops with no record of sales.

Are these social benefits or do they create unexpected perverse consequences?

SECOND Amendment
as defined by the founding fathers

SECOND Amendment
as defined by the NRA

DAVE GRANLUND © www.davegranlund.com

4. Kerug et al., "Firearm Related Deaths in the U.S. and 35 Other High- and Upper Income Countries."

5. Follman, "The True Cost of Gun Violence in America." See also Cook and Ludwig. *Gun Violence.*

QUESTIONS

1. Discuss what Dave Granlund's cartoon suggests. What issues about guns might the Founding Fathers have debated or overlooked?

2. Give examples of ways that the US Constitution has been improved and clarified over time.

3. Does the Second Amendment provide room for federal regulations to promote gun safety?

4. Do you think that the Second Amendment has been abused? In what ways?

15

The Ridiculous State of America's Gun Laws

Whenever a state legislator or member of the US Congress proposes even the most minimal regulation on guns, gundamentalists shout from the housetops, "We don't need any new laws about guns, just enforce the one's we have." Perhaps you have noticed a subtle change in their predictable protests. Gone is the phrase "*enforce the twenty thousand laws we have on the books already.*" It has almost completely disappeared from their repertoire because it was so specious. Stay tuned. They'll be back soon with more lies and misinformation to keep the guns flowing.

Nevertheless, when we speak of guns and gun laws, the American people must confess we are incredibly uninformed about them, and we are even more in the dark about the governmental agency whose work is to oversee the manufacture, distribution, sale, and ownership of guns in America. We call that agency the Bureau of Alcohol, Tobacco, Firearms and Explosives. For short, the ATF.

Their work officially began in 1972 with 2,500 agents charged with inspecting all the gun dealers in America. At its founding, the FBI had 8,700 agents, the Drug Enforcement Agency (DEA) had 1,500, and there were 1,900 US Marshals. Today, the FBI has 13,000 agents; the DEA, 5,000; and there are 3,300 US Marshals. ATF today remains at 1972 levels—2,500 agents. They are responsible for enforcing gun laws (as well as laws governing tobacco and alcohol) in all 50 states with fewer agents than the NYPD employs to enforce the laws of New York City alone. There are presently

60,000 gun dealers and an ATF inspection is likely to take place *every 8 years.*[1]

Michael Bouchard, retired former Assistant Director for Field Operations for ATF, said in testimony before the Sub-Committee on Crime, Terrorism, and Homeland Security, on February 28, 2006, "We were always given just enough food and water to survive. We could barely just keep going. The ATF could never get that strong, because the gun lobby would get too concerned."[2]

In addition to the Tiahrt Amendment signed by President George W. Bush in 2003, let's consider some of the egregious laws Congress has put in place to keep ATF weak and ineffective and that literally make it impossible for them to do a good job in their assigned task.

The Gun Control Act of 1968 gives the ATF authority to check gun dealers for illegal sales, but *only once every twelve months.* In the year 2015, only 7 percent of gun dealers were checked.

The identities of US dealers who sold guns seized at Mexican crime scenes are to be removed from public view.

If the ATF forces a corrupt gun dealer out of business, (a very unlikely event), he can employ the "fire sale loophole" and dispose of his stock without imposing background checks on any purchasers.[3]

Licensed gun dealers must keep specific records of firearms sales, but the ATF cannot use those records to compile a database of gun owners.[4]

In 2003, Congress passed a law that bars federal law enforcement from releasing any information to the public that links guns used in crimes to the original purchaser or owner.[5]

When firearm dealers close they are required to box up all records and send them to the National Tracing Center in Martinsburg, West Virginia. Police and law enforcement agencies throughout the country regularly ask the Center for information, but their employees cannot get to it. In 2009 there were 12,000 boxes stacked up to the ceiling waiting *to be copied by hand because the Center is prohibited from using computers.*[6] (I do not

---

1. Fallis, "The Hidden Life of Guns."
2. Ibid.
3. Pompilio, "States With Weak Firearm Laws Lead In Crime Gun Exports."
4. Fallis, "The Hidden Life of Guns."
5. *New York Times,* The Sorry State of Gun Control"
6. Fallis, "The Hidden Life of Guns."

know how many boxes are there today, but the center needs more pens and pencils.)

The 2010 Appropriations Bill for major law enforcement agencies reveals the limits Congress imposes on the ATF. For the FBI there are nineteen lines of congressional direction; for the DEA there are ten; for ATF there are eighty-seven lines including the requirement to *keep gun-tracing databases hidden from the public.*[7]

The NRA is indebted to a public that asks them and their puppets in Congress very few embarrassing questions about the farcical gun laws they have written. But how can citizens ask questions about these laughable laws when their representatives go to such inordinate lengths to hide their effects from the public? If a gun shop in your area is engaged in the lucrative business of trafficking illegal guns, shouldn't you as a citizen have a right to know about it? It's beyond strange that the agency commissioned to investigate such illegality is *by law* required to say nothing about it. Only gundamentalists can be proud of such chicanery, or does that constitute tyranny? Next time you hear the NRA or politicians on the far right speak about the tyranny of *big government,* remind them of the subterfuge of the Gun Lobby, which insists that the public be kept in the dark about crime and the guns that perpetuate it. Apropos is Jesus' story of the man who had such great vision he could see a "tiny speck in his neighbor's eye, but was unable to see the log that was in his own eye" (Matt 7: 3–5). *Why* is Congress hiding? *What* are they hiding? *Who* are they hiding? The public has a right to know.

To be honest the NRA, the Gun Empire, and gundamentalists are not the least bit interested in passing laws that keep youth, criminals, domestic abusers, or terrorists from getting guns. On the other hand, they *are* intensely interested in selling more and more guns to them. Their hypocritical pretensions declare these sales undergird "freedom" and they argue that *how any* purchaser chooses to use his/her gun is a *private matter.* It is not society's business, nor is it the business of government. Can you see more clearly how the Gun Empire is able to protect the sale of guns, but not people?[8]

---

7. Ibid.

8. For a list of other ludicrous gun laws and policies see chapter 15 of my book, *America and Its Guns.*

CONCEALED CARRY

Handgun sales increase with every mass shooting as fear grips those who imagine they or their loved ones might be the next victims. Twenty years ago carrying a concealed weapon was illegal in twenty-two states and less than five million Americans had a concealed carry weapons permit (CCWP). Since then every state has some form of concealed carry. Thirty-three states are "shall issue states" where law enforcement is required to supply a CCWP if a citizen passes a background check and applies for one. Most reasonable people assume getting a permit to carry a lethal weapon would call for a thorough examination. But, this is America and when it comes to guns, the fewer requirements and laws the better. "Requirements," it is said, "are a ploy by *big government* to take our guns." There *are* no restrictions or requirements to get a CCWP and holders now number 12.8 million.[9]

My friend Andy Goddard reveals how easily one can get a CCWP. When the Virginia Legislature, for the convenience of its citizens, opened a website for CCWP applications, Andy logged on, filled out the required data, sent in his payment by credit card, and in a few minutes had his license. Convenient, yes, but Andy has *never even once* held a gun in his hand.

The state of Florida is as slipshod as Virginia in issuing permits. A *South Florida Sun-Sentinel* analysis of state records found loopholes, errors, and miscommunication that gave hundreds of criminals access to a permit. Among the roughly 410,000 Floridians licensed to carry a hidden gun were 1,400 people who pleaded guilty or no contest to felonies; 216 people had outstanding warrants for arrest; 128 people had active domestic violence injunctions; 6 were registered sex offenders.

"I had no idea," said Baker County Sheriff Joey Dobson, who sits on an advisory panel for the state's Division of Licensing, which issues the permits. "I think the system, somewhere down the line, is broken. I guarantee you the ordinary person doesn't know (that) . . . and I'd venture to guess 160 legislators in Florida don't know that, either."[10]

CCWP holders are nevertheless the very people the NRA touts as "America's most trustworthy citizens." In truth, the screening process for a

9. Osnos, "Making a Killing," 36.
10. *Gainesville Sun*, "Felons Exploit Loopholes in Fla Concealed Weapons Law."

permit is almost non-existent. The Violence Policy Center in state-by-state analyses found several permit holders who committed mass murders.

Being open and accepting of all persons is a cultural and spiritual value for me, but I draw the line at giving a CCWP to a sex offender, domestic violence abuser, one who stalks an ex-spouse or one's children, or a mass murderer. Neither do I think one with impaired vision should have a CCWP. But, some states declare such limitations should not disqualify a good citizen from getting a permit and offer assistance in filling out their application forms. Others require applicants with impaired vision to hit a target at a gun range before authorization. Iowa, on the other hand, grants a CCWP to those who are *completely blind*.

Advocates for those with impaired vision and Iowa law enforcement may disagree whether it's a good idea for a totally blind Iowan to have such a weapon, but the governing principle is: "You are blind? So what? You say you need a gun for protection. Who are we to stand in the way of a good law-abiding citizen exercising his/her Second Amendment rights?"[11]

Many states have reciprocal laws, which allow citizens with permits to carry a concealed weapon in other participating states. Who knows? There may be further questions when totally blind Iowans want to travel to reciprocal states and carry their Glocks with them. If you are shopping at Kroger's, would you feel more secure knowing one who is completely blind is packing heat?

Other states have opted for open carry. But is that any better? Josh Horwitz, the Executive Director of the Coalition to Stop Gun Violence, examines the response of the Colorado Springs Police Department to a 911 call placed by Naomi Bettis on Halloween Day in 2015. It shows the high price of normalizing open carry. Bettis saw gunman Noah Harpham walking down the street with a rifle and handgun just minutes before he opened fire and killed three innocent Americans. She called 911, but dispatch did not send officers to the scene because Colorado had an open carry law. "Well, it is an open carry state, so he can have a weapon with him or walk around with it," the dispatcher told Bettis. After a second 911 call by Bettis, the police sent officers to the scene, but that was *after* the shooting started and one man lay dead in the street and two more were waiting to die.[12]

11. Clayworth, "Iowa Grants Gun Permits to the Blind."
12. Horwitz, "The Price of Normalizing."

STAND-YOUR-GROUND LAWS

People have a right to defend themselves from a threat in their home or on their property. This is commonly referred to as the Castle Doctrine as in "a man's home is his castle." Today's stand-your-ground laws are significantly expanded to include any place you may lawfully be. Further, these laws ignore what is central in biblical law and tradition where one who is in a threatening situation has a responsibility to retreat, if at all possible, in order to avoid the spilling of blood. Such a response affirms the value and dignity of each human life. In Jewish daily prayers people are enjoined to *seek and pursue peace and preserve human life (pikuach nefesh)*. This obligation takes precedence over almost all other commandments.[13]

In 2005, Florida was the first state to fundamentally reject the idea one had a personal responsibility to avoid bloodshed. When Governor Jeb Bush signed the first stand-your-ground -law into Florida Statute #776.013, it said, "a person has no duty to retreat and has the right to stand his or her ground" if he or she thinks deadly force is necessary to prevent death, great bodily harm, or the commission of a forcible felony like robbery."

Law enforcement asks only three questions in stand-your-ground cases. 1) Did the defendant have a right to be there? 2) Was he/she engaged in a lawful activity? 3) Could he/she reasonably have been in fear of death or great bodily harm? Dependence of the law on one's *feelings or perceptions* is crucial to understanding *how* the law will be enforced. One claiming protection through these laws takes the "evidence of one's *feelings*" to court where gundamentalists maintain "I'd rather be judged by twelve than carried by six," an aphorism of gun writer, Jeff Cooper, an enthusiastic former Board Member of the NRA.

Because some form of stand-your-ground laws are applicable in thirty-three states, the American Bar Association (ABA) commissioned a study of them. Conclusions were: stand-your-ground laws, which vary from state to state, obstruct and confuse law enforcement personnel and disproportionately affect minorities. The laws have been responsible for increasing homicide rates that encourage a shoot-first mentality. "I don't like the looks of that guy," can easily become a "lawful reason" to open fire.

Dr. Jerry Ratcliffe, chair of the Department of Criminal Justice at Temple University, regards the ABA report as unequivocal: "If our aim is to increase criminal justice system costs, increase medical costs, increase

13. Steinberg, "Conflict Prevention and Mediation in the Jewish Tradition."

racial tension, maintain high adolescent death rate and put police officers at greater risk, then this is good legislation," Ratcliffe said. "There is no reliable, credible evidence to support laws that encourage 'stand your ground.'"[14]

These laws mark a significant and highly troubling departure from America's traditional self-defense guidelines. We are nurturing gun slingers who retreat from no one. To retreat or stand down from a confrontational situation sounds unmanly to gundamentalists and others who consider themselves tough. Too many tough guys are out there itching to pull the trigger because they believe, *"real men stand their ground."*

You know something is wrong when our gun laws provide more leniencies for civilian use of firearms than is available to law enforcement or to American soldiers in a war zone. Military personnel returning from Iraq and Afghanistan have fewer restrictions imposed on them back home than they had in combat.

The ABA report also found stand-your-ground laws reinforce racial bias due to cultural stereotypes. In instances where a white shooter kills a black person, that homicide was 350 percent more likely to be ruled as justified under stand-your-ground law, than if a white shooter killed another white person. There is widespread opposition from law enforcement towards these laws, which speak volumes about a dreadful shoot first, ask questions later attitude. But it is rapidly becoming a norm in the United States. Most Americans do not want to go where these stand-your-ground laws are slowly but surely taking us.

Firmin DeBrabander lists another unintended social consequence of these laws. He writes, "Citizens must now live in fear of their armed neighbors in addition to prospective criminals. What if someone who spies *you* walking down the street thinks *you look suspicious?* What if *you* become a target for a would-be George Zimmerman? Or what if the man you argue with, may insult or offend you, even unintentionally, is armed and irascible—and the argument escalates?"[15]

That scenario played out in a dimly lit theatre in Florida. Chad Oulson, a forty-three-year-old father texted his young daughter during the previews and that offended a retired seventy-one-year-old police officer Curtis Reeves seated directly behind him. Reeves asked Oulson to stop texting. An argument ensued and voices were raised, which led the young father to throw popcorn at his adversary, who took out a hand gun and killed him.

14. Li, "Report Links Stand-Your-Ground Laws to Higher Homicide Rates."
15. DeBrabander, "How Gun Rights Harm the Rule of Law."

Reeves is invoking the protection of stand-your-ground laws because he felt threatened and needed to defend himself. The former cop could have stood up and moved to another seat. But, the Florida legislature told him, "he didn't need to retreat."[16]

I found a clue last summer in a shopping mall in Harrisonburg, Virginia about our cultural enthusiasm for standing our ground in confrontational situations. It was on a young man's T-shirt. Across his chest was a big American flag and underneath were five words in bold: "These colors do not run."

Sitting right next to this young man, I thought back to the first time I saw our flag and these five words together. It was around 1942 or 1943 in the midst of the Second World War. I walked into a post office with my mother and there on the wall was a poster with a huge American flag and underneath were the words: "These colors do not run."

As a seven- or eight-year-old, I was thrilled, proud, and greatly comforted to see that. My sister's boyfriend was fighting the Germans; my best friend's brother was a fighter pilot in the South Pacific; my future brother-in-law was going to be an Army doctor. That poster assured me we were going to win the terrible war because our soldiers would never back down before anybody. No matter how tough the fight, our soldiers would not retreat. They would stand firm.

How often, especially during our subsequent wars, have the flag and those five brave words given confidence to our citizens and soldiers and justified our military ventures? That kind of bravery is in our DNA. We are a kick-butt country and proud of it. Our military doesn't back down; our police don't back down; and my neighbor with his Glock 17 will not back down. Other nations or peoples may be willing to deescalate a situation, and not stand their ground, but to walk away from a tense situation sounds un-American.

Next time you hear stand-your-ground laws explained at a community gathering or at a PTA meeting, *listen carefully* to the language that is used. Every time I have heard these laws explained by a government official or a police officer, they use the words, *"You do not have to retreat."*

We don't retreat in America; that is not what we do; that is not who we are. As we sing "The Battle Hymn of the Republic," what some call our national hymn, we are even proud of Jesus who "has sounded forth the

16. Almany, "One Piece Still Missing from Puzzle of Fatal Theatre Shooting: Why?" CNN Jan. 14, 2014.

trumpet that shall *never* sound retreat."[17] Those of us who are enamored with stand-your-ground laws, or want to flaunt our power, whether with a policeman's badge, an imposing physique, or a gun on the hip, promote *an excessive need* to finish the job and show everybody that we are in charge (see chapter 17, "Policing in the Inner City").

DOING THE NUMBERS

When you see the suffering and pain that legislators have visited upon our entire nation with laws that protect gun sales instead of citizens, you have to be blind, insane, or a coward to accept it. To our own peril we permit their short-sighted laws to become norms in the United States. One of the most popular slogans of the Gun Empire is "Guns Save Lives," but doctors and coroners who sign death certificates 33,000 times a year testify the cause of death was a gun.

Looking at our population and gun death rates as a whole, we have only a relative few anecdotal accounts where guns have actually saved lives. When we look holistically at the nation, the only scientific conclusion that is believable is "guns take lives." Simply do the math that compares the deaths of Americans in our most recent war in Iraq with those who were killed on our own streets and in our own homes by firearms. In the seven and a half years of war in Iraq we buried approximately 4,500 military personnel. In that same period of time we laid to rest 220,500 American civilians.[18]

In August of 2015, Major Cities Chiefs Association sponsored a conference of police chiefs from across the country in Washington, D.C., to talk strategy over America's increasing numbers of homicides, particularly in our larger cities. D.C. Police Chief Cathy Lanier said, "We have not seen what we are seeing right now in decades."[19] Surveys of all its members showed there are more guns now on our streets that lead to more killings and there is a rise in violent crime.

Chicago, at the beginning of August 2015, had the most slayings with 235. Even though their police seized 3,400 illegal firearms through July, the shootings continued. Among the recommendations coming out of the

17. "Battle Hymn of the Republic," verse 2.

18. Department of Defense and Center for Disease Control statistics.

19. Greenberg, "Police Chiefs from Around the Country Meet in D.C. to Discuss Violent Summer."

summit were calls for more stringent gun laws, including harsher penalties for gun crimes and for using high-capacity magazines.[20]

We cannot ignore the fact that the numbers of persons *who are shot* every year is going up just as the ages of those doing the shooting is going down. One hundred and seventeen thousand Americans are shot every year.[21] Because of quick response from EMTs and the expertise of medical personnel in our hospital emergency rooms, not all those who are shot die. I have spoken, however, to several paraplegics who wish they had died. One described his daily routine to me: "The first thing I do when I wake up every morning is to remove my feces by hand from my anus." He lived to tell the story, but he is a joyless victim.

We can examine these horrible numbers till our eyes glaze over, so it is imperative to remind ourselves that statistics are simply human stories with all the blood washed off.

QUESTIONS

1. Do you have a concealed carry or open carry license? Does anyone close to you have one? Does it make you feel safe?

2. Where would you draw the line on who should be entitled to such licenses and who should not? Should anyone be permitted to carry openly? Or concealed?

3. Of current gun laws, many are designed to shield the Gun Industry from responsibility and to make gun violence investigation more difficult for law enforcement. Do you think the general public is aware of this? Why or why not?

4. Ideally, the U.S. military has strict rules for all personnel on when a gun can be used even in attack areas. Why would 30 states provide its citizens more permissive use of assault weapons and "Stand Your Ground" laws than are allowed by the military in war zones? What cost does America pay for Stand Your Ground Laws and the idea that "we don't need to retreat?"

5. Why does Congress ignore the pleas of law enforcement for more sensible gun regulation?

20. Greenberg, "Cities Confront A Summer of Bloodshed."
21. www.smartgunlaws.org.

16

The Gun Empire's Plan
to Arm Everybody

We hear a great deal today that America is slip-sliding away from being the greatest and most powerful of the nations. It makes good
copy when politicians promise to make America great again. Hearing such
bluster, I'm reminded of Luke's account of Jesus the Savior-King's entry into
Jerusalem on a donkey. The people exclaimed, "Blessed is the king who
comes in the name of the Lord. Peace in heaven and glory in the highest heaven." But instead of reveling in their applause, King Jesus sat down
and wept over the city: "If you, even you, had only recognized on this day
the things that make for peace. But now they are hidden from your eyes"
(Luke 19:38–41). If only those who yearn for the greatness of yesteryear
could understand Jesus' insistence that those who want to be great, must
first become servants.

Millions of Americans and a majority of gundamentalists consider
us a nation in decline. They are convinced the decay began when *"they"*
removed morning devotionals and assemblies from public schools and
banished prayer and God himself from our classrooms. The onslaught continued as the Ten Commandments were taken off the walls of courtrooms
and town councils voted against Christmas crèches on courthouse squares.

For those who hunger for those "good old days," it is grossly inad-
equate to hear, "We must respect people of all religions" as our Constitution
proclaims. The words sound insipid to "real patriots" who yearn for those
"good old days" when privileged Christians were "in control" of things and

life made a lot more sense. Isn't that the way it is supposed to be? Actually, President John Adams declared in 1797 with the unanimous consent of Congress that "the United States was not a Christian nation any more than it was a Jewish or a Muslim nation. We welcome persons of any religion or no religion."[1]

My wife and I found the doctrine of the separation of church and state to be an unexpected gift to us when we served as Christian missionaries in Japan from 1965 to 1974. After World War II, American occupation forces insisted that the Japanese Diet write a new Constitution in which the nation rejected the establishment of a state religion, which was at least partly responsible for the rise of Japanese militarism and eventually led to World War II.

When we enrolled our children in the local public elementary school in Tokyo, they were the only blue-eyed Christian children among 1,500 students. We taught the Christian faith to them in the best learning environment: our home and our local church. We were very grateful Buddhist and Shinto prayers were not uttered in their school assemblies or classrooms. Their Christian identity was respected, while Buddhism and Shinto remained the country's principal religions.

Whenever there is talk of decline in our country—and it seems there always is—the *one* thing that appears to be lacking is a meaningful standard of change. How can we know where we are today if we don't really know where we stood in "those good old days"? But, one thing we do know is when we start talking about decline in America, many people grow nervous, even though we are by any standard the most powerful country in the world.

Marilynne Robinson's essay "Fear" focuses on the general fearfulness of our culture today, which is in a constant state of flux. She cites Leviticus 26 that describes the state the people of Israel would find themselves in if they no longer were loyal to God: "The sound of a driven leaf shall put them to flight, and they shall flee as one flees from the sword, and they shall fall when none pursues. They shall stumble over one another, as if to escape a sword, though none pursues."

She says, "Numbers among us today with weapons would blast that leaf to atoms and feel brave as they did it, confirmed in our alarm by the fact that there are so many leaves." Those who "forget God . . . make irrational responses to their irrational fears." The greatest threat of our fearfulness is

1. The Treaty of Tripoli.

that it "obscures the distinction between *real* threats on one hand and on the other the terrors that beset those who see threats *everywhere*. . . . Granting the perils of the world, it is potentially a very costly indulgence to fear indiscriminately, and to try to stimulate fear in others, just for the excitement of it, or because to do so channels anxiety or loneliness or prejudice or resentment into an emotion that can seem to those who indulge it like shrewdness or courage or patriotism. But no one seems to have an unkind word to say about fear these days, un-Christian as it surely is."[2]

The pace of change in today's world, where many of us work for starvation wages, and all of us must deal with globalization, global warming, instantaneous communication, the technological revolution, and "the browning of America" that will soon render Caucasians a minority, is turning America upside down and inside out. These undeniable phenomena are revving up both our fears and our trust in carrying concealed weapons so we can cope with all the risks and uncertainties. Meanwhile, the Gun Empire scrambles to write one gun law after another to support the myth that those who carry guns are America's best and most loyal citizens. They are the ones who are protecting themselves and their families and are keeping the country "the way it was, and the way we want it to be world without end, Amen."

Journalist Fareed Zakaria sees our anxieties as the outgrowth of "a new kind of nationalistic identity based on fear, insecurity, and anxiety." In such times people turn to God, greed, or guns to try and hold on to the privileges they once thought were spelled out in their birthright, but today are questioned and/or claimed by minorities and others who did not inherit them.[3]

Our computers and smart phones give us an instantaneous power to get in touch with everyone on the planet, but we do not seem interested in what "the other" thinks or feels. The larger question is do we even *care* what they think or feel? We ask instead, should we expend the effort to understand them when we are capable of protecting ourselves from them?

Gundamentalists claim our freedom is best expressed in our ability to buy a gun of choice, but that kind of *freedom* is turning our nation into selfish armed tribes, competing for resources and dominance. Understanding one another is far down the list of our priorities, but it must move to the top of the list if we want to live in peace, or even survive, by trusting in

2. Robinson, "Fear," 2. New York Review of Books, Sep. 24, 2015.

3. Zakaria, "People Driven By Identity, Not Ideology."

an even greater power . . . the power of a welcoming open hand instead of a clenched fist.

Recently I crossed paths with a young man who made no pretense of wanting to know what others beyond his own tribe are thinking or feeling. He draws his own lines and confesses his own faith and proudly displays it on his bumper sticker: "When in doubt, empty the magazine." Only one who is inordinately afraid would publicize such a philosophy. He is fearful someone from another tribe will sneak up on his turf and take what he considers his alone. He is a true gundamentalist; he is the one most likely to keep a bullet in the chamber of his gun at all times so he can be fully prepared to defend himself and his loved ones from dangerous people. I find it difficult to reach out to a guy like that who is so afraid, but doesn't even know it.

Such palpable fear, propped up by testosterone, fuels America's gun sales, gun shows, gunshots, and gun deaths and is behind the rush to put in place concealed carry and stand-your-ground laws that protect skittish gun owners when they meet a Muslim, immigrant, or someone else who is different. These laws give restless individuals the discretion to judge the intentions of other people by what they look like or the religions they profess, along with the "right" to shoot first and ask questions later.

We don't have to look very far down the path to see what is in store for America if we listen to their counsel, arm everybody, and abolish "gun-free zones," which they call "killing scenes" because that is where terrorists would choose to go and be unimpeded. We don't have to be clairvoyant to recognize where cave-man instincts will take us if we listen to those who drum up fear and hate even from the pulpits of so-called Christian churches and universities.

To be frank, I wouldn't want to live in a college dormitory that overnight could become a fortress for gundamentalists. Nor do I want my grandchildren to live in an America where everybody and their brothers are armed. When public school teachers from kindergarten through high school, preachers in the pulpit, ushers in movie theatres, bartenders, bus drivers, child care providers, waitresses in pizza parlors, and nurses in hospitals are all packing heat, our nation is soon going over the cliff. This is not hyperbole; nor is it pretty. It is a real danger to our republic. Just two months after Idaho's legislature legalized guns on campus, an Idaho State

University Chemistry Professor shot himself in the foot while teaching a lab.[4]

Those "with eyes to see" the chaos brought by these unintended consequences must open their eyes to what is happening to us as a people and we must demand moral leadership from our faith communities and political courage from our legislators. We must demand a safer and saner country.

BLAMING VICTIMS FOR THEIR OWN DEATHS

In their quest to arm us all, gundamentalists are heralding a new approach: blaming the victim of gun violence for his/her own death. The deceased cannot hear such diatribes, but the survivors can, and that is the goal of those who use these despicable measures to spread more fear and sell more guns. For years it has been standard practice to blame victims of sexual assaults and rape for their own trauma. Gossips go to work and people whisper numerous assumptions when such crimes are committed: "She was asking for it." "Her blouse showed cleavage." "Her skirt was too tight." "She smiled too much and the assault was her fault."

Today, in the wake of more mass shootings, gun apologists are increasingly using the same shameful *blame the victim tactics*. They say, "If they only had a gun they would be alive today. Why weren't they carrying?" You probably remember after the Sandy Hook Elementary School massacre how gundamentalists all over the country denounced gun control supporters, saying, "the blood of children is on their hands" and doubled down on their campaign to arm all teachers. The most famous of their speeches was given by Wayne La Pierre at the Willard Hotel in Washington, D.C. on December 21, 2012.

After the gruesome massacre at Emanuel AME Church in Charleston—where nine members of a Bible Class lost their lives, including South Carolina State Senator Rev. Clementa C. Pinckney—NRA board member Charles Cotton declared, "[Senator] Pinckney voted against concealed carry. Eight of his church members might be alive today if he had expressly allowed members to carry handguns in church. Innocent people died because of his position on a political issue."[5] Why wasn't he packing heat?[6]

4. Schwartz, "Idaho Professor Shoots Himself in the Foot."

5. Ingraham, "An NRA Board Member Blames the Pastor Killed in Charleston for the Deaths of His Members."

6. Ingraham, Christopher, Washington Post Workblog, June 19, 2015.

Every few years the Gun Empire comes up with a new approach, some new catchphrase, some tactic that might inspire more people to buy guns. Blaming the victims for being killed is the current guiding precept. It makes no difference if the shooting was in a kindergarten, a school, church, college campus, a pitch black theatre, or an army or navy base, the charge is always the same: "No one had a loaded gun, which would have stopped the killing or the *extent* of the bloodshed." After the rain of death at Fort Hood and the Washington, D.C. Navy Yard, where a combined twenty-four service personnel died and thirty-four were injured, on military bases brimming with guns, Wayne La Pierre's accusation became, "They didn't have *enough* guns."[7]

Then there was the tragedy that befell Monica Butler Johnson on August 9, 2015, when her ex-husband murdered her after systematically stalking her and their two sons for months. Ascension Parish, Louisiana, Sheriff Jeff Wiley blamed Johnson for getting killed. He claimed she could have stopped her ex-husband had she been armed. What makes this kind of advice even more disturbing is that Sheriff Wiley was appointed chair of the Louisiana Commission on Law Enforcement by Governor Bobby Jindal. The commission's stated purpose is to "promote public safety by providing progressive leadership and coordination within the criminal justice community." Wiley evidently sees no contradiction between his mission for public safety and his public advocacy that all citizens should be armed.

The sheriff said, "Domestic abuse victims have to be willing to use guns against their abusers, when the legal system doesn't work. Get your concealed weapons permit. Ladies, learn how to safely handle a weapon, learn how to safely store a weapon, and when you're in a situation like this, shoot him in your back yard before he gets in your house. Drop him. I mean, I'm serious. Take the extremes necessary to live a life where you don't have to worry about your kids and your life."[8]

Subsequently, Sheriff Wiley said he would not criminally charge domestic abuse victims who kill their abusers. That may sound big-hearted to some, but it fails to take into account that black women like Ms. Johnson and Latina women are far more likely to be charged with murder, manslaughter, or other crimes when killing an abuser, according to the Michigan Women's

7. Shen, "NRA's Wayne La Pierre: 'There Weren't Enough Good Guys with Guns at Navy Yard Shooting.'"

8. Merlan, "Sheriff: Domestic Violence Victim Could Have Prevented Her Own Murder if She'd Just Had a Gun." *Jezebel*, Aug, 11, 2015.

Justice and Clemency Project, which works to free women prisoners who were convicted of murder, but who acted in self-defense against their abusers. *Not a single study to date has shown that the risk of any crime including burglary, robbery, home invasion, or spousal abuse against a female is decreased through gun ownership. Though there are examples of women using a gun to defend themselves, they are few and far between, and not statistically significant.*[9]

Those who study domestic violence agree that "just get a gun" is very bad advice. "It is always highly concerning when a person introduces a weapon into a violent situation," Katie Ray-Jones, CEO of the National Domestic Violence Hotline, told *Jezebel* in a statement. "While someone may be trained to use and carry a firearm, there is always a possibility that the weapon could be used against them by their abusive partners. We encourage domestic violence victims and survivors to use the resources and tools available, like The Hotline, to create a plan for their safety that is tailored to their individual situation."[10]

Research on guns and domestic violence is conclusive: injecting a firearm into *any* situation involving domestic abuse is adding fuel to a fire. One study of women physically abused by current or former intimate partners found a "five-fold increased risk of the partner murdering the woman when the woman owned a firearm."[11]

The shameful tirades of "blaming the victim for not being armed" is widespread in the rhetoric of the NRA. In response to an editorial in The University of North Carolina's *Daily Tar Heel* written on March 22, 2015, that argued "guns are not the solution to campus sexual assault," NRA News host Cam Edwards replied, "I hate to tell the editors here of the *Daily Tar Heel*, but the burden of stopping that assault is not going to be on the person committing that assault, not at that moment in time. The burden of stopping that assault is on the victim. It is on the victim."[12]

After the Charleston shooting, South Carolina State Senator Bill Chumley remarked, "These people sit in there, waited their turn to be shot.

9. Michigan Women's Justice and Clemency Project, umich.edu/-clemency.

10. Merlan, "Sheriff: Domestic Violence Victim Could've Prevented Her Own Murder If She'd Just Had a Gun." The National Domestic Violence Hotline can be reached any time at 1–800-799-SAFE.

11. Johns Hopkins Bloomberg School of Public Health Fact Sheet, "Intimate Partner Violence and Firearms."

12. Johnson, "NRA News Host Lectures College Students: Burden of Stopping Sexual Assaults 'Is on the Victim.'"

That's sad. But somebody in there with the means of [armed] self-defense could have stopped this. And we'd have less funerals than we're having."[13] Senator Chumley has a 92 percent rating from the NRA and voted last year to authorize the carrying of concealed firearms in bars.[14]

Says Josh Horwitz, "The nine innocent Americans murdered in Charleston were exercising their fundamental freedom to worship in a manner of their own choosing. Because they chose to pray without weapons does not mean they were 'waiting for it.' It means that they were trying to live their lives as the Constitution envisions — in 'domestic tranquility.'"[15] Blaming the victim for a rape or one's own murder is deplorable, no matter what the circumstances. When we dig a little deeper in the NRA's blame the victim campaign, we realize it is a smokescreen for the Gun Lobby to keep us from having an honest dialogue about the problems caused by easy access to so many guns. When we chase what we in the South call "rabbit trails" and don't talk about the real issue, three things will occur: 1) The violence will continue; 2) More guns will be sold; 3) *Sooner or later they will go off.* We can count on it.

QUESTIONS

1. Fear is a constant theme in America. What are daily fears in your community? What are effective ways to help people who live in constant fear?

2. Imagine our culture if everyone carried a firearm. Would the omnipresence of guns be a deterrent to their use or an enabler of use?

3. Do you think that the new NRA marketing strategy of "blame the victim for not carrying a gun" will be successful in bringing millions more Americans into gundamentalism?

4. Like suicide, domestic violence is a crisis where gun use is likely, if one is available. What can we do as a society to de-escalate domestic violence and better protect victims without arming families?

13. Griffin, "S.C. Lawmaker Apologizes for Saying Charleston Victims Waited Their Turn to be Shot."

14. Griffin, Drew. CNN Politics, June 25, 2015.

15. Horwitz, "The Charleston Victims Weren't Asking For It."

17

Policing the Inner City

Whenever city officials discuss guns, the police department must be at the table, and saving the lives of countless African Americans must be the most important item on the agenda. Murders by guns are the number one killer of young black men between the ages of fifteen and thirty-four and the reason why they are often called an endangered species. These young men are four times more likely to be shot and killed than to die in a car accident.[1]

Police who daily put their lives on the line to keep social order in our inner cities are well aware of this reality. Having large numbers of guns that are frequently used in a particular neighborhood makes law enforcement nervous. No one claims that everyone has a gun, but it *feels* that way to both residents and the police.

Whenever the police are dispatched to resolve a domestic dispute in a well-to-do neighborhood, they are anxious. Their angst is compounded when they go to low-income neighborhoods where people are desperate, feel exploited, and have little or no hope for a better tomorrow. It is said police sergeants routinely tell their officers their most important job is to make it home safely. First responders know the implications of poverty; they are aware danger escalates when one who is suspected of a crime feels

1. Schrager, "The Very Stark Numbers on Young Black Men and Gun Violence."

156

"the man" represents a system that is rigged against him, thinks he has nothing more to lose, *and happens to have a gun.*

My parents taught me early on that the police were my friends. I was told to go to them any time I needed help. I trusted them implicitly and on one occasion, as a ten-year-old, I persuaded one to take me home in his patrol car because I just finished watching the movie *Frankenstein Meets the Wolfman* and was afraid to go home by myself.

Parents of color deliver vastly different messages to their children. They are told to be respectful of the police, but not to ask for any favors. If they are stopped by the law for any reason, their instructions are be polite, obey all orders, and *never* argue because police are representatives of a system and a culture that has not been kind to their parents. Consequently, African-American or Latino children grow up to fear police, or at least, be guarded around them. They are wary with good reason.

Police know there are lots of guns in the inner city, and they are used when people feel threatened or angry. Experience tells them *some* of the men who congregate in front of the local liquor store or 7–11 are armed. While numerous law enforcement officers testify they have never drawn their gun in a confrontation, those who work in volatile neighborhoods in our inner cities cannot make such a claim. In a confrontational situation, they are trained to draw their guns for self-protection. Contrary to the gun press, their guns, however powerful *in such moments* do not provide confidence, poise, or self-control; the guns they draw often make them more anxious. There is a saying in law enforcement, "When a gun is drawn, there is an inclination to use it."

Law enforcement's anxiety is compounded today because communities are resentful over excessive force and the large numbers of young black men who have been shot unnecessarily. The Black Lives Matter movement is insisting, and rightly so, that police must have good reason for shooting at a suspect. Police also are mindful the cameras that many of them are now wearing do not lie. As never before, they are being held responsible for excessive force. Every African-American neighborhood in our inner cities is sensitive to unnecessary or rough treatment at the hands of police. They understand it as a sign of systemic racism.

It was manifest long before the spate of horrific events in the summers of 2014–2015 in places like Ferguson, Missouri, Baltimore, and New York City. It was present in Charleston, South Carolina, when a fifty-year-old black man, Walter Scott, tried to run away from officer Michael Slager, who shot five times and killed him. Scott's death took place at the most frequent point of interaction between police and citizens: a traffic stop. In Scott's case, a broken tail light assembly precipitated his death. Perhaps Slager's *excessive force, all caught on camera by a passer-by,* was a precursor for the mass murder at the Emanuel African Methodist Episcopal Church in downtown Charleston three months later. We will never know, but we should all feel confident in declaring, "Violence begets more violence." It always has, it always will.

The *Washington Post* for years suspected fatal police shootings were under-reported, so they directed a year-long national project to track them. Their findings indicate the 986 police killings in 2015, are over twice the rate previously reported by the FBI in any previous year. Five hundred and sixty-four of those killed were armed with a gun at the time. About a quarter of them (243 persons) were in the throes of a mental or emotional crisis; 266 persons were killed while fleeing. Fifty percent of those killed were white; 26 percent were black; 17 percent Hispanic; and 8 percent were from other races. Between 2005–2014, 47 officers were indicted (about 5 per year) for shooting deaths; while last year, 2015, 18 officers were indicted. These figures do not include police shootings of black women, or police killings that did not involve gunfire, or deaths while in custody.[2]

My heart goes out to those living in poverty but also to law enforcement who are often forced to make split-second decisions on the amount of force to use to restore order in explosive situations. With 350,000,000 guns in the country and counting, the training police receive is grounded in one reality: the overwhelming presence and fear of guns. In the most unpredictable circumstances, when a "suspect" reaches for his pocket, particularly if his movement is abrupt, police, already nervous, have a tendency to open fire. Too many times, after firing, they have discovered the "suspect" was reaching for his cell phone, wallet, pillbox, or inhaler. Such a mistake is not uncommon. A person holding a gun is more likely to misperceive an object in another person's hand to be a gun.[3] The predictable result is often death or injury to suspects, increased anger and despair among the residents, and frequent bouts with PTSD and emotional struggles for those who did the shooting. This whole scene is because of the overwhelming presence of guns.

2. Kindy et al., "Officers Fatally Shoot 965."
3. Osnos, "Making a Killing," 43.

These shootings represent as well an ongoing dilemma for law enforcement, especially when the identity of police officers who do the shooting is seldom revealed to the community. In 2015, 210 persons were fatally shot by police officers who have not, as yet, been publicly identified by their departments. With further analysis the following were given by departments throughout the country as reasons why shooters remain unidentified:

14—If divulged, the officer's life would be endangered.

17—The office releases names only when charges are filed.

22—It is department policy not to release names.

32—Other reasons.

60—Investigations are pending.

65—No response from the police departments.[4]

There is strong public support for requiring police to wear body cameras, which, it is believed, will significantly reduce excessive force that has become a huge national problem and a source of rioting throughout the country. The public continues to call for more transparency whenever force of any kind is used on citizens. Officers automatically are not given the benefit of the doubt these days if force is used. Citizens are demanding accountability.

In Chicago where violent crime, including murders and police shootings of offenders, are on the increase, police unions have been a powerful voice against releasing the names of officers in fatal shootings. Chicago police killed nine persons last year but their contracts with the city clearly prohibit the department from identifying an officer to the media unless the shooting results in criminal or administrative charges.

There is a grim and growing toll of citizens who are shooting police officers at random in retaliation for what is perceived as unjustified shootings.[5] During the first three months of 2016, the number of police officers shot and killed by angry citizens had more than doubled from the same period last year. Retaliation, however, reached fever pitch in Dallas, Texas, on July 8, the day after two separate police shootings of black men in Louisiana and Minnesota.

4. Sullivan et al., "In Fatal Shootings by Police, 1 in 5 Officer's Names Go Undisclosed."
5. Berman, "Police Are Dying by Gunfire at Over Twice Last Year's Rate."

Thirty-seven-year-old Alton Sterling was killed when two Baton Rouge police officers shot him as he appeared to be held down, according to cell phone footage that captured the shooting. A day later, Philando Castile, thirty-two years old, was shot during a traffic stop and his girlfriend Diamond Reynolds broadcast the aftermath on Facebook Live.

A huge Black Lives Matter protest was staged in downtown Dallas, but that was not enough for Micah Xavier Johnson, who snapped and reached into his large arsenal of guns and bomb-making materials and grabbed a powerful sniper weapon he was trained to use while serving in Afghanistan. He wrote a note saying that he wanted to kill white people, particularly white police officers. He killed five of them and wounded twelve others. It was the deadliest attack for law enforcement since seventy-two officers were killed in the 9/11 attack. It brought the number of officers killed in firearms related incidents so far this year to twenty-six, or a 44 percent increase over the same time in 2015.[6]

Does the public's right to know who did the shooting in every case trump the risk of public retaliation against on duty policemen and women? It is a predicament. Law enforcement cannot shoot or arrest its way to safe cities, and even those who feel the most exploited must not assume every police shooting is totally unjustified.

The quandary is exacerbated because of another vicious circle . . . the weaponization of citizens and the militarization of police forces. The American people are bombarded at every turn by the Gun Empire and urged to buy a firearm for protection from the bad guys in the neighborhood *and from the cops who are known to shoot people of color without good cause.* In volatile sections of our cities these perceptions quickly become mandates to get a gun while one's neighbors, whom God commands us to love, are regarded as threats.

Micah Johnson felt he had such authorization and had been collecting the tools of war to use on the streets of Dallas for some time. After the devastation, authorities found in his home the well-known tools of mass murder: bomb-making and ballistic materials, and lots more guns and ammunition. What we see in Dallas is evidence of the great distortion racism brings to everybody and everything in the city. It is proof that our hopeful vision of a post-racial America is at least further down the pike.

President Obama, in addressing Dallas and the American public said, "When incidents like this occur, there's a big chunk of our citizenry that

6. Zoroya, "26 Police Killed So Far in 2016, up 44% from 2015."

feels as if, because of the color of their skin, they are not being treated the same, and that hurts, and that should trouble all of us. This is not just a black issue, not just a Hispanic issue. This is an American issue that we all should care about."[7]

Paul Jannuzzo, former chief of American Operations for Glock, the Austrian gun company, declared, "Every time a bomb goes off somewhere, every time there's a shooting somewhere, sales spike like crazy."[8]

The geography of where the carnage occurred matters little. The bloody details will be broadcast to every nook and cranny in America. When people are fearful they could be next on the hit list of some madman, more and more guns will be flying off the shelves of gun stores. In spite of research that reveals gun purchases bring *far more risk to owners than protection,* these guns will be stashed away in dressers, closets, and glove compartments, and sooner or later, they will go off in murders, assaults, suicides, and accidents. *There is strong evidence they will not be used against criminals, or terrorists, those of another race or religion, but against family, friends, or acquaintances, or in suicides, or accidents.*

Simultaneously, as more people buy, trust, and use their guns on one another, and death tolls increase, particularly in the inner city, police themselves will feel more vulnerable when they are called to go and settle disturbances there. Police also fear for their lives and need to protect themselves. They don't want to be easy targets for gang members and/or desperate people.

Some city and state police departments are in conversations with the Army and Marines and are tempted to further militarize their peacemaking equipment, especially when the materiel they are offered is free and comes with no strings attached. Our military has an abundance of armaments like assault weapons, grenade launchers (that can also be used to fire tear gas canisters over long distances), and .50 mm rifles that can shoot five miles and one mile accurately. In addition, they have dozens of armored vehicles and troop carriers that are no longer needed to fight foreign wars and are simply rusting away on bases somewhere. Doesn't it make sense to transport our courageous first responders by armored personnel carriers? We do that for our soldiers in foreign lands. Why not protect our courageous policemen and women on our city streets?

7. Fears, "Racism Twists and Distorts Everything."
8. Osnos, "Making a Killing," 36.

Some jurisdictions, fearful of riots and civil unrest, have accepted these gifts without much thought as to how they would be used or perceived. Nor have they given much thought to the question: against whom would they be deployed? What would it look like to have the city's cops show up for a disturbance in certain neighborhoods in armored personnel carriers brandishing assault weapons? Some officials have said plainly, "Thanks, but no thanks." They have decided the free armored vehicles on their city streets would only increase the suspicions of an already beleaguered community, which historically has not trusted the white power structure or the intentions of law enforcement. Those law enforcement entities that have refused the complimentary war materiel have correctly anticipated these impressive additions would not bring healing to their cities, but only deepen its wounds. Power does have its limits.

WHAT CAN WE LEARN FROM ENGLAND'S BOBBIES?

Excessive force is a problem that crops up at least every now and then within law enforcement in countries all around the world. Keeping order requires the use of force. In other industrialized nations police do not face imminent danger of being shot, which is quite possible in America. While long guns for hunting and sports shooting are usually allowed, defensive or military style guns are not. Public access to lethal handguns and assault weapons is denied. Without the mystique of a Second Amendment, police can protect people instead of firearms, which has become a norm in America. As a result, both police and the general public are relatively free from gun violence in all of the industrialized countries of the world except our own. In a much safer environment, England has had a long and respected tradition of maintaining an unarmed police force.

In recent years, however, with guns smuggled into the country and increasing threats of terrorism, the national police force has made adjustments to their proud tradition and armed a small, elite cadre of officers who, in spite of being issued powerful handguns, hardly ever use them. England's approach to training this cream of the crop of officers provides a methodology that would, without a doubt, reduce police killings in the United States. All police in Britain, whether armed or unarmed, are taught to back away from situations that might otherwise escalate. They do not feel they must "win" every confrontation. With this philosophy in place, on average, the few British police who are armed open fire only five times a year.

Their training is grueling with regular physical and psychological trials, including long hours at the firing range and frequent exercises, which challenge them to find creative ways out of confrontations. Griff White writes, "Sir Denis O'Connor, a former police chief who later served as a royally appointed independent overseer of British police work, said cops in Britain take seriously the idea of 'policing by consent.' They see themselves as working for the public, he said, rather than for the state itself." Their fear is getting it wrong and being criticized by a judge. "Cops in the U.S. fear getting shot and killed. Those are two very different worlds." With an overabundance of guns accessible to our citizens, law enforcement may not be able to adopt every strategy the British Bobbies use, but they can still learn a lot from their colleagues in England, particularly if they can be trained how to "back away from some confrontations and learn they do not have to 'win' every altercation."[9]

TRAUMA IN THE POLICE FORCE

Before he became pastor of the Second Presbyterian Church of Richmond, Virginia, Alex Evans was pastor of the Blacksburg Presbyterian Church and chaplain of the Blacksburg, Virginia Police Department. When a mentally ill student slaughtered thirty-three students and professors and wounded twenty in the massacre at Virginia Tech in 2007, Alex, along with clergy from the community, ministered to the survivors and to victim's families.

Experiencing the same trauma of his friends and colleagues on the Blacksburg Police Department and the University Police Force, he asked his seminary classmate, Eric Skidmore, the Chaplain for the South Carolina Law Enforcement Assistance Program, to help him found a Virginia chapter to give support to law enforcement personnel who experience almost daily shock and psychological pain from gun incidents.

My respect and gratitude for first responders quadrupled in the fall of 2014 when Alex invited me to attend a "Post Critical Incident Seminar" of his chapter's annual meeting at Massanetta Springs Conference Center, near Harrisonburg, Virginia. The conference hall was full of police officers who had endured what the Law Enforcement Assistance Program (LEAP) describes as "a critical incident" in their careers, i.e. any event that results in an overwhelming sense of vulnerability and/or loss of control. These include line-of-duty shootings, getting shot or seriously hurt on the job, high

9. White, "For Gun-less Bobbies: Training is a Better Weapon."

speed pursuits that end in tragedy, events that bring prolonged and critical media attention, personal tragedies, and the like. Officers can discuss such incidents with those who have been there, supported by trained counselors and police chaplains. These discussions promote normalization and recovery from the trauma and pain of such encounters. The FBI has used this format since 1985.

These men and women, many of whom wrestle with PTSD, came from as far away as Missouri, and were eager to be with colleagues who have experienced similar trauma and endure the same recurrent bad dreams. I recall an especially poignant moment in the plenary. A large man was in tears; his shoulders heaved as he recounted the day he was ordered to investigate a domestic dispute.

He entered the house to find the husband screaming at his wife. When the policeman turned and saw him standing there, he picked up something shiny from the table and walked menacingly towards him. The policeman drew his gun and ordered the man to stop and lower his arms, but he kept coming at him. He fired his gun and killed his would-be assailant. The shiny object in his hand turned out to be a butter knife.

His colleagues understood his distress. He had killed another person whose weapon could not have severely injured him. But how was he to know that? In several places in this book I have been critical of police using excessive force particularly on African-American citizens. I stand by those statements. Nevertheless, I confess my blindness to the strains and stresses of those instantaneous judgment calls our first responders must make on a regular basis. Such strains take their toll and on their families as well. Nor was I aware of the meager salaries police officers earn in maintaining law and order on behalf of us all.[10]

One police officer reflecting on his time at the seminar said, "We are taught to take care of our uniforms, vehicle, equipment, etc. It's about time we learn to take care of ourselves and each other." Said another, after attending a LEAP Conference in South Carolina: "Two weeks before attending the class I was at a point of taking my own life. I entered the class not sure of the outcome. Seeing people just like me showed me I'm not alone, and you all have given me the tools to deal with past, present, and future problems—these things, along with many of the peer team's words, pats on the back, and smiles give me a new lease on life. . . . Now I know I can do my

10. Vick, "What's It Like to be a Cop in America," 38.

job and am good at my job. The past is not coming back now when I think about the shooting incident. I know that I am O.K. and not alone."[11]

Our society cannot function without police. By and large they do an exceptionally good job. Like all other people, they make mistakes and should be held accountable for them, but the nation also needs to show genuine appreciation to those who put their lives on the line for us. We need to understand the pressures of what it is like to be a cop. The FBI wants us to know some of the realities faced by those who work in law enforcement.

- Job-hopping is common.
- Five to ten percent of officers experiencing a traumatic event will develop moderate to severe PTSD.
- Law enforcement resignation rates are high.
- Law enforcement divorce rate is 15–25 percent higher than the general population.
- Twice as many police officers commit suicide as are killed in the line of duty dealing with felons.
- Law enforcement personnel have twenty-two deaths per one hundred thousand compared to twelve deaths per one hundred thousand in the general population.

A recent study at Radford University found that:

- Police have a much higher mortality rate from cancer and heart disease.
- An officer's life expectancy is twelve years shorter than civilian counterparts and five years shorter following retirement.[12]

11. SCLEAP.org/groupcrisisintervention.

12. www.VALEAP.org/Homepage.

QUESTIONS

1. Reflect on your own life experience of encounters with police. What stands out?

2. Do you think Atwood finds a correct balance between concern for black lives and concern for police?

3. Especially since Congress allowed the Assault Weapons Ban to expire, gundamentalists and police have found themselves in a kind of "arms race," with more and more powerful weapons available. Should the gun and ammunition industry be allowed to profit from this "arms race"?

4. Do you think local and state police departments should use excess US military weapons and equipment?

5. Do you know of families or individuals who have experienced gun trauma and PTSD? What can citizens do to help these individuals?

18

Fighting Crime and Gun Violence in Urban America

We have made some remarkable progress in race relations in the United States. We've come a long way from separate bathrooms and drinking fountains labeled for white and colored. If nothing else, we have twice elected an African American to the highest office in the land. Nevertheless, we are just one or two incendiary events away from greater racial strife. The reality is too many young black and brown men are dying needlessly in our inner cities and scores of people of color wonder aloud if black and brown lives really matter. Police shot and killed almost one thousand men in 2015; they were disproportionately black. This number is far more than the FBI has ever reported before.

Colbert King, African-American columnist for the *Washington Post*, puts the question directly to middle-class America: "Has the annual racking up of homicides by the dozens made us phlegmatic to murder? Or is it something else too terrible to admit? Do we simply not care about homicides when they occur in parts of town we don't frequent and the victims belong to a group we either don't like or care much about?"[1]

The late Tony Auth, cartoonist for the *Philadelphia Inquirer*, once portrayed a couple reading the evening paper. The wife asks, "What is the solution to our ghettoes? The husband replies, "Honey, the ghettoes *are* the solution." I know lots of people who agree with that sentiment where

1. King, "Where is the outrage?"

powerful people and impregnable power structures work to keep some people out of sight and out of mind.

A close African-American friend cautioned me about using the term *ghetto* in this book. He said, "Some blacks would consider a white man's use of the word 'racist' and disparaging of those who live in the lowest socio-economic area of the city." In light of what I have written in the previous pages about justice and God's love for us all, I will take the risk and use the word. After all, it has been around a long time and all of us, racists and non-racists alike, know its meaning and implications. I use the term, however, with profound respect for those persons who suffer because of prejudice and economic exploitation and are forced to live in determined sections of any big city. I use the word, only as the dictionary defines it: "Any section of a city in which members of some minority group live, or to which they are restricted, as by economic pressure or social discrimination." I remind the reader, the definition itself acknowledges the area is built on injustice, and exploitation.

Not only do we find the highest unemployment there, but the most illiteracy and school dropouts; the most unwed mothers; the most homes without fathers; the highest rates of alcoholism; the most communicable disease; the highest levels of lead poisoning; the highest rates of incarceration and drug use; and the most crime.

Nor can we ignore one significant reality. Our inner cities are full of guns, gunshots, and gun deaths. Mass shootings, unsurprisingly, drive the national debate on gun violence, which is intentionally stimulated by disinformation and easily morphs into myth. As horrific as these massacres are, they are not indicative of America's high rates of gun deaths. Our astronomical numbers are not because of places like Newtown, Columbine, Virginia Tech, and the Pulse Nightclub in Orlando. They are fueled by the ruthless killings of young black men in our inner cities. More than thirty Americans are murdered with guns every day and roughly half of them are black men although blacks constitute only 18 percent of our population.[2]

Looking past this terrible imbalance *without seeing it* has disastrous consequences for the country, especially when twenty years of government-funded research has provided us with several hopeful strategies to prevent so many deaths. These approaches include passing some very promising

2. Lopez, "The UCLA Shooting Exposes How We Often Ignore the Most Common Forms of Gun Violence."

gun laws and new emphases in training police officers on how to de-escalate tense situations.

Having the political will to address the injustice and exploitation one finds in urban America means much more than cautioning law enforcement to be more circumspect about shooting people of color. It means building a new culture, which must begin by acknowledging law enforcement cannot arrest its way to a peaceful city or by throwing the book at low income people for petty crimes.

Every single American must insist we put an end to this racist approach to policing in African-American neighborhoods. This is not simply a black problem; it is a *city* problem. It is a human problem. It is an American problem. Police must spend as much time and energy solving black on black murder in the inner city as they do white on white murder in the suburbs.

Jill Leovy spent years researching the details that surrounded the murder of a mixed race teenager in the Watts neighborhood of Los Angeles and the subsequent conviction of his murderers. She confronts the racist attitudes and procedures that heretofore prevailed among law enforcement in Los Angeles when there was a gun homicide in Watts.[3]

She argues the Los Angeles power structure is predominantly white. They regard the ghetto itself as the solution to racial issues, such as with the late Tony Auth of the *Philadelphia Inquirer,* cited earlier. This is also true of most large cities throughout America. She maintains this perspective continues to set the stage for the racist atrocities of Southern law that are somewhat better known to Americans—the stacked courts, fee systems, and chain gangs—abuses so systematic that across the South, black people dismissed the whole framework as "the white man's court."

In modern cities today, Leovy alleges officials frequently look the other way when a poor black man is killed by another poor black man in the city center. Little is done to search out the murderer. The unmistakable message sent to the community is that black lives don't matter all that much and extreme violence will continue to be tolerated.

When officials look the other way on the most serious of black on black crime, it means gangs and drug dealers will dispense their own kind of justice and revenge. Dismissing the intrinsic value of poor black men by refusing to devote time and resources to find their killers and bring them to justice, brings instead a harvest of factionalism, informal systems

3. Leovy, *Ghettoside.*

of discipline and self-policing, terrifying etiquette restrictions, witness intimidation, vigilantism, rumors, arson, lynching, and a homemade system of order based on relationships—the whole dreary cornucopia of informal justice. In this system, law enforcement crushes small crimes, but big crimes are indulged.

Says Leovy, it may not appear self-evident that impunity for white violence against blacks would engender black on black murder, but when people are stripped of legal protection and placed in desperate straits, they are likely to turn on those closest to them. Says Leovy, "Allowing people to kill and face no consequences is an aspect of enmity toward them."[4]

Leovy praises her role model, Detective Sal La Barbera, whose observations over years of service in south Los Angeles, convinced him that catching killers was what *built law*—that successful homicide investigations were the most direct means at the cop's disposal of countering the informal self-policing and street justice that is the scourge of black populations.[5]

Leovy accuses Los Angeles police of frequently driving around the edges of the ghetto where they are told to "be proactive," focus on "suppression," or practice "crime control, nuisance crime, and prevention," conduct consent searches, run license plate checks, and drive around some more.[6] Such tactics are not limited to Los Angeles. Recall, it was the broken tail light housing that led officer Slager to pull over Walter Scott in Charleston and ultimately kill him as he tried to run away.

I learned a bit about "nuisance crime" back in 1956–1957, when I worked as a chaplain's assistant at the Virginia State Penitentiary in Richmond. I interviewed many prisoners to ascertain if they knew the reasons why they were incarcerated and what was the nature of their offense. I was dumbfounded to record large numbers of young African-American inmates, who were to be known henceforth and forever as felons, because they were found guilty of the crime of "throwing rocks at railroad cars." I don't recall interviewing any new white felons with similar charges. I didn't say anything about it at the time as *I didn't have the authority to "question the system."* It wasn't my job. God, forgive me. I'm sure throwing rocks at railroad cars today still qualifies in the minds of legions of people as a "nuisance crime" and they want law enforcement to "throw the book at the offenders."

4. Ibid., 154–55.
5. Ibid., 58.
6. Ibid., 156–58.

Then there is the persistent problem of law enforcement: usually white officers singling out black men for arrest and using excessive force against them. That's why we hear a common cry from the inner city: "Who do you call when those who are paid to protect you are killing you?" In July of 2014, the choking death of Eric Gardner in New York City who repeatedly said, "I can't breathe, I can't breathe" while lying face down on the sidewalk raised the ire of African Americans and those concerned with "excessive force" nationwide. Then, as if on cue, there were the fatal shootings of eighteen-year-old Michael Brown in Ferguson, Missouri, and Walter Scott in Charleston, South Carolina. Three months later nine persons were slaughtered by a young white supremacist in Charleston's Emanuel AME Church at a Bible study. These murders and other well-publicized police incidents have been the catalyst for more national discussion of racism, to the irritation of many whites: "Who, me? I'm not racist. I've got lots of black friends."

In February of 2015, the Director of the FBI, James Comey, made public research that shows that people in a community where the majority is white, unconsciously react differently to blacks. In those areas where non-whites commit a majority of the crimes, law enforcement officers have let their prejudices formulate mental shortcuts that lead them to more closely scrutinize members of minority groups.[7]

Don't think for a minute blacks are surprised by the FBI's findings. How they keep on keeping on in the midst of such bigotry is way beyond me. How they live dignified lives and give so much to this country when they are constantly suspected, distrusted, watched, and presumed guilty, and even feared because of their skin color is baffling to me. I've never experienced such intolerance and injustice and I wonder if I could stand it. Perhaps keeping records of how many times they and their friends have been stopped by police for DWB (driving while black) helps them keep their equilibrium.

J. Herbert Nelson, of the Presbyterian Church, USA, Washington office, just before the trial of Darren Wilson, the policeman who shot Michael Brown, wrote, "It is not enough for us as Christians to be appalled or sad when viewing Ferguson, Missouri, as a place beyond our own reality. We must be clear that the issues of this shooting are deeper than anything one trial can resolve. Yes, it is about the shattered hopes of a family that has lost a loved one, a loss, which will reverberate for generations. But it is also

7. Schmidt, "FBI Director to Give Speech Addressing Relations Between Police and Blacks."

about the social sin of prejudice, bigotry, and institutional racism, which is embedded in our social structures, our justice system, and the laws by which we claim to offer freedom to each other."[8]

Nelson continues, "Perfect love casts out fear, says the Scriptures, but we know how risky it is to try and establish relationships with those whom we have previously feared, dismissed or discounted, or never even noticed. Why has it taken Americans so long to come together at a table to discuss why there is so much violence in our cities and how we can best work together to stop it? Why has it taken us so long to eat from a common loaf and drink from the same communion cup?"[9]

To pretend we can enjoy life surrounded by members of our own tribe, on an island of prosperity in a sea of poverty and avoid taking the risks of learning to love others whom we once considered unlovely, is an exercise in futility. We are like the horse that clings to a burning barn because it is the only security he knows.

Make no mistake, America's barns *are* on fire; the places we considered secure are being dismantled. Science, the Internet, college educations for thoughtful youth, globalization, and technology, are coalescing to expose the rickety structures of our tribal identities. If our *human race* is to survive, let alone flourish, our worn-out, outdated racist systems must be demolished if for no other reason than we want to survive.

When there is little hope there will be more respect or love tomorrow, and the squalor is ignored, desperate people frequently turn to the solution they see on TV—guns. As we await more social analysis to trickle in from Ferguson, New York City, Cleveland, Charleston, Chattanooga, Chicago, and elsewhere, we have learned a lot more than we wanted to know about excessive force and racist attitudes. Hopefully, we will learn that more white communities are waking up to the realities of racism and demanding democratic policing for all of urban America because it is in everyone's self-interest to live in a just society.

This is a mandate for a new style of professional and democratic policing. "The anger that spilled into the streets from these horrific events in Ferguson, New York and elsewhere, reflected not only the devaluing of black lives but the grim recognition that African Americans find themselves

---

8. Nelson, "A Call For More Than Judicial Remedies to the Killing of African American Boys and Men."

9. Ibid.

hemmed in between the dangers of crime and the perils of those whom other communities can trust to protect them from it."[10]

"The Cop," a profile of Darren Wilson, whose non-indictment for the shooting death of Michael Brown sparked intense, ongoing rioting in Ferguson, Missouri, is a compelling rendition of what is happening. It puts a human face on the strains and stresses of law enforcement personnel who work in our inner cities; explains the legitimate complaints of the black community and supports their demands for respect and human dignity; while offering a telling critique on the need for more democratic policing throughout the nation, and particularly in our city centers.

Wilson reached out for help to Mike McCarthy, a ten-year veteran of the Ferguson Police Force because he really wanted to understand and communicate with the African-American community. McCarthy, who was raised in the area, was not surprised with Wilson's difficulties and mentored him for several months, saying he was one of the best officers on the force, if for no other reason than he had an earnest desire to learn and understand. McCarthy expressed his dismay at the training police cadets are receiving. They spend many hours firing weapons and learning how to apprehend suspects but they spend very little time in establishing common ground with people whose life experiences are totally different. McCarthy bemoaned the recent survey by the Police Executive Research Forum, which revealed police cadets usually receive fifty-eight hours of training in firearms, forty-nine hours in defensive skills, ten in communication skills, and eight in de-escalation tactics.[11]

English cops are good at de-escalating tense situations because they are trained to do that; American police in nail-biting situations are trained to draw their guns and be decisive. They are told that to "back down" in confrontational situations is perceived as showing a lack of resolve, and could be seen as a sign of weakness. If police were habitually seen as "backing down" the community would think they are not "in control" of the situation. This is a cultural inclination; it is not only a police problem. It is an American predicament. The bravado belongs to us all. It is reflected in the recent flurry of states rushing to adopt stand-your-ground laws *where one does not have to retreat.*

Reverend Starsky Wilson was the co-chair of the Ferguson Commission, whose members were asked by Missouri Governor, Jay Nixon,

10. Cobb, "The Talk of the Town: Crimes and Commissions."

11. Halpern, "The Cop."

to study what factors might have contributed to the rioting. In his view, "the moment when Darren Wilson first spoke with Michael Brown was enormously consequential. It frames the engagement and sets a tone for the relationship." In a place like Ferguson, police officers needed to spend more time in the schools, getting to know disadvantaged students, and they had to learn to treat more residents as allies. He asks us to consider what might have happened if Darren Wilson had known Brown, or Brown's grandmother, and was able to say, "Does Miss Jenny know you're out here?" Such a question has a more potent authority than saying, "Use the f———sidewalk, not the middle of the road."[12]

In October 2015, I was privileged to be a part of a summit called, "Subverting the Gospel of Guns" at Andover-Newton Theological Seminary in Boston. Keynoters were Boston Mayor Martin Walsh; Maura Healey, Attorney General of Massachusetts; and William Gross, Superintendent in Chief of the Boston Police Department. They all spoke of Boston's extensive democratic policing efforts that have earned great praise from the White House, the Justice Department, and other agencies of government. "Operation Home Front" is a good example of the collaboration between the Boston School Police Unit, school safety, and social service agencies, and faith-based organizations, that all believe the family is the first line of defense against gang activity, truancy, and violence.

Police and clergy are teamed up to frequently walk the streets, meet neighbors, and build trust in the inner city. They visit homes where there are youth at risk of gang involvement or detrimental behavior. These visits are initiated on a school-by-school basis when a serious incident takes place or there is an escalating level of issues that may adversely affect school safety. This initiative provides a crucial link for parents, students and teachers to gain leverage in preventing social problems.

Boston police officers have earned a wonderful reputation for playing ball with kids and driving ice cream and hot dog trucks to distribute treats to the youth in troubled sections of the city.

Boston is a long way from being the City of God, but every officer on the force is frequently reminded that "law enforcement cannot arrest its way to a peaceful city." It requires human interaction, human compassion, and human cooperation. It was an epiphany for me to hear these interdisciplinary leaders speak about their collaborative strategies for democratic policing.

12. Ibid., 55.

The implications of such approaches are being addressed all over the nation even though some police departments are slow to come on board. Old habits die hard. Some academies still promote a hyper-aggressive style of policing that reaches back to the turbulent 1960s and 1970s, when federal and local officials declared a "War on Drugs" and promised to "get tough on crime." In the late '60s, after Los Angeles created the first SWAT team, hundreds of other cities and even small towns followed suit. Swat teams became a recruiting tool for new cops looking for adventure. Then with open markets for criminals to get guns there was an arms race between drug cartels and law enforcement to see who could gain the advantage. Mark Lomax, Executive Director of the National Tactical Officers Association, said, "It used to be an officer had a flashlight, maybe a nightstick, and their hands and mouth. They learned to be good with their verbal skills. When you add a gun to officer's belts, they will be prone to use it."[13]

Sue Rahr is the Executive Director of the Washington State Criminal Justice Training Commission that is leading efforts in her state to retrain police from being Warriors to Guardians. She warns some police academies are still preparing new officers to "go to war with the people we are sworn to protect and serve." While a minority of recruits do not buy into the program, her efforts are making headway as new first responders see the wisdom and long term benefits of cooperative interaction with the public, and are anxious to learn listening skills.

Over the past three years Rahn's commission has trained about 2,000 new recruits and transfers, or about 20 percent of the 10,000 officers estimated to be working in local departments throughout the state. Rahn says, "It's going to take a generation to establish a new culture." May God speed the day![14]

---

13. Kindy, "New Style of Police Training Aims to Produce 'Guardians' not 'Warriors.'"
14. Kindy, "Creating Guardians, Calming Warriors."

QUESTIONS

1. Does your city have a neighborhood where minority persons are expected or forced to live? Do you live there or near there? Do you have friends there? Have you ever visited your friends there?

2. Atwood details how black-on-black murders often receive less investigation priority than murders involving whites. Over time, how do these cumulative unsolved murders impact black communities?

3. As the white population becomes a non-majority, will white Americans be more open to an honest discussion about race or less open? Where do you experience honest dialogue about race and racism in America?

4. Atwood states that over thirty Americans are murdered by guns every day and half of them are young black men, even though blacks make up only 18 percent of the population. If you are a black American reading this, how do you keep up your spirit with this level of violence, including police-related violence? How can we reduce or end this level of gun violence?

5. Atwood lifts up the city of Boston as a model for successful community policing and race relations. In the prior chapter 17, he suggests that the unarmed English Bobbies have training in de-escalation that would benefit American police forces. Do you see this approach as a benefit? Why or why not?

19

Good Gun Laws Work

Although in days past I used the term extensively, I no longer call my work "gun control." Neither does the CSGV, the Brady Group, Every Town for Gun Safety, Moms Demand Action, and practically all others. We speak of *"preventing gun violence" or "gun safety."* Those terms more accurately describe what we are about. We are not interested in controlling guns. We are committed to saving lives. If you share those goals, I invite you to start using these more accurate terms.

Another factor in adopting this language is it is harder for gundamentalists to reach the same level of scorn when they hear preventing gun violence. When they hear the term gun-control it automatically conjures up images of *big government* confiscating weapons. That image renders them incapable of joining in rational dialogue. Nevertheless, the most "hard core zealots" will say, "So what?" "A rose by any other name." *"Gun control will never work,"* they shout. They are wrong. Good gun laws work well in reducing the availability of handguns to criminals and others who should not be able to get their hands on them.

A consistent theme of the gun lobby is "when guns are outlawed, only outlaws will have guns." They insist any regulation on guns punishes law-abiding people who would obey the law, while criminals would ignore it. As a result, good people would be at the mercy of criminals. Criminals or terrorists do not always obey stop signs or speed limits either (to be honest, neither do I), but no one suggests doing away with them. That would not be a good idea.

The experience of Great Britain and Japan throws a different light on the gun lobby's claims. These countries confidently reply: "When guns are outlawed, very few outlaws will have guns." Gun crime in Japan and England is virtually nonexistent compared to American standards. In fact, 60 percent of the time when a firearm is used in England, the "firearm" is a dummy replica or a bluff.[1] Good gun laws work and they do it without infringing on anyone's Second Amendment rights.

States that have implemented strong, intentional laws to keep guns out of the hands of dangerous people have been very successful. To illustrate how effective they are, consider the last two states to join our union in 1958 and 1959, Alaska and Hawaii. Respectively, they have the weakest and the strongest state gun laws. Correspondingly, the death rates by guns per one hundred thousand citizens are the highest and the lowest of all our states. In 2014, Alaska, with its weak gun laws, has a death rate per one hundred thousand persons of 19.2 while Hawaii, with its strong laws, has a death rate per one hundred thousand of 2.6.[2] Good gun laws work. What follows are a few examples of good gun regulations that if codified would reduce gun deaths in each of our states.

BACKGROUND CHECKS FOR ALL GUNS SOLD

Ninety percent of Americans support this background checks: Republican and Democrat, North and South, East and West, gun owner and non-gun owner alike. This figure includes 85 percent of gun owners and members of the NRA.[3] At present, only licensed gun dealers must conduct an instantaneous background check when they sell any of their guns. At America's 5,000 gun shows and on the Internet "those *who are not in the business of selling guns for a living*" are not required to ask any buyer for identification or background information, even though they may have access to large stashes of firearms. Their sales are strictly cash and carry.[4]

---

1. Armedwithreason.com/debunking-the-five-most-important-myths-about-gun-control/.

2. Henry J. Kaiser Foundation: State Health Facts, "Numbers of Gun Deaths Due to Injury by Firearms."

3. Luntz, National Poll of Gun Owners.

4. Department of the Treasury, Bureau of Alcohol, Tobacco, and Firearms, "Following the Gun: Enforcing Federal Laws Against Firearms Traffickers," 17.

It should be more difficult for those who are a danger to themselves and others to acquire a lethal weapon. Having a background check before one can purchase and own a gun makes the country safer. Background checks have blocked 2.1 million sales to dangerous people since the inception of the Brady Handgun Violence Prevention Act in 1993. The data includes an additional 352,000 gun sales blocked to criminals, felons, domestic abusers, fugitives, and others since 2010, according to Brian Malte, of the Brady Group. He estimates 358 purchases are blocked every day. "Unfortunately," he said, "in the majority of states, criminals and other people not allowed to own or buy guns legally are still able to avoid background checks by making purchases online or at gun shows."[5]

Just after the report was issued in December of 2014, an ex-convict in West Virginia was able to buy a gun on Facebook, which he used to kill four people and himself. Clearly, Congress needs to finish the job on background checks by expanding the Brady Law to cover all online and gun show sales.[6]

BANNING ASSAULT WEAPONS

These are weapons designed specifically for military use to kill as many people in a confined space as possible. That is their purpose. They are the weapons of choice for mass murderers. Extended magazines, easily attached to the gun, enable shooters to fire up to one hundred rounds of ammunition in one minute and the bullets are so powerful they can go right through the walls of our homes. Why would any good law-abiding citizen need such a powerful weapon? It has no social redeeming purpose. It is the only firearm interfaith communities have asked to be banned for the sole reason that it is a military gun for soldiers to use in combat. It is not needed in a crowded apartment house or on a city street. And should one take an assault weapon to the woods during deer season, fellow hunters will give you a very wide berth. You have to stretch the English language to label such a gun a sporting weapon. It has no place in our communities. We need to petition Congress to once again ban this killing machine.

5. Lowery, "2.1 Million Gun Sales Stopped by Background Checks in 20 Years Brady Report Finds."

6. Horwitz, "Price of Normalizing." Brady Campaign, "Dangerous People."

RESTORE FEDERAL FUNDING FOR RESEARCH INTO GUN VIOLENCE

Earlier in this book I wrote of the nation's need for accurate information about gun violence, which is profoundly lacking. Despite many good ideas from advocates for gun violence prevention there is little scientific evidence as to what measures would actually work and how well. The Gun Empire once again proposes *mandatory ignorance* as the best option for the nation. Once again, the enemy for gundamentalists and those on the extreme right, is science. They fear the facts that research might set free.

Even though Congressman Jay Dickey, Arkansas-R wrote the provision to stop CDC research on guns and gun violence, he has had a change of heart and now urges its repeal. He wrote in an op-ed that, unlike health researchers studying car accidents or infectious diseases, "U.S. scientists cannot answer the most basic question: what works to prevent firearm injuries?"[7]

Once again we see the excessive pronouncements and arrogant overreach of gun zealots who believe they have the knowledge and authority to tell scientists what areas of human interaction they should be studying and how they are to conduct their research. Furthermore, they show their incredible bias as they say, "knowing how many people are dying and by what means is irrelevant to government, law enforcement and/or to the practice of medicine." In chapter 4, I wrote about the NRA's suit against psychologists, psychiatrists, and pediatricians for asking suicidal persons and curious children if there is a gun in the house. The claim that such questions are political in nature and are irrelevant to the practice of medicine is ludicrous. As Antisthenes, the Greek philosopher and student of Socrates, said, "The most useful piece of learning in life is to unlearn what is untrue."

MAKING GUN TRAFFICKING A FEDERAL CRIME

Every gun in American begins as a legal gun manufactured or imported and is distributed to and through legal dealers. But over the years many of these legal guns have become part of a highly profitable illegal gun market. According to ATF, over 400,000 gun crimes every year come from what the Brady Campaign calls, "Bad Apple Gun Dealers." Nine out of ten of these guns used in crime can be traced to just 5 percent of America's gun dealers.

7. Williams and Ferris, "Fight To End Gun Research Ban Fizzles."

These scoundrels engage in straw purchasing and gun trafficking; turn off video surveillance cameras to falsify sales records, and ignore tell-tale signs of criminal behavior such as one customer purchasing 85 guns in one visit. Sales from these "Bad Apple Dealers" victimize 1,300 Americans each and every day.[8]

That astonishing statistic literally begs for increased surveillance and penalties for straw-man purchases where one who cannot pass a background check can get a firearm by hiring someone else to buy the gun and deliver it to him. Only recently, the Supreme Court upheld a federal ban on straw-man purchases even when the intended recipient could legally have bought the gun himself. Today, if you get a gun, you must buy it yourself. That is a good law and any kind of gun trafficking should be a federal crime.

Gun traffickers move guns from states with weak laws, particularly in the South and Southwest to states or districts that have stronger laws like Illinois and the District of Columbia. Many of these states have large inner city populations and high crime rates. Gundamentalists say, "See, gun control doesn't work. Look at all the laws these states have and just take a look at the high crime rates in D.C. and Chicago. They are off the charts." Have you ever heard that?

Of course you have! Chicago is not an island. Interstate gun trafficking is a major source of street guns in the city. Between 2009 and 2013, 60 percent of guns recovered in crimes in Chicago were originally purchased in other states like neighboring Indiana, and far-away Mississippi that have very weak laws. In addition, just outside Chicago's city limits, but still in Illinois, gun stores are not subject to the same strong laws, adding to the ease with which illegal guns are bought and sold in those locations.[9]

When I think of how easy it is to engage in gun trafficking, I'm reminded of my college days at Florida State University in the 1950s. The university itself was in Leon County, which, at that time, was a dry county that forbade the sale of alcohol. Do you think that was a big problem for enterprising young men with automobiles who knew Georgia was only sixteen miles away? These guys made an amazing discovery: just over the state line was a liquor store called, State-Line Liquors. Suffice it to say, there were plenty of spirits on the FSU Campus in Tallahassee, and most of the students I hung around with were proud to attend a great "party school."

---

8. #StopBadApples, The Brady Campaign. Fact Sheet.

9. Gerney, "Chicago: Cesspool of Gun Crime or Victim of Lax Gun Laws in Neighboring States."

Today enterprising gun dealers station their shops just over the city limits and state lines of bordering states with strong gun laws. They welcome anyone who wants a gun. The money is the same color. Even though there is a law against interstate purchases of handguns, if one really wants to buy a gun, *something* can be arranged. You can always pick up a gun from rogue dealers just across the state lines and take it back into your city with its strong laws. Gun trafficking needs to be a federal crime.

GUN VIOLENCE RESTRAINING ORDER

I am very proud of the work of the CSGV staff in drafting and promoting the Gun Violence Restraining Order Law (GVRO), which recently was enacted in California under the signature of Governor Jerry Brown. This legislation holds enormous promise for any state that wants to stop another mass shooter before he can pull the trigger. The law itself is based on the same principle as a domestic violence restraining order. It allows family members and/or law enforcement to go before a judge and request that guns be temporarily removed from one who is a danger to oneself and/or others, while allowing for due process.

Notably, a GVRO does not rely solely on mental illness as a marker for violence. Research shows the overwhelming majority of the mentally ill will never be violent toward others. The risk of self-harm is far greater. The stronger indicators of risk include a history of violent behavior, domestic violence, drug and alcohol abuse, and statements made to others indicating a violent outbreak.

The GVRO became law in California following the 2014 mass shooting at the University of California-Santa Barbara in Isla Vista. The gunman, Elliott Rodger, had been given a personal welfare check by authorities and was considered to be a danger, but law enforcement had no authority to remove his guns. Soon thereafter he killed six students and wounded fourteen others. If the GVRO had been in place, those six Californians would be alive today. And perhaps the Pulse Nightclub shooting would not have taken place in Orlando.

HANDGUN PURCHASER LICENSING ACT OF 2015.

Another example that good gun laws work was revealed on June 11, 2015, by Daniel Webster, a researcher at Johns Hopkins Center for Gun Policy and Research. His study of Connecticut's Handgun Purchaser Licensing Law implemented in 1995, shows that requiring a buyer to give a fingerprint, has *reduced homicide rates by 40 percent in the state.*[10] Meanwhile, and since 2007, the Missouri State Legislature has step by step weakened their state's similar handgun licensing law. Their efforts to weaken this law to please the state's gundamentalists, have resulted in dozens of murders and a *25 percent increase in its homicide rates.*[11] The state of Maryland enacted a similar law in 2013, narrowing the legal route to gun ownership. The NRA threatened to take the matter to a referendum, but backed down when polling revealed wide support for the law.[12]

Licensing laws work because they make it much harder for a person who is prohibited from owning a gun to get one. Licensing also deters the temper-driven purchase of a gun. If someone is angry and threatens the life of another licensing can help him cool off. These kinds of fatal shootings are far more common than the dramatic killings we can recite by name and number and city. These handgun purchaser laws close many of the loopholes that exist in our current federal background check system by requiring all sellers, both licensed and unlicensed to sell handguns to individuals with a valid permit or license. Similar national legislation soon will be introduced by Maryland representatives Chris Van Hollen and Elizabeth Esty and Senators Richard Blumenthal and Chris Murphy. It deserves wide support.

REPEAL THE PROTECTION OF LAWFUL COMMERCE ACT OF 2005

In late 2005, the US Congress and President George W. Bush passed the Protection of Lawful Commerce Act (PLCA), which blocks access to the courthouse for the families of gun victims. This law denies victims of gun violence the right to sue manufacturers, distributors, or dealers for *negligent, reckless, or irresponsible conduct.* No other industry in America enjoys such blanket immunity and protection from irresponsible actions.

This law protects firearms manufacturers and dealers from being held liable when crimes have been committed with their products. However, both manufacturers and dealers can still be held liable for damages

10. Richinick, "Handgun Law in Connecticut Helped Decrease Gun Homicides."

11. Tavernise, "Fewer Gun Restrictions and More Gun Killings."

12. Smith, "Why Gun Control Advocates Keep Trying."

resulting from defective products, breach of contract, criminal misconduct, and other actions for which they are directly responsible in much the same manner that any US-based manufacturer of consumer products are held responsible. They may also be held liable for negligence when they have reason to know a gun is intended for use in a crime. The PLCA is codified at 15 U.S.C. §§ 7901–3.

The PLCA is not a paper tiger. It has sharp teeth and destroys the most vulnerable among us. Ask Sandy and Lonnie Phillips about that. Their twenty-year-old daughter was gunned down by James Holmes in the 2012 Aurora, Colorado, theatre massacre. Sandy and Lonnie brought suit against the online ammunition retailer and three others who sold Holmes the ammunition and other gear he used to carry out his attack that killed eleven others in addition to their daughter while wounding seventy others. Their case did not even make it to trial. A federal judge ordered the Phillip's family to pay $200,000 in legal fees to the ammunition dealers. Adding insult to injury, the judge's order will likely bankrupt them. To explain his ruling the judge wrote: "Those who ignore a fire should be responsible for the cost of suppressing it before it becomes a conflagration." Repealing this huge unjust law would help restore at least some faith in our court system and gun laws.[13]

The above are only examples of good gun laws. They do not exhaust the possibilities for good legislation. As citizens and legislators use their energy, intelligence, imagination, and love they will give birth to other good laws that will save lives and maintain a treasured concept in America— equal justice under the law.

MAKE GUN VIOLENCE A PUBLIC HEALTH ISSUE

A public health issue is not a law; it is an approach to a specific problem. Imagine what our country would look like if we had the national and political will to simply admit we had a problem with guns and wanted to make our country safer. Just admitting we have a problem would be a giant step toward wholeness; just as the first step toward recovery for one with an alcoholic or drug addiction, is to acknowledge there is, in fact, a problem. A simple course correction is needed.

Public Health approaches operate with three core concepts: (1) prevention is preferable to treatment; (2) alterations in the environment are

13. Brock and White, "Family to Pay Price for Trying to Sue Ammo Dealer."

more likely to be effective than attempts to change individual behaviors; and (3) multiple strategies directed toward different risk factors are necessary to solve the problem. These principles can be used to structure programs and approaches that would prevent firearm deaths and injuries.[14]

The public health approach is not moralistic or preachy; it does not place blame, or make recommendations to remove guns from the market. It simply focuses on data and follows the data for safer use. Think how the safety of automobiles has improved over the years as such things as seat belts, better brakes, lights, air bags, safety glass, and collapsible steering columns have been introduced along with changes to highways and traffic lights, etc. Making small, incremental changes to firearms would reduce America's gun deaths. Declaring gun violence a public health concern is an idea whose time has come.

ENCOURAGING REPUBLICAN VOTERS TO VOTE FOR GOOD GUN LAWS

Linking the NRA and America's nonsensical gun laws with the Republican Party is not to disparage a valued political party; it is simply to state the facts. Let's be honest: The NRA and the Republican Party have a common enemy: *big government*. We hear from gundamentalists and Republicans on a regular basis that the Federal Government wants to confiscate all of America's 350,000,000 guns and take away Second Amendment rights. Consequently, after every mass shooting, the gun manufacturers, through their trusted allies in the NRA, will urge gun zealots to buy another gun "while they still can." Many Democrats as well have bought into perpetuating such paranoia and have also received A Ratings from the NRA along with nice checks; but it is no secret the organization's most loyal disciples are Republicans.

- In 2014 alone, the NRA spent nearly $30 MILLION to influence elections—nearly all of it to elect Republicans.

- The NRA has received over $10 million from the Koch Brothers' network.[15]

---

14. Powell, Sheehan, and Cristoffel, "Firearm Violence Among Youth: Public Health Strategies for Prevention."

15. *Common Cause,* "5 Facts You Didn't Know About The NRA's Political Spending."

- NRA's coffers remain full with at least $1,000,000 in yearly contributions from manufacturers like Beretta, Brownell, Smith and Wesson, Pierce Bullet Seal Target Systems, Springfield Armory, and Midway USA. Their endowments have a balance of roughly $14 million.[16]

I grew up as a Republican, and I love family and friends who have remained loyal to the party. What is baffling to me is that almost all of them are aghast at the nation's gun deaths and absurd gun laws, but they continue to vote for representatives who never vote against the NRA's wishes. Whenever a reasonable or even minimal restriction on guns is proposed in a state or national legislative body, they listen to those who shout those "abracadabra words": "Freedom," "Second Amendment," "Constitution," and "gun rights." Uttering these shibboleths, at least in the Valley of Virginia where I live, renders reason obsolete. One is led to believe freedom, the Second Amendment, the Constitution, and gun rights are in grave danger. That is simply not so. *Not one of these cherished American concepts is in any danger whatsoever from any common sense gun law.* Would that my Republican family and friends could understand that and would listen to the reasoned voice of their sainted leader, Ronald Reagan!

The former president favored gun regulations that included mandatory waiting periods for gun purchases. He said in a *New York Times* op-ed in 1991, "Every year, an average of 9,200 Americans are murdered by handguns. This level of violence must be stopped." He added, "If tighter regulations "were to result in a reduction of only 10–15 percent of those numbers (and it could be a good deal greater), it would be well worth making it the law of the land."[17] If Republicans, who are as tired of our obscene levels of gun deaths as Democrats, would get in touch with their legislators and tell them how tired they are of the carnage, we would soon have reasonable, common-sense gun laws in this country and would no longer be the laughing stock of freedom-loving countries around the world.

16. Hickey, "How the Gun Industry Funnels Tens of Millions of Dollars to the NRA."
17. Reagan, "Why I'm For the Brady Bill."

QUESTIONS

1. Ninety percent of the general public and 85 percent of gun owners support universal background checks, including gun show and on-line sales. Can you think of any other issue on which 85–90 percent of the American public agrees?

2. In this chapter the author lists several common-sense gun laws that would save lives. Do you agree with him or not? Do any of these laws fundamentally undermine the Second Amendment?

3. Making gun trafficking a federal crime would curtail "straw purchases" and allow states with strong gun laws to be protected from guns coming from states with weak laws. Do you see any downside to this legislation?

4. What might be the long-term result of repealing the special immunity of the gun industry from consumer lawsuits?

5. If you are a Republican, what in your opinion holds back rank-and-file Republicans from supporting laws to reduce gun violence? Were you aware of Ronald Reagan's support for good gun laws?

20

A Grass Roots Social Movement

The most feeble people I meet are those who, when informed that ninety Americans die every day at the barrels of guns, hang their heads and heave a huge sigh, saying, "The only thing we can do is pray." That is code for there is nothing we can do about it. Such a defeatist attitude reveals a belief that it is God's will that we repeat our tragedy day after day and year after year, world without end. What an abysmal understanding of God's plans for the world! What a rejection of God's love! What a renunciation of God's will for our country! What a denial of the power of God in our lives!

Prayer, unaccompanied by hard work to stop the violence and killing, is at best, the mouthing of pious platitudes and a childish belief that God loves gibberish. I'm inviting you to engage in real prayer that is "subversive and seeks to overthrow and ruin the pyramids of callousness, hatred, opportunism, and falsehood."[1] I'm inviting you to join an energizing spiritual, moral, ethical awakening and grassroots movement to stop gun violence. I'm inviting you to get on the bandwagon and raise your voice. Don't forget, bandwagons don't stay around long. You must get on board while you still can. Bandwagons are always on the move to give others a chance to participate.

Having worked for forty-one years to prevent gun violence, I am thrilled to say we, at last have a movement! That is something we have never had before. Oh, we've had a few successes every now and then: the Million Mom March; some one-gun-a-month laws; a few states enacted good laws

1. Waskow, "Continuing Heschel in Our Lives."

that continue to save lives; there was an assault weapons ban for ten years. But, we have never had a grassroots, nation-wide movement to keep efficient killing machines out of dangerous people's hands, but today, we, at long last, have a grassroots movement!

In 1975, when this issue became my driving passion, very few people wanted to talk about it. I often felt I was howling at the moon. Just a few years back, gun violence was the elephant in the church parlor. No one wanted to acknowledge it was even there. Not today! Even in the Bible Belt, after untold numbers of senseless mass murders and horrible tragedies have seared their way into our consciences, we meet thousands of committed, hard-working advocates who have joined the movement. They are working for safe communities because they don't want repeats of our terrible mass murders.

Those of us in the movement were certain that the slaughter of those twenty first graders with a military assault rifle in Newtown, CT by a mentally challenged young man would be the tipping point to rally the whole nation behind sensible gun regulations. We were wrong. Old habits and old sins die hard. In spite of 90 percent of the American people supporting background checks on all guns sold, a vocal minority of gundamentalists persuaded their puppets in Congress to hold the line against placing any restrictions on firearm sales whatsoever. If the US Senate in its present configuration can't vote for new laws, we must elect new lawmakers who can.

When it comes to political change, things move at glacial speed. We've been here before, taking two steps forward and one step back. But, it is a different playing field today. Even though gundamentalists and the NRA's cronies in the Senate voted down common-sense legislation on June 20, 2016, there is no doubt, sensible measures will soon be back on the table. Perhaps we won't win in the next round either, *but we are ultimately going to win. It is no longer a matter of if, it is a matter of when.* The handwriting *is on the wall.* Even though the minority of gun extremists still hold the reins, they have been backed into a corner and cannot evade responsibility indefinitely. Reasonable gun regulations are on the way.

Since 9/11, gundamentalists have been working overtime to stop *any* proposal that would place any restriction on any gun of any kind in any place. They work very hard telling the nation we need more guns so we can protect ourselves from terrorists and other "bad guys."

If one really believes we need to protect ourselves from dangerous individuals, the next question is: should we make it even easier for them and other bad guys to get firearms with no questions asked at one of our 5,000 gun shows or on the Internet? If persons are being kept off our airliners because they *may* have ties to radical groups, why would we permit them to legally buy guns and explosives? That is absurd. Sooner, rather than later, we are all going to rejoice when reason once again makes an appearance in the halls of Congress.

Not only activists, but heretofore uncommitted people are hungry to know the truth about America's gun pandemic. They want to understand why and how we remain the only country in the democratic world to permit the slaughter of 33,000 of our citizens every year as extremists declare their deaths are the price we must pay for freedom.

Present absurdity cannot hide the fact that we are witnessing a *kairos* moment when we see the hand of God at work bringing about desperately needed changes to America's gun laws, which used to protect guns instead of people. There are rumblings from coast to coast that portend a great eruption of reason. People across the country have started thinking about guns. When people *really think*, and not simply rearrange their prejudices, great things can happen. The prophet knew that. Listen to the invitation from Isaiah's God: "Come now, let us reason together says the Lord." I like the NRSV translation even better: "Come now, let us argue it out" (Isa 1:18–20).

When people start "arguing it out" others will soon be brought into the conversation. When preachers use their moral authority and preach on the topic and Sunday school classes debate the rights and risks of having a gun in the home, when lay leaders discuss the latest gun tragedy, or the last headline about a mass shooting, and folks at potluck suppers talk about the dangers their young people face because so many guns are out there . . . a grassroots movement is gaining steam.

Let no one say that is just talk. Just words. Even Almighty God needed words to create the world. "Let there be light," the Creator decreed, and creation came into being. Creation always happens, for good or ill, when words are spoken. Every war, every movement to exploit or degrade people by nation, race, ethnicity, or sex began with words. Likewise, every movement to establish justice, build safe streets, show mercy, and promote unity among the human race; every movement to save human lives, free the captives, stop wars, and begin the work of peace, began with words.

Words are never the end of our witness, but our movement begins and is sustained as caring people *talk* about the need for change. When we no longer lose 90 persons every day to gunshots, when we no longer bury 33,000 people a year, when America no longer suffers 87 percent of the developed world's children killed by guns, it will be because people of faith and good will are talking about preventing unnecessary deaths. That is happening all over America, today! Thanks be to God.

A safer and saner vision of society is coming into focus. People are coming together and "arguing it out." Even in Montana and Mississippi people are talking about Constitutional rights to live with domestic tranquility without fear of being shot. They are realizing God's will is about love and peace and safe city streets. People are starting to insist on their inalienable rights to pursue life, liberty, and happiness in safety.

Skeptics are still around who mock the idea that we have a movement. "Look at all the killings that continue day after day." "How can you talk about a movement?" they ask. We remind all doubters and skeptics that movements *never* begin with victories; they start with defeats, oppression, many deaths and too many tears. Calamities and thousands of God's people dying unnecessarily are what give birth to movements.

Remember that first bloody march for civil rights from Selma, Alabama to Montgomery? It ended in defeat. Chaos reigned as police on horseback beat marchers with night sticks and turned dogs and water cannons on the defenseless. That trouncing was captured on film for all the nation to see. It made people sick. It was the beginning of a spiritual awakening in America. Those were the moments when it became crystal clear that our national documents had teeth, and every human being was indeed born with "certain inalienable rights." We recall other movements— the crusade that brought big tobacco to its knees and the fruitful efforts of Mothers Against Drunk Driving, who changed our laws about driving under the influence, insisting that offenders take responsibility for irresponsible behavior.

Since Newtown, at least a half a dozen new national organizations to prevent gun violence have sprung up. Companies like Target, Starbucks, Jack-in-the-Box, Wendy's, Chipotle, Chili's, Applebee's, and other large chains, including Trader Joe's and Whataburger in Texas, even in Texas, have posted signs that open carry is not permitted in their establishments. *People* magazine issued a call to action urging readers to contact their representatives and demand they do something to stop the madness. In numerous cities, vigils are held whenever there is a shooting or a death. Thousands of churches, synagogues, mosques, and businesses are placing signs on their doors that guns are not allowed inside. Even the National Basketball Association sponsored ads with their biggest stars urging the nation to stop gun violence. This has not happened before.

On June 2, 2016, Gun Violence Awareness Day, thousands of Americans wore orange to call attention to gun violence prevention efforts throughout the country and 125 skylines and iconic landmarks turned their cities and venues orange. When the Empire State Building and Niagara Falls are bathed in orange light, you know something big is brewing.

Muslims, Christians, and Jews are meeting and organizing interdenominational and interfaith conferences. People are learning how they have been bamboozled by the NRA and how a small minority of extremists write dozens of absurd laws that protect guns but put people at risk. Simply put, Americans are not happy with our levels of gun deaths. Our people do not like the direction gundamentalists are taking our country and are demanding a course correction.

During the civil rights struggles of the sixties, one elderly woman was heard to say, "I'm sick and tired of being sick and tired." We are hearing the same today. The nation is sick and tired of hearing an endless recital of gun deaths that are totally unnecessary. Think back. The American people stopped a foolish war in Vietnam because we were sick of all the deaths. We united and shouted out, "Enough! Enough! Not one more!" and our soldiers packed up their gear and came home.

Some of the most encouraging signs about the vitality of the movement are from the faith community, which is finally recognizing gun violence is a profound spiritual issue. I'm still puzzled as to why it took us so long to comprehend that every single gun fatality in America is a person born in God's image; a precious child of God; a brother or sister in God's human family; a neighbor whom God commands us to love; and one whose body is "a temple of the living God." Every religion in the world has a golden rule and the command: "Thou shalt not kill." What other scriptural authority did they need? There is not another social movement with stronger biblical, theological, moral, and ethical principles than preventing gun violence.

Today we are hearing sermons about America's guns from pastors, priests, rabbis, and imams who have never preached on the subject before. Perhaps they realize being silent in the midst of a plague is to vote for death. Perhaps they have discovered if they always take the middle of the road, sooner or later they will be run over.

One common complaint I hear from lazy, over-indulged disciples is: gun violence is a political matter and preachers and religious leaders should avoid it. Two hundred years ago the same complaint was leveled at churches and clergy who addressed the evils of slavery that many considered a political and economic issue, but not a spiritual one. We hear the same murmurings whenever one of our wars or its tactics is challenged by a patriot who seeks peace, or one of God's people confronts racism, sexism, environmental concerns, LGBT issues, or a host of other sins to which the human spirit is heir.

I heard someone say, "We practice passover in our church." "I didn't know you were Jewish," a friend replied. "Oh we're not. What I mean is when a controversial subject is raised, we all keep quiet until the need to discuss it passes over." Make no mistake. People of faith cannot practice this kind of passover and pretend to love our city, our neighbors, or our God. You can't love people without caring about that which is killing so many every year. We cannot talk about loving one another and ignore the heartache of ninety American families that are ripped apart by a firearm every single day.

Gun violence is no more a political issue than arson or driving under the influence. To the contrary I believe it is the greatest religious, spiritual, ethical, and moral issue before our nation. And the depth of our nation's heartbreak has only increased because the faith community has in the past listened tenderly to those who have whined about their gun rights instead of hearing the voices of victim's families who continue to weep at their gravesides and will never be the same.

I have a lover's quarrel with the Christian church in America. I love it, but I'm far from pleased with it. Maybe you also have a lover's quarrel with it, or with another faith community. Maybe you have a lover's quarrel with the Republican or Democratic Party to which you have looked for leadership on this issue and have found their attention wanting.

The church is, in fact, a *giant,* brim-full with the potential power of God, yet it tiptoes around the city hoping not to offend anyone as it timidly prays about the bloodshed on America's streets. My *giant* is tempted to remain neutral on gun violence because there are those in the congregation who will label the issue "political" even when it is thoroughly non- partisan. Guns kill Republican and Democrats and Independents, every day. The victims are Jews, Christians, Muslims, Sikhs, Buddhists, atheists, agnostics, whites, blacks, Latino, Asian, men, women, boys, girls, young, old, gay, straight, rich, poor, rural and urban, gun owners and non-gun owners. No category of human being is immune to a bullet.

It is impossible for any faith community to be neutral about a pandemic, especially when God promises to give us a spirit of confidence, love, and self-discipline. To be timid about our gun epidemic is to proclaim, through our silence, God is pleased with our status quo. Not to decide to speak out is to cast a vote for more suffering and death.

Part of the church's mission is to promote social righteousness in the world. But today, people of faith are often intimidated and bullied by a small minority of religious gundamentalists who proclaim guns are more important to America's future than loving our neighbors and living in domestic tranquility. I reject that. I denounce that. It is heresy. It is idolatry. I'm angry about that, and I refuse to keep quiet about it.

I'm calling on you as well, to be bold and vocal. I implore you to challenge your church's leadership, both clergy and lay. Perhaps you might assemble some kindred spirits to meet with your priest or pastor and governing body and inform them of your convictions.

Now is the time to express your belief that Jesus' church must do more than pray for the families whose loved ones have been slaughtered by guns. We must do more than support an ambulance service to pick up the wounded and rush them to the hospital, or a cemetery. Tell them you believe God calls your church to help build a safe and peaceful city where little children are not afraid to go to a public park for fear of being shot. Tell your leaders you expect educational and worship opportunities around the subject as well as concrete actions members can take to build "the beloved community."

One thing we know: The gun manufacturers and NRA want to keep gun violence strictly a political issue. They hope the faith community will not talk about it, let alone study it. But the day is soon coming when the church and other faith communities will recognize that violence of any kind is an affront to God. Once people of faith are claimed by that spiritual, moral, and ethical power, our gun violence pandemic will end.

I trust that you, the reader, will devote energy, intelligence, imagination, and love and act boldly to remove the idolatrous mask from gundamentalism as you follow God's promised paths to justice and peace. May it be so!

QUESTIONS

1. Do you sense public arousal on the need to reduce gun violence? Do you know of anyone in your community working on common-sense gun laws?

2. Do you agree with Atwood that words and communication about gun violence are the way to jump-start change? What can you do to help start that conversation?

3. Were you aware of the corporations that prohibit carrying firearms on their property? Do you want to criticize them or thank them?

4. Whether you are a person of religious faith or not, what role do you think the religious community needs to play to reduce gun violence?

5. Atwood refers to a "*kairos* moment," the New Testament concept of a time when an issue can no longer go unheeded, a time when divine spirit intervenes and helps. Do you see God's hand at work in the movement to prevent gun violence? Is so, what is required of us?

Assignment: Visit websites listed in the bibliography of this book and see where they lead you: perhaps to a national organization working on common-sense gun laws . . . perhaps to a group in your community working to reduce gun violence . . . or perhaps to the courage to find a friend or two or ten to start such a group.

Appendix

Helpful Websites on Gun Violence

Advocating for Children: American Academy of Pediatrics:
https://www.aap.org/enus/advocacy-and-policy/federaladvocacy/pages/
aapfederalgunviolencepreventionrecommendationstowhitehouse.aspx

Brady Campaign www.bradycampaigntopreventgunviolence.org

Children's deaths and injuries: Protect Children Not Guns Report
http://www.childrensdefense.org/campaigns/protect-children-not-guns/

Coalition to Stop Gun Violence www.csgv.org

Domestic Abuse statistics and how to counteract it
http://smartgunlaws.org/domestic-violence-firearms-policy-summary/

FBI Uniform Crime Report in US, https://www.fbi.gov/about-us/cjis/ucr/ucr

Gun Violence Archive a non profit for current statistics for all gun violence concerns
www.Gunviolencearchive.org.

Guns and Violence Against Women
http://everytownresearch.org/reports/guns-and-violence-against-women/

Guns: Bizarre shootings and/or deaths

Violence Policy Center. http://concealedcarrykillers.org/

Gun laws by state: Law Center to Prevent Gun Violence Website
http://smartgunlaws.org/search-gun-law-by-state/ crazy laws

Guns and Suicide: The Hidden Toll
http://www.hsph.harvard.edu/magazine-features/guns-and-suicide-the-hidden-
toll/

Suicide Research at Harvard Injury Control Research Center
http://www.hsph.harvard.edu/hicrc/firearms-research/gun-ownership-and-use/

Gun injuries, deaths, and suicides: CDC WISQARS Tool (Center for Disease Control) ;
http://www.cdc.gov/injury/wisqars/

International comparisons : http://www.gunpolicy.org/

Weapons used in murders and suicides: www.infoplease.com

NRA Website

NRA Board of Directors statements on women, race, LGBT, government/ Pres. Obama, democrats, etc. www.csgv.org/archives/NRAontherecord

Presbyterian Church USA policy www.pcusa.org/resource/gun-violence-prevention (Most other denominations have similar sites)

Presbyterian Peace Fellowship www.presbypeacefellowship.org/toolkit

Bibliography

Achenbach, Joel. "Always on Alert." *Washington Post,* February 3, 2013.

Albright, Madeline. *Memo to the President: How We Can Restore America's Reputation and Leadership.* New York: Harper, 2008.

Alexander, Keith. "Boy Who Shot Sister Didn't Realize He Had Killed Her." *Washington Post,* December 12, 2015.

Almany, Steve. "One Piece Still Missing from Puzzle of Fatal Theatre Shooting: Why?" CNN, January 14, 2014.

Almasy, Steve, and John Newsome. "Florida Mother Shoots Daughter She Thought Was Intruder." CNN, December 31, 2015.

American Foundation for Suicide Prevention. AFSP.org/about-suicide/statistics.

Annals of America, the. Vol. 12, edited by William Benton. NY: Encyclopedia Britannic, Inc. 1976.

"The Armed Citizen." *American Rifleman.* November, 2014.

Atwood, James. *America and Its Guns: A Theological Expose.* Eugene, OR: Cascade, 2012.

Auchter, Bernie. "Men Who Murder Their Families: What the Research Tells Us." *National Institute of Justice Journal,* No. 266, May, 2010. http://www.nij.gov/journals/pages/archive.aspx.

Ayoob, Massad. "Trend Crimes and the Gun Dealer." *Shooting Industry,* March 1993.

Barden, Mark and Jackie. "Bernie Sanders is Wrong About Our Gun Lawsuit." *Washington Post,* March 20, 2016.

Benton, William, ed. *The Annals of America.* Vol. XII. New York: Encyclopedia Brittanica, Inc., 1976.

Berman, Mark. "Police Are Dying by Gunfire at Over Twice Last Year's Rate." *Washington Post,* April 3, 2016.

Bienaime, Pierre. "The Russian Navy Is Aiming to be Much Larger than the US Navy." *Business Insider,* September 24, 2014.

Bowerman, Mary. "Virginia Man Who Died in Police Custody Tased Repeatedly." *USA Today,* November 12, 2015. http://www.usatoday.com/story/news/nation-now/2015/11/12/man-police-custody-tased-over-20-times-virginia/75638054.

Bowers, Matthew. "Chesapeake Marine Guilty of Accidentally Killing Infant Child." *Virginian-Pilot,* June 25, 2010.

Borger, Julian. "Gun Lobby Claims it would 'workout of President Bush's office.'" *The Guardian,* May 4, 2000.

Brady Campaign to Prevent Gun Violence. "Dangerous People." December 9, 2014.

———. "Stop Bad Apples." Fact sheet.

Bibliography

————. The Winter Report 2011.

Brock, Sam, and Rachel White. "Family to Pay Price for Trying to Sue Ammo Dealer." NBC News Bay Area, August 3, 2015.

Brose, Marla. "Funeral for New Mexico Girl Killed in Road Rage Dispute." *Albuquerque-Journal,* October 28, 2015.

Brueggemann, Walter. "*Deadly Illusion.*" Book Review. *Christian Century,* August 5, 2015, 36.

Bureau of Alcohol, Tobacco, Firearms and Explosives. *Firearms Commerce in the United States Annual Statistical Update 2012.* Public paper.

"The Bureau of Alcohol, Tobacco, Firearms and Explosives reports America has more Gun Stores than Subway, McDonalds, and Starbucks Combined." http://rare/us/story/america-more-gun-stores-than-subway-mcdonalds-and-starbucks-combined.

Burggraeve, Roger. *Desirable God: Our Fascination With Idols, Images, and New Deities.* Leuven, Belgium: Peeters, 2003.

Caruso, Kevin. "Suicide by Cop Suicide Prevention, Awareness, and Support." Web Paper. www.Suicide.org.

CBS News. "Family, Friends, Bid Final Farewell to Harrison Sisters Killed by Father in Murder-Suicide." February 27, 2015.

CDC and Department of Defense.

Chan, T. H. "Guns and Suicides: The Hidden Toll." The School of Public Health, Harvard University. Public Paper, December 4, 2012.

Chandrasekaren, Rajiv. "A Legacy of Pain and Pride." *Washington Post,* March 29, 2014.

Chang, Alvin. "Evidence Suggests 2015 Will Be Record Year For Gun Sales" *Vox,* December 27, 2015.

Circuit Court of Lafayette, Missouri. *Janet Delana v. CED Sales, Inc. Odessa Gun and Pawn.*

CNN. "American Deaths in Terrorism vs. Gun Violence in One Graph." October 2, 2016.

Clayworth, Jason. "Iowa Grants Gun Permits to the Blind." *Des Moines Register,* September 8, 2013.

Cobb, Jelani. "The Talk of the Town: Crimes and Commissions." *The New Yorker,* December 6, 2014, 16–17.

Collman, Ashley. "Man, 53, shot dead his 34-year-old wife and pet parrot because 'they talked too much'" Daily Mail.com, May 8, 2014.

"Columbine Shooter Eric Harris' Journals and Writings." http://www.acolumbinesite.com/eric/writing/journal/journal.html.

Common Cause. "5 Facts You Didn't Know About The NRA's Political Spending," December 7, 2015.

Cook, Philip, and Jens Ludwig. *Gun Violence: The Real Costs.* New York: Oxford University Press, 2000.

Cooper, Michael. "Census Officials, Citing Increasing Diversity, Say U. S. will be a 'Plurality Nation.'" *New York Times,* December 12, 2012.

Cosgrove, Christine. "Murder-Suicide in Elderly Rise." Depression Health Center. WebMD Feature Archive.

Cox Newspaper Services, Florida, 1981. Cited by Tom Diaz. Powerpoint Presentation, Stony Point, NY, September 16, 2008.

Dahl, Julia. "Empire State Building Shooting Sparks Questions About NYPD Shot Accuracy." CBS, August 29, 2012.

Daily Mail. "3-year Old Girl Accidently Shot Herself Dead After Finding Father's Gun." www.dailymail.co.uk/news/article. February 12, 2015.

Davidson, Osha. *Under Fire: The NRA and the Battle for Gun Control.* Iowa City, IA: University of Iowa Press, 1998.

DeBrabander, Firmin. "How Gun Rights Harm the Rule of Law." *The Atlantic,* April 1, 2015. http://www.theatlantic.com/politics/archive/2015/04/how-gun-rights-harm-the-rule-of-law/389288/.

Dees-Thomases, Donna. *Looking for a Few Good Moms: How One Mother Rallied a Million Others Against the Gun Lobby.* New York: Rodale, 2004.

Defilappis, Evan, and Devin Hughes. "Gunfight or Flee: New Study Finds No Advantages to Using a Firearm in Self-Defense Situations." *The Trace,* January 19, 2016, www.thetrace.org.

Department of the Treasury. Bureau of Alcohol, Tobacco, and Firearms, "Following the Gun: Enforcing Federal Laws Against Firearms Traffickers." June 17, 2000.

Diaz, Tom. *Making a Killing: The Business of Guns in America.* New York: The New Press, 1999.

———. Powerpoint Presentation at the Gun Violence/Gospel Values Conference Stony Point, Center, Stony Point, NY, September 16–18, 2008.

Dionne, E. J. "Making Gun Safety (Politically) Safe." *Washington Post,* December 10, 2009. A-17.

———. "The Right to Be Free from Guns. *Washington Post,* June 26, 2015.

Divakaruni, Chitra Banerjee. *The Unknown Errors of Our Lives.* New York: Doubleday, 2001.

"Domestic (Intimate Partner) Violence Fast Facts." CNN Library, May 4, 2016.

Dunlap, Charles. "Revolt of the Masses and the Insurrectionary Theory of the Second Amendment." *Tennessee Law Review,* vol. 62:643 (1997) 643–77.

Ebert, Joel. "Tennessee Lawmaker Giving Away AR-15 Receives 'Death Threats.'" The Tennessean.com, June 13, 2016.

Economist. "When Lawsuits Make Policy." November 19, 1998, 255–88.

Elliott, Steve. "Why I Destroyed My Handgun." *Washington Post,* October 18, 2015.

Esler, G. "Logic Which Makes Guns Safe But Shopping Trolleys Lethal." *Scotsman (Edinburgh),* November 30, 1998.

Estes, Adam Clarke. "3-D Printer Guns Are Only Getting Better and Scarier." GunsMagazine.com.

Fallis, David. "The Hidden Life of Guns." *Washington Post,* October 26, 2010.

Fears, Darryl. "Racism Twists and Distorts Everything." *Washington Post,* July 9, 2016.

Field and Stream. "Use Pepper Spray Instead of Guns to Stop a Charging Grizzly." Public paper.

Follman, Mark. "The True Cost of Gun Violence in America." *Mother Jones,* April 15, 2015. http://www.motherjones.com/politics/2015/04/true-cost-of-gun-violence-in-america.

FoxNews.com. "Al Qaeda Urges American Muslims to Buy Guns for Terror Attacks." June 4, 2011.

Frankel, Todd. "Why The CDC Still Isn't Researching Gun Violence Despite the Ban Being Lifted Two Years Ago." *Washington Post,* January 14, 2015.

Frum, David. "Do Guns Make Us Safer?" www.CNN.com/2012/07/30/opinion/frum-guns.

Bibliography

Gainesville Sun. "Felons Exploit Loopholes in Fla Concealed Weapons Law." January 29, 2007.

Gerney, Arkadi. "Chicago: Cesspool of Gun Crime or Victim of Lax Gun Laws in Neighboring States." *ThinkProgress,* May 24, 2014.

Gokavi, Mark. "Family of Man Shot at Wal-Mart Wants an Answer." *Dayton Daily News,* August 11, 2014

Greenberg, Andy. "The Bullet That Could Make a 3-D Printed Gun a Practical Deadly Weapon." *Security,* November 5, 2014.

Greenberg, Will. "Cities Confront A Summer of Bloodshed." *Washington Post,* August 4, 2015.

———. "Police Chiefs from Around the Country Meet in D.C. to Discuss Violent Summer." *Washington Post,* August 3, 2015.

Griffin, Drew. "S.C. Lawmaker Apologizes for Saying Charleston Victims Waited Their Turn to be Shot." *CNN Politics,* June 25, 2015.

Grimaldi, James, and Sari Horwitz. "Industry Pressure Hides Gun Traces; Protects Dealers from Public Scrutiny." *Washington Post,* January 22, 2011.

Grossman, Dave. *On Killing: The Psychological Cost of Learning to Kill in War and Human Society.* New York: Back Bay Books, 2009.

Hall, Gary. "Gun Violence Prevention Laws Save Lives: Conversing With Your Congregation About Gun Violence." Faiths United to Prevent Gun Violence, September, 2014.

Halpern, Jake. "The Cop." *The New Yorker,* August 10 &17, 2015, 44–55.

Harris, Eric. "Columbine Student's Writings and Journal."

Healy, Jack, et. al. "One Week in April Four Toddlers Shot and Killed Themselves." *New York Times,* May 5, 2016.

Heller v. District of Columbia, 2008.

Hemenway, David. *Private Guns–Public Health.* Ann Arbor, MI: University of Michigan Press, 2010.

———. "Does Owning a Gun Make You Safer?" *Los Angeles Times,* August 4, 2015.

Henley, William Ernest. "Poems by William Ernest Henley." Forgotten Books: Classic Reprint Series. July 15, 2012.

Herbert, Bob. "A Culture Soaked in Blood." *New York Times,* April 24, 2009.

Heston, Charlton, NRA Convention Speech, in Philadelphia. 1998.

Hickey, Walter. "How the Gun Industry Funnels Tens of Millions of Dollars to the NRA." *Business Insider,* January 16, 2013. www.businessinsider.com/gun-industry-funds-nra-2013-1.

Horwitz, Josh. "The Charleston Victims Weren't Asking For It." *Huffington Post,* June 29, 2015.

———. "The Price of Normalizing." *Huffington Post,* http://www.huffingtonpost.com/josh-horwitz/the-price-of-normalizing_8521488.html.

———. "The Racial Double Standard on Gun Violence." *Huffington Post,* October 9, 2014.

———. "When Violence Trumps the Constitution, Democracy Is in Peril." *Huffington Post,* June 6, 2016.

Horwitz, Joshua, and Casey Anderson. *Guns, Democracy, and the Insurrectionist Idea.* Ann Arbor, MI: University of Michigan Press, 2009.

Ingraham, Christopher. "There Are Now More Guns Than People In the US." *Washington Post,* October 5, 2015.

———. "Dog Shoots Man." *Washington Post,* November 1, 2015

————. "From 2004 to 2014, Over 2,000 Terror Suspects Legally Purchased Guns in the US." *Washington Post,* November 16, 2015.

————. "An NRA Board Member Blames the Pastor Killed in Charleston for the Deaths of His Members." *Washington Post Workblog,* June 19, 2015.

Ingraham, Christopher, and Carolyn Johnson. "CDC Study: Gun Deaths Catch Up To Car Deaths." *Washington Post,* December 19, 2015.

Jacobson, Louis. "Fact Checking US Politics." *Politifact,* July 23, 2012

————. "Do 100,000 People Get Shot Every Year in the US?" *Politifact,* July 23, 2012

James, Susan. "Suicide Rate Spikes in Vietnam Vets." ABC News, May 3, 2012

Jewett, Robert. *The Captain America Complex: The Dilemma of Zealous Nationalism.* Philadelphia: Westminster, 2003.

Johns Hopkins Bloomberg School of Public Health, "Intimate Partner Violence and Firearms." Public paper.

Johnson, Timothy. "NRA News Host Lectures College Students: Burden of Stopping Sexual Assaults 'Is on the Victim.'" Mediamatters.org, March 31, 2015.

Jones, Julia, and Eve Bower. CNN, October 2, 2015.

Kaiser, Henry J, .Foundation. "State Health Facts: Numbers of Gun Deaths Due to Injury by Firearms."

Kansas City Star. "Flush Arrogant Gun Policy," September 25, 2013.

Kaplan, Sarah. "N. C. three-year-old finds gun in dad's store. He shoots himself dead." *The Washington Post,* January 15, 2016.

Kastor, Elizabeth. "The Power of Pow: The Debate Rages On." *Washington Post,* December 19, 1991.

Kellerman, Arthur, et.al. "Injuries and Deaths Due to Firearms in the Home." *Journal of Trauma,* 1998. Vol. 45 (1998) 263–67.

Kelly, Erin. "TSA Finds Record Number of Firearms in Carry-on Bags." *USA Today,* January 23, 2015.

Kerr, Dara. "Ghost Gunner Lets People Make Untraceable Homemade Guns." *Sci-Tech,* October 1, 2014.

Kerug, E. G., et al. "Firearm Related Deaths in the U. S. and 35 Other High- and Upper Income Countries." *International Journal of Public Opinion Research* (1998) 214–21.

Kiely, I. "Gun Rhetoric vs. Gun Facts" Factcheck.org. December 21, 2012.

Kindy, Kimberly. "Creating Guardians, Calming Warriors." *Washington Post,* December 11, 2015.

————. "New Style of Police Training Aims to Produce 'Guardians' not 'Warriors.'" *Washington Post,* December 10, 2015.

Kindy, Kimberly, et al. "Officers Fatally Shoot 965." *Washington Post,* December 27, 2015.

King, Colbert. "A Life is Lost. Does Anyone Even Care?" *Washington Post,* February 7, 2015.

————. "Pray for the District, Too." *Washington Post,* November 21, 2015.

Kleck, G. *Targeting Guns: Firearms and Their Control.* Hawthorne, NY: Aldine de Gruyter, 1997.

Klimas, Liz. "Look Closely: Can You Tell These Cellphones Are Actually Weapons in Disguise?" *Blaze,* April 12, 2013.

La Pierre, Wayne. *Guns, Crime, and Freedom.* Washington, DC: Regnery, 1994.

————. NRA Speech, March 11, 2009. You Tube.

————. Speech at The Willard Hotel, Washington, DC. December 21, 2012.

————. You Tube. September 19, 2013.

Langford, Adam. NPR Radio, On Point, "Stop the Paralysis." August 31, 2015.

Langford, Steve. "Family, Friends, Bid Final Farewell to Harrison Sisters Killed by Father in Murder-Suicide." CBS News, February 27, 2015.

Lazo, Luz, and Greg Miller. "Ex-Official with CIA Arrested at BWI," *Washington Post,* August 8, 2015.

Lee, Peggy. "Luzern County D. A.: Man Killed by Suicide by Cop." www.WNEP.com, August 11, 2015.

Leovy, Jill. *Ghettoside: A True Story of Murder in America.* New York: Spiegel and Grau, 2015.

Leshner, A. L., et al. *Priorities for Research to Reduce the Threat of Firearms-Related Violence.* Washington, D.C.: National Academies Press, 2013.

Li, Victor. "Report Links Stand-Your-Ground Laws to Higher Homicide Rates." *The American Bar Association Journal,* October 1, 2014, 1–56.

Lipschitz, A. "1995 Suicide Prevention in Young Adults (age 18–30)." *Suicide and Life-Threatening Behavior,* 25 (1995) 155–70.

Leshner, A. L., et al. *Priorities for Research to Reduce the Threat of Firearms-Related Violence.* Washington, D.C.: National Academies Press, 2013.

Levin, Jeffery. "In Defense of the Right to Bear Flintlock Muskets." *Los Angeles Times,* March 14, 2001.

Lopez, German. "The UCLA Shooting Exposes How We Often Ignore the Most Common Form of Gun Violence." Vox.com/policy-and-politics/2015/.

Lourim, Jake. "Darryl Hamilton, Killed in Apparent Murder-Suicide." *USA Today,* June 22, 2015.

Lowery, Wesley. "2.1 Million Gun Sales Stopped by Background Checks in 20 Years Brady Report Finds." *Washington Post,* February 28, 2014.

Lowy, Jonathan. "She Begged Them Not to Sell Her Daughter a Gun." The Brady Campaign to Prevent Gun Violence, December 3, 2014.

Luntz, Frank. National Poll of Gun Owners, Including NRA Members. Sponsored by Mayors Against Illegal Guns. July 2012.

Martinez, Luis, Joseph Rhee, and Mark Schone. "No More Jesus Rifles," ABC News, January 21, 2010.

Matsakis, Aphrodite. *Vietnam Wives.* Lutherville, MD: Sidran, 2001.

Mauch, Ernst. "My Gun, Your Choice." *Washington Post,* May 19, 2014.

McGuire, F. "Gun Stocks Shooting Profits," www.newsmax.com/Finance/StreetTalk/gun-stocks-shooting-profits/2015/12/03/ID/704450/.

Melber, Ari. "Man Tased, Shackled, and Driven to Hospital, Dies in Police Custody." www.msnbc, November 11, 2015.

Mencken, H. L. "The Divine Afflatus." *New York Evening Mail,* November 16, 1917.

Merchant, Carolyn. *Radical Ecology: Search for a Livable World.* New York: Taylor and Francis Group, 2005.

Merlan, Anna. "Sheriff: Domestic Violence Victim Could Have Prevented Her Own Murder if She'd Just Had a Gun." *Jezebel,* August 11, 2015.

Michigan Women's Justice and Clemency Project. umich.edu/-clemency

Miller, Patrick. *The Ten Commandments.* Louisville: Westminster John Knox, 2009

Misra, Tanvi. "Mapping the Sale of Firearms vs. Frappuccinos." The Atlantic City Lab. http://www.citylab.com/crime/2016/01/map-gun-dealers-starbucks/423801/.

Moore, Stewart, et al. "Charges Likely for Grandmother in Sam's Club Shooting." WISTV. com, June 9, 2008.

Bibliography

Morlino, John. "Guns make the Difference." Letters to the Editor, *Washington Post,* June 28, 2015.

Motoko, Rich. "NRA Envisions 'A Good Guy with a Gun' In Every School." *New York Times,* December 21, 2012.

Mount, Harry. "Was Einstein Right?" *Daily Mail London,* January 28, 2015.

Mount Holyoke School of Education. "John Adam's Warning Against The Search for Monsters to Destroy." www.mtholyoke.edu/acad/intrel/jqadams.

Nelson, Libby, and Javier Zarracina. "A Shocking Statistic About Gun Deaths in the US." *Vox: Policy and Politics,* December 4, 2015.

Nelson, J. Herbert. "A Call For More Than Judicial Remedies to the Killing of African American Boys and Men." Office of Public Witness, Presbyterian Church USA. Public Paper, August 21, 2015.

New York City Mayor's Office. "Ted Cruz's Call for Muslim Patrols Angers N. Y. Police," YouTube. March 23, 2016.

New York Times. "The Sorry State of Gun Control." October 31, 2010.

Nolan, Jim. "Senate Panel Votes Down Gun Control Bills." *Richmond Times,* January 26, 2015.

Norton, Rob. "Unintended Consequences." In David R. Henderson. *Concise Encyclopedia of Economics.* 2nd ed. Indianapolis: Library of Economics and Liberty, 2008.

NPR. "The Day One Man Decided to Give Up His Gun." www.npr.org/2015/04/24/401711396/the-day-one-man-decided-to-give-up-his-gun.

———. "Twelve Year-Old Boy Carrying Replica Gun Dies." www.npr.org, November 23, 2014.

NPR Science Friday. "Is Gun Violence a Public Health Issue?" December 4, 2015

Obama, President Barack. Speech at Memorial Service for Charleston shooting victims

Osnos, Evan. "Making a Killing." *New Yorker,* June 27, 2016, 36–45.

Pane, Lisa Marie. "James Bond Meets Samuel Colt; Seeking to Build a Safer Gun." http://phys.org/news/2016-05-james-boond-samuel-colt-safer.html.

Pavao, Esther. "Slavery and the Founding Fathers." www.revolutionarywar.net/slavery.

Pearle, Lauren. "Kids and Guns: By the Numbers." ABC News, January 29, 2014. http://abcnews.go.com/blogs/headlines/2014/01/kids-and-guns-by-the-numbers/.

Pew Charitable Trust. "One in 31 U. S. Adults are Behind Bars, On Parole, or On Probation." A Public Safety Performance Project. April 1, 2010.

Pompilio, Natalie. "States With Weak Firearms Laws Led in Crime Gun Exports," *Philadelphia Daily News,* September 28, 2010.

Potok, Mark. Interview on the Diane Rehm Show, NPR Radio, March 31, 2010.

Powell, E. C., K. M. Sheehan, and K. K. Cristoffel. "Firearm Violence Among Youth: Public Health Strategies for Prevention." *Annals of Emergency Medicine* 28 (1996) 204–12.

Presbyterian Church in the United States of America. 202nd General Assembly Minutes, 1990.

Presbyterian Outlook, February 18, 2013.

Reagan, Ronald. "Why I'm For the Brady Bill." *New York Times,* March 29, 1991.

Reeves, Richard, and Sarah Holmes. "Guns and Race: The Different Worlds of Black and White Americans." The Brookings Institute, Social Mobility Memos, December 15, 2015.

Reich, Robert. "Tribalism is Tearing America Apart." http://media.salon.com/2014/01/Robert_reich.jpg.

Reisenweber, Brandi. "What's this Business about Chekhov's gun?" Writer Magazine of Gotham Writers Workshop, Inc. https://www.writingclasses.com/toolbox/ask-writer/what's-this-business-about-chekhovs-gun.

"Remarks by the President on Common Sense Gun Safety Reform." The White House: Office of the Press Secretary, January 5, 2016.

"Report: Chicago Gun Violence Costs 2.5 billion a Year." *Chicago Tribune,* March 3, 2009.

Rich, C. L., D. Young, and R. C. Fowler. San Diego Suicide Study: "Young vs. Old Subjects. *Archives of General Psychiatry* 43 (1986) 577–82.

Richinick, Michele. "Handgun Law in Connecticut Helped Decrease Gun Homicides." www.newsweek.com, June 11, 2015.

Robinson, Marilynne. "Fear." *New York Review of Books,* September 24, 2015, 1–3.

Rogers, Paul. "Photo of Streisand home becomes an Internet hit." *San Jose Mercury News,* mirrored at californiacoastline.org, June 24, 2003.

Ross, Jeffery Ian. "In Gun Control Debate, Imposed Access Control is Best Short-Term Solution." *The Hill,* November 16, 2015.

Rowen, James. "Guns in Homes Pose Greater Risk to Families than Intruders, Data Shows." *Milwaukee Journal,* December 20, 2012.

Samuels, Dorothy. "Gun Deaths Versus Car Deaths." Violence Policy Center, July 16, 2014.

Schmidt, Michael. "FBI Director to Give Speech Addressing Relations Between Police and Blacks." *New York Times,* February 11, 2015.

Schrager, Allison. "The Very Stark Numbers on Young Black Men and Gun Violence." *Bloomberg Business,* August 20, 2014.

Schwartz, Hunter. "Idaho Professor Shoots Himself in the Foot." *Washington Post.* September 4, 2014.

Shaull, Richard. *Naming the Idols: Biblical Alternatives for US Foreign Policy.* Oak Park, IL: Meyer-Stone, 1988.

Shen, Aviva. "NRA's Wayne La Pierre: 'There Weren't Enough Good Guys with Guns at Navy Yard Shooting.'" *ThinkProgress,* September 22, 2013.

Smith, Fraser. "Why Gun Control Advocates Keep Trying." *Maryland Daily Record,* July 24, 2015.

Smith, Morgan. "Gun Rights Advocates to Build Weapons at Capitol." *Texas Tribune,* January 6, 2015.

Smith, Tom, and Stephen Herrero. "Efficacy of Firearms for Bear Deterrence." *Journal of Wildlife Management,* March, 2012, 1021–27.

Solzhenitsyn, Alexander. Acceptance Speech for Nobel Prize for Literature, 1970.

Somerset, A. J. *Arms: The Culture and Credo of the Gun.* Biblioasis.Com, 2015.

Schrager, Allison. "The Very Stark Numbers on Young Black Men and Gun Violence." *Bloomberg Business,* August 20, 2014.

South Carolina Law Enforcement Assistance Program. SCLEAP.org/groupcrisisintervention

Steinberg, Gerald. "Conflict Prevention and Mediation in the Jewish Tradition." *Jewish Political Studies Review,* 12 (Fall 2000) 3–4.

Stern, Melissa. "Mom Files Suit Against Gun Dealer Over Sale to Mentally Ill Daughter." FoxKC.com, March 12, 2014.

Suen, Brennan. "Fox News Revives 'Black on Black Crime Canard to Dismiss Black Lives Matter.'" http://mediamatters.org/research/2015/09/03/fox-news-revives-black-on-black-crime-canard-to/205364.

Sullivan, John, et al. "In Fatal Shootings by Police, 1 in 5 Officer's Names Go Undisclosed." *Washington Post,* March 31, 2016.

Tavernise, Sabrina. "Fewer Gun Restrictions and More Gun Killings." *New York Times,* December 21, 2015.

Thompson, Cheryl and Mark Berman. "Stun Guns: 'There was just too much use.'" *Washington Post,* November 27, 2015.

Thompson, Mark. "Unlocking the Secrets of PTSD." *Time,* April 6, 2015, 41–43.

Thoreau, Henry David. *Walden and Other Writings.* New York: Barnes and Noble, 1992.

Treaty of Tripoli.

Turkel, Dan. "Guns Have Killed More Preschoolers than Police Officers in the Line of Duty." *Business Insider,* October 14, 2015.

U.S. Department of Veterans Affairs/PTSD. https.//maketheconnection.net/conditions/ptsd.

Vernick, J. S., et. al. "I Didn't Know the Gun Was Loaded: An Examination of Two Safety Devices That Can Reduce the Risk of Unintentional Firearm Injuries." *Journal of Public Health Policy* 20 (1999) 427–40.

Vick, Karl. "What's It Like to be a Cop in America." *Time,* August 24, 2015, 38.

Violence Policy Center. "License to Kill: More Guns, More Crime." Public Paper, June 2002.

Virginia Law Enforcement Assistance Program. VALEAP.org

Wallis, Jim. "Bush's Theology of Empire." *Sojourners,* December 19, 2003, 20–26.

Ward, Karla. "Five year-old boy accidently shoots, kills 2-year-old sister in Cumberland County." *Lexington Herald-Leader,* April 30, 2013.

Washington Post. "More Shootings, More Death," August 27, 2015.

Washington Post. "Not a Toy," June 6, 2015.

Washington Post. "Straight Shooting," May 10, 2014.

Washington Post. "Why Are You Trying to Kill Me, Man?," November 6, 2015.

Waskow, Arthur, Rabbi. "Continuing Heschel in our Lives: Prayer as Politics, Politics as Prayer." The Shalom Center.org. https://theshalomcenter.org/node/175.

White, Griff. "For Gun-less Bobbies: Training is a Better Weapon." *Washington Post,* June 12, 2015.

Wilkinson, D. L., and J. Fagan. "The Role of Firearms in the Violence 'Scripts': The Dynamics of Gun Events Among Adolescent Males." *Law and Contemporary Problems* 59 (1996) 55–89.

Williams, Katie, and Sarah Ferris. "Fight To End Gun Research Ban Fizzles." *The Hill,* December 13, 2015.

Wink, Walter. *Engaging the Powers: Discernment and Resistance in a World of Domination.* Minneapolis: Fortress, 1992.

Wintemute, Garen, et al. "Mortality Among Recent Purchasers of Handguns." *New England Journal of Medicine,* November 18, 1999, 1583–90.

Witkin, G. "Handgun Stealing Made Real Easy." *U.S. News and World Report.* June 9, 1997, 34–35.

Wolfson, Andrew. "Ky. Baptists Lure Unchurched to God at Gatherings to Give Away Guns." *Louisville Courier Journal,* March 2, 2014.

Wu, Annie. "When Toy Guns Cause Real Harm." *Epoch Times,* March 3, 2015

Young, Emma. "Bullet Hole Causes Huge Alaskan Oil Spill." *New Scientist,* October 9, 2001, 1.

Zakaria, Fareed. "Change Your Gun Laws, America." *Washington Post,* July 30, 2015.

Bibliography

———. "People Driven By Identity, Not Ideology." *Washington Post*. July 4, 2014.

Zandrozny, Brandy. "He killed a Pregnant Mom, but he still gets a Gun." *The Daily Beast*, March 21, 2016.

Zatat, Narjas. "More Gun Shops Than Starbucks, MacDonald's, and Supermarkets Put Together." *Indy 100 Independent*. June, 2016

Zoroya, Gregg. "26 Police Killed So Far in 2016, Up 44% from 2015." *USA Today*, July 9, 2016.